Public Housing
and Urban Renewal

Richard D. Bingham

Public Housing and Urban Renewal

An Analysis of Federal-Local Relations

PRAEGER SPECIAL STUDIES IN U.S. ECONOMIC, SOCIAL, AND POLITICAL ISSUES

Praeger Publishers   New York   Washington   London

Library of Congress Cataloging in Publication Data

Bingham, Richard A
    Public housing and urban renewal.

    (Praeger special studies in U. S. economic, social,
and political issues)
    Bibliography: p.
    Includes index.
    1. Public housing--United States--Case studies.
2. Urban renewal--United States--Case studies.   3. Public
housing--Social aspects.   4. Federal-city relations--
United States--Case studies.   I. Title.
HD7293.B55   301.5'4'0973   74-19822
ISBN 0-275-05810-7

PRAEGER PUBLISHERS
111 Fourth Avenue, New York, N.Y. 10003, U.S.A.

Published in the United States of America in 1975
by Praeger Publishers, Inc.

Printed in the United States of America

This study was undertaken in an attempt to fill a vacuum in our knowledge concerning the adoption and effects of federal grants to local government. Most prior work in this area consisted largely of aggregate analysis of grants in general with a concern for their effects on the expenditure patterns of local government or of detailed case studies concerning the use and effects of particular grants on particular cities. In spite of the fact that grant programs, and specifically federal-local programs, have been with us for a number of years, very little is actually known concerning either factors determining their adoption by local government or the effects the specific grants have had on the community. Both the aggregative approach and the case studies approach fail to detect regularities in grant use and distort much of the real meaning of modern federalism.

Two federal grant programs were examined in some detail, attempting to answer two basic questions: (1) Why do some cities make extensive use of federal grants while other cities virtually ignore them? (2) What impact have federal grants actually had on cities? To this end, public housing and urban renewal grants were selected for analysis. Quantitative analysis covered all incorporated U.S. cities with 1960 populations of 50,000 or more. In addition, the study incorporated field studies of six cities selected through the use of a regression model. The case studies were expected to add insight to the variance explained by the quantitative analysis and to suggest explanations for the remaining unexplained variance.

The study initially identified five underlying dimensions of U.S. cities through the use of factor analysis. These dimensions, along with a number of variables defining the political system, were used with substantial success to explain grant use. The analysis showed the overwhelming importance of two of the city dimensions as determinants of grant use. This is not to say that the other variables are unimportant; the political system, for example, was shown to have substantial intervening influence.

The effects of housing and renewal grant use were examined in four general areas: local business and economic health, government and politics, city land use patterns, and social conditions. Housing and renewal grants were not found to be related to the short-term economic health of the community, although there was some evidence that public housing construction had a small effect on employment. The findings generally suggest that if renewal and housing grants do promote economic vigor, the time lag necessary for the grants to produce any measurable change is much longer than was heretofore believed.

Both housing and renewal were related to low levels of government employment--again suggesting that both programs are used to improve local conditions. The research conclusively shows the ability of urban renewal to increase city revenues and improve the local tax base. Public housing, on the other hand, did not prove to be the drain on the public coffers that some critics suggest. Although urban renewal and public housing are both considered volatile local issues, successful use of these programs had little effect upon stability in the mayors' offices. Other factors, such as type of local government, appear to be more important determinants of local political stability.

One of the apparent side effects of urban renewal has been its use in changing patterns of land ownership. Renewal was found to be a highly successful tool for shifting land from private to public uses.

And finally, the study explodes a number of myths concerning the pricing and quantity of low-income housing in the city. While urban renewal is often blamed for destruction of low-cost housing, there appear to be other programs (for example, highway construction) that are the real contemporary villains. The same is true of both public housing and renewal and improved housing conditions. Neither program has the dominant role in upgrading housing conditions that was once suspected.

The study thus concludes that public housing and urban renewal meet only some of their espoused goals while both programs had certain spillover effects. Public housing, however, did not exhibit the societal deficiencies associated with urban renewal. While public housing is suffering from a certain "hardening of the arteries," the program is basically beneficial to all segments of urban society. Urban renewal, on the other hand, is not. Certain basic changes in the program structure are deemed necessary before the program can operate to the advantage of all groups within the city.

The comprehensive analysis of individual grants, such as urban renewal and public housing, should reveal something about the nature of grants in general. It is imperative that we know more about why cities adopt particular grants as well as attempt to determine the effects of grant programs. As was suggested here, the spillover effects of some grant programs may, in the long run, be more important than the programmed effects.

ACKNOWLEDGMENTS

I wish it were possible to acknowledge all of the individuals and organizations assisting me in this study, but space does not permit proper acknowledgment of all those whose assistance was so valuable. I owe a special debt of gratitude to F. Ted Hebert, Samuel A. Kirkpatrick, and David R. Morgan for their assistance and helpful suggestions during the design and execution phases of this project as well as their many helpful suggestions during manuscript preparation. I also owe a special thanks to all of those local officials and administrators whose cooperation and assistance during the field studies aided immeasurably to any contribution this study may make.

Special thanks goes to the Bureau of Government Research of the University of Oklahoma for computer assistance and administrative support. A debt of gratitude goes to Vickie Craig for her many hours of keypunching and to Martha Bingham and Judie Grove for careful and painstaking editing and typing. The study could never have been accomplished on its present scale without the financial support of the Woodrow Wilson National Fellowship Foundation. The stipend they provided me and the expense allowance for the field studies made this project possible.

And finally, I wish to thank my family, Martha, Connie, and Paul, for two years of patience while I was immersed in this project.

CONTENTS

LIST OF TABLES

LIST OF FIGURES

Public Housing
and Urban Renewal

1

FEDERAL GRANTS IN
AN INTERGOVERNMENTAL
PERSPECTIVE

There is no question but that federal grants-in-aid have become a dominant concern of both scholars and practitioners of intergovernmental relations. Federal grants are a fact of life--they are here to stay. The proliferation of grants during the past 40 years has had a profound effect upon the character of American federalism. By 1968 per capita federal grants amounted to exactly $90.00 for every man, woman, and child in this country. These grants accounted for 19.4 cents of every dollar of total state and local revenue. In other words, almost 20 percent of all state and local revenue was received from the federal government.[1] Federal grants as a percent of state and local revenues ranged from a low of 14.7 percent in Indiana to an astonishing high of 71.3 percent in Alaska. Those states with the lowest per capita income generally appear to benefit the most from federal grant programs. In the 17 states with the lowest per capita income between 1965 and 1967, the federal government added grants of 36 cents to each state and local dollar as compared to 23 cents for all states.[2]

A BRIEF HISTORY

Federal grants had an inauspicious beginning in 1802 when Ohio was admitted to the union. Congress allowed 5 percent of the proceeds from the sale of public lands in Ohio to be applied to the construction of roads within the new state. In 1818 Congress broadened the law to provide that all states be given 5 percent of the proceeds of land sales within their borders. They further required that 3 percent be used for the "encouragement of learning" with one-sixth of the 3 percent designated exclusively for a college or university.[3]

Some sources credit the Morrill Act of 1862 with the practical beginning of the modern grant system.[4] The Morrill Act was designed to assist states in establishing and maintaining the land-grant college system. The grant was in the form of federal land rather than money; however, states were allowed to sell or lease the land but were required to use the money to support a state land-grant college. The act placed certain conditions on the use of the revenue derived from the land sales and required annual reports. Thus the pattern was established; needed resources were provided by the federal government in exchange for state acceptance of a national program coupled with certain minimum standards.

In the late 1800s federal aid took the form of direct monetary payments rather than contributions of land. The first along this line was a program passed in 1887, the Hatch Act, to establish agricultural experiment stations. Congress also enacted grant programs for highway construction and for vocational education and rehabilitation.[5]

The depression of the 1930s brought on a new wave of programs --programs in the areas of welfare and economic security. Major areas of emphasis included grants for low-rent public housing, improved health services, Social Security, etc. The increasing number and complexity of these grants brought on more extensive supervision by the national government.[6] Direct intergovernmental transfers from federal to local governments also originated with the depression of the 1930s. Most were administered by ad hoc agencies: the Federal Emergency Relief Administration, Public Works Administration, Works Progress Administration, etc.[7] These agencies were liquidated during the early years of World War II and the grants ceased, but they had established the trend of things to come.

Following World War II Congress initiated a new series of grants for health care, education, and for renewal of the physical environment of urban areas. The era was characterized by increasing emphasis on social programs with new grants for education, special assistance to depressed areas, the "war on poverty," and "model cities." All of these programs were designed to fight significant aspects of what is popularly known as the "urban problem."[8]

CURRENT TRENDS

During recent years certain trends in federal grant programs have been identified. These trends include (1) large-scale growth, (2) excessive categorization and widespread proliferation, (3) direct federal-local relations, and (4) increased use of project grants.

The amount of money allocated for federal grants to state and local government has been rapidly increasing. Federal grants have

recorded continuous increases in every year since 1948 with the
annual increase in grants-in-aid from 1949 through 1970 averaging
almost 13 percent.[9] Some credit this growth to the nature of federal-
state-local fiscal relations. John Kenneth Galbraith, for example,
notes a serious imbalance in the revenue capabilities between federal, state, and local governments. One consequence, he believes,
is a constant pressure on the federal government to utilize its superior revenue position to help redress the balance at lower levels.[10]

The Advisory Commission on Intergovernmental Relations contends that the most striking characteristic of the recent trend in the
federal grant program has been not only growth, but widespread
proliferation and excessive categorization.[11] The most commonly
cited example is the case of water and sewer grants--four separate
grants administered by four separate agencies, and all for the same
purpose. Nowhere is this trend more evident than by glancing
through one of the federal government's grant catalogs. The 1970
Catalog of Federal Domestic Assistance, for example, alphabetically
lists 1,013 programs by title and contains more than 1,040 pages.[12]

A third trend has been the expansion of direct federal-local
relationships. The concept is frequently referred to as "direct federalism." Though not a recent concept (the low-rent public housing
program of 1937 was the first direct federal-local grant program),
large-scale bypassing of the states is characteristic of the 1960s.[13]
Of the 38 programs in which the state plays no part (as of 1967), 23
were passed between 1961 and 1967. The Advisory Commission on
Intergovernmental Relations notes several distinguishing characteristics of direct federalism:

> First, to some extent it is a response to the problems
> of big cities thought to be neglected by States, and as
> such reflects the independent political role of large
> urban centers. Second, however, direct Federal-
> local grants have never been limited to the big cities;
> such grants as public housing, urban renewal, educa-
> tion and airports have substantially aided small local-
> ities and suburbs as well. Third, direct federalism
> is a way of pinpointing target areas. It is a reaction
> to the more conventional system of distributing Fed-
> eral funds through State governments and reflects
> growing impatience with State and local boundaries.
> Finally, in most programs, national control of local
> performance is relatively close.[14]

The main categories of direct federal-local transfers are in education, housing and community development, airport construction,
waste treatment facilities, and other miscellaneous grants.[15]

Figure 1.1 illustrates the growth trend by functional category from 1940 through 1968.

Many credit the states with the development and growth of direct federalism. Richard Leach believes that direct federalism can be considered a direct outgrowth of the failure of the states either to assist local government or to remove the shackles that make them "too weak and inept" to accomplish their purposes. A vacuum had been created and the federal government stepped in by default.[16]

Terry Sanford also points an accusing finger at the states. He cites the states with failure to cede to the cities adequate powers to tax, zone surrounding areas, regulate housing, provide mass transportation, and acquire open space.[17]

James Maxwell, too, blames the states for direct federalism:

> But the fact is that most state governments have not been interested in urban renewal, low rent public housing, airport construction, and the war on poverty programs. Irresponsive to urban needs, the states did not resist federal-local action. Accordingly, a direct federal-local relationship developed, federal aid being provided on a contractual basis to numerous local agencies without an intervening state authority; the interests of the state in the activity, as well as its responsibility to its local governments, were sidetracked.[18]

Finally, another recent trend has been the expanding use of project grants. In 1962 approximately two-thirds of the federal grants in effect were of the project type. By 1966 this figure had increased to three-fourths. In part the increase in the use of project grants is related to the growth of the direct federalism concept. Project grants are typically used extensively in urban areas. As direct federal-local relationships have increased, the project grant has been a primary vehicle for that increase.[19]

TYPES OF GRANTS

There are a number of ways that grants may be described. They are often categorized either by the administrative procedures involved in their distribution or according to the conditions attached to their use. Utilizing classification according to administrative procedures, grants might be designated either as formula grants or project grants. A formula grant is a grant that is distributed to all states, cities, or other units of government in accordance with a

FIGURE 1.1

Federal Grants-in-Aid to State and Local Governments,
by Major Functional Categories, 1940-68

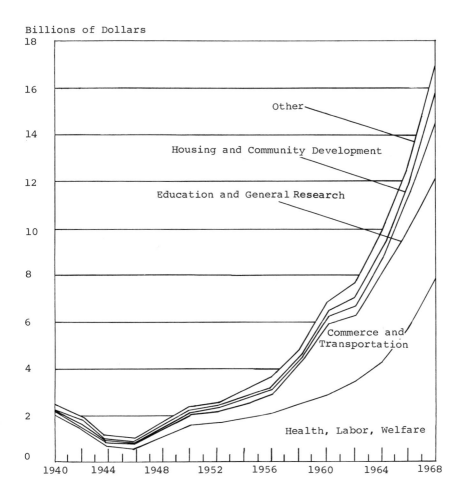

Source: Advisory Commission on Intergovernmental Relations, Fiscal Balance in the American Federal System, vol. 1 (Washington, D.C.: Government Printing Office, 1969), p. 147.

formula written into the enacting law. These grants then become a matter of right and not of privilege. Project grants, on the other hand, are grants to meet specific problems and are not necessarily spread uniformly.[20] For example, two states as of the mid-1960s never passed the enabling legislation necessary to allow localities to receive assistance for public housing construction, although the program has been in effect since 1937.[21]

Both types of grants generally require some type of matching, whose requirements may be of two kinds: variable matching, which reflects the differing abilities of the recipient unit of government to support the aided function, and a fixed matching ratio, under which each of the receiving units is required to share the same percentage of the program costs.[22]

According to conditions of use, grants might be considered either categorical grants or block grants. "Categorical grants are made for narrowly circumscribed purposes determined by the Congress to be of national concern. . . . Block grants are either unconditional fiscal grants to a specified level of government, or grants restricted to a broad program purpose. . . ."[23] An example of the latter might be the Partnership in Health Act of 1966, a block grant for health purposes. Figure 1.2 presents a diagram of the types of grants based upon conditions of use and the administrative procedure involved in the grant distribution.

FIGURE 1.2

Relationship between Grants Categorized by Conditions
of Use and by Administrative Procedure
Involved in Grant Distribution

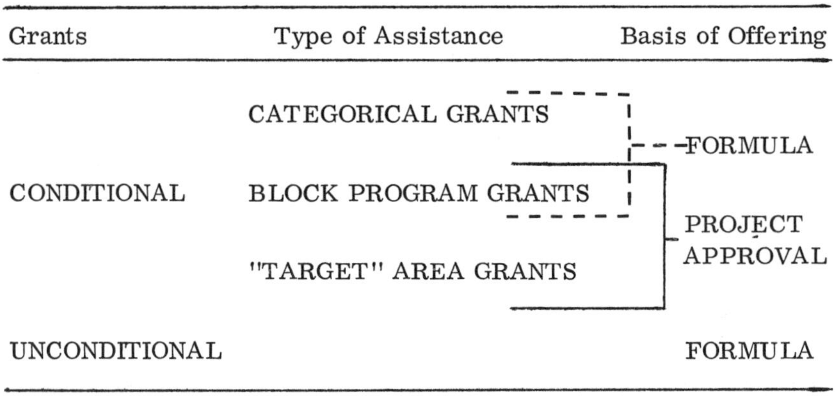

Grants	Type of Assistance	Basis of Offering
	CATEGORICAL GRANTS	
		FORMULA
CONDITIONAL	BLOCK PROGRAM GRANTS	
		PROJECT APPROVAL
	"TARGET" AREA GRANTS	
UNCONDITIONAL		FORMULA

Source: Selma J. Mushkin and John F. Cotton, Sharing Federal Funds for State and Local Needs (New York: Praeger, 1969), p. 22.

Selma Mushkin and John Cotton describe grants according to condition of use under the following four typologies:

1. Categorical (or conditional) matching grant, open-end. A grant offering limited to use for a specified objective--requiring the recipient to match a fraction of the grant; no upper limit on the offering.
2. Categorical (or conditional) matching grant, closed-end. Same as above except that there is an upper limit to the offering to each state.
3. Categorical (or conditional) grant, no matching, closed-end. A grant offering limited to use for a specified objective of determined magnitude for which no matching on the part of the recipient is required.
4. General unconditional grant. A grant offering that the recipient is free to use as he desires and that has no matching requirement. [24]

Figure 1.3 illustrates the fiscal tradeoffs officials might make between two programs, program X and program Y, under the aforementioned categories. In all cases line AB represents the tradeoff options between the two programs in the absence of grants. In all cases program X will receive the grant. Also in all cases point 1 represents the decision maker's judgment as to the best combination of programs X and Y to purchase with a given dollar without grants.

An open-end categorical matching grant changes the budget constraint AB to AC. The decision maker then selects the new best combination of programs. A selection of point 2 would produce an increase in both programs X and Y while selecting point 2' would decrease program Y while substantially increasing program X.

The closed-end categorical matching grant is identical in operation to the open-end grant up to a level where the allotment for program X is exhausted (point D). Up to point D, changes in the levels of X and Y could be determined by the combination of substitution and income effects as with the open-end grant. Beyond D there is an income effect only and the grant acts merely as an unrestricted addition to income.

The categorical grant with no required matching would produce budget line AFG. In this case, F of program X is received at no cost to the local jurisdiction. Note also that program Y is increased through a substitution effect.

Finally, the unrestricted fiscal grant merely shifts the budgetary decision line from AB to HI and has a pure income effect. The suggested effect would be to increase the magnitude of all programs. [25]

FIGURE 1.3

Fiscal Effects of Grant-in-Aid Programs

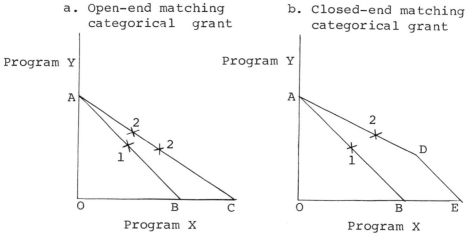

a. Open-end matching categorical grant

b. Closed-end matching categorical grant

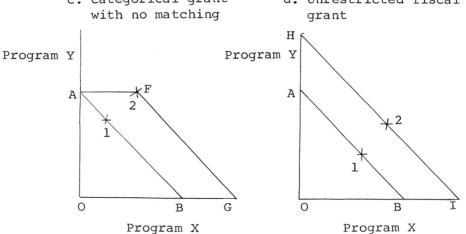

c. Categorical grant with no matching

d. Unrestricted fiscal grant

Source: Selma J. Mushkin and John F. Cotton, Sharing Federal Funds for State and Local Needs (New York: Praeger, 1969), p. 34.

GRANT OBJECTIVES

Grants, then, are designed with certain effects in mind--effects that go far beyond the narrow purpose of the specific grant. Implicit in all grants is the attempt by the granting authority to modify in some way the behavior of the grantee through the use of a "carrot and stick approach." Grants, at least theoretically, have a number of specific objectives that may be regarded as independent or as potentially complementing each other. Mushkin and Cotton present an excellent summary of these objectives.[26]

One objective is the promotion of national standards for programs that concern the nation as a whole. Within this guideline there are three types of issues:

1. Activities affecting the nation's security and defense.
2. Activities at the local or state level that if carried out (or if not carried out) would have significant impact on jurisdictions outside the state of origin--for example, education, pollution control, transportation.
3. Services considered to be part of the birthright of citizens of this nation--for example, programs to ensure that all American citizens have adequate opportunity for individual growth and for a decent standard of living (based on income, health care, housing, and so on).[27]

The mitigation of benefit spillover is a second objective that has received emphasis in recent years: the premise being that a state or local governmental unit, when making an expenditure or taxation decision, will make the decision based exclusively on the interest of the citizens in its jurisdiction. However, these decisions have effects beyond the government's jurisdiction. Presumably, this series of independent suboptimal decisions do not produce an optimum allocation of resources from a national viewpoint. Grants, then, can provide a correction for such spillover. Since grants attempt to influence subunit spending, presumably they tend to offset the spillover effect.

A third function advanced for grants-in-aid is that of narrowing interstate financial differences. Through the use of formulas, usually based upon a measure of wealth such as per capita income, the "poor" states are often allocated a higher per capita amount than the "rich" states. Attempts are made to equalize in a number of areas. Among them is the attempt to equalize public revenues: Certain grants are designed to reduce the gap in per capita revenues between the states. Closely related is the attempt to equalize public services. The notion of equalizing effort to achieve some desired minimum level of services is probably more feasible politically than equalization of revenues. Finally, a much less ambitious and more probable goal is that of equalization to achieve national program standards. This is based on the contention that resolving explicit problems or providing certain minimum standards should not place a differential burden on taxpayers in different states. There is probably general consensus, for example, on certain minimum benefits for the handicapped or on minimum standards for sewage treatment.

Finally, a fourth proposed function of the grant-in-aid system, and one that is obviously more controversial than the other three, would use grants to change the balance of resources between the public and private sectors. For example, the national revenue system could draw revenues from the wealthy suburban sector of our metropolitan areas and redirect them to the central cities. It might also be used to foster a national policy concerning population movement or industrial location.

THE SYSTEMS APPROACH

Any further discussion of grants must now move from generalities to the specific. Having thus far examined the grant-in-aid from a historic perspective, and having briefly examined some of the more common economic models, it is necessary to examine grants in relation to their environment and to devote some attention to their effects. Perhaps the most widely utilized "method" of recent years devoted to quantitative analysis of government outputs has been public policy analysis. The major impetus to this systematic and quantitative movement undoubtedly came from scholars in the field of economics. A major pathfinder in this area was Solomon Fabricant's The Trend of Governmental Activity in the United States Since 1900, published in 1952.[28] Fabricant used multiple correlation analysis to study the relationship between three factors (per capita personal income, population density, and percent of the population living in urban places) and the interstate variations in the level of 1942 operating expenditures of state and local governments. He found that these three variables "explained" 72 percent of the variation in expenditures for the various functions analyzed.

This type of analysis was not solely limited to economic studies; in the early 1960s other academic disciplines recognized the utility of this analysis and were quick to adapt it to their own use. Of substantial interest is a 1963 study by two political scientists, Richard Dawson and James Robinson, analyzing the relationships among interparty competition, socioeconomic conditions, and measurements of welfare policy in the United States.[29] They found significant rela-

10

tionships between each pair of the three sets of variables until they held socioeconomic conditions constant. They then noted that the relationship between interparty competition and welfare expenditures was substantially reduced. They thus concluded that interparty competition was not as influential a determinant of welfare policy as were socioeconomic characteristics. One writer credits Dawson and Robinson with creating a renewed interest in state and local politics.[30] Their contribution to the development of studies in policy analysis is significant for several reasons. Most important was the use of aggregate data. Their analysis was over all states and not merely a comparison of a few. These writers were also among the first to systematically explore the relationships between public policy outputs (welfare), socioeconomic variables, and political characteristics of the states.[31]

Of equal importance in the early 1960s was the genesis of an analytical framework that would prove useful in giving theoretical meaning to analysis of public policy. David Easton's application of a systems approach to the study of political science is often credited with providing such a framework.[32] Thomas Dye developed a model based upon Easton's systems approach that he used as a basis for a major study published in 1966.[33] Dye's model assumed that environmental inputs operated through the political structure to produce outputs in terms of policy actions. Outputs, then, were the dependent variables while environmental inputs and the political structure were the independent variables. Dye used simple, partial, and multiple correlation analysis to test his model. He used four socioeconomic characteristics of the state's population as his environmental inputs: median family income, industrialization, educational level, and urbanization. He also selected four variables to represent the political system of the state: voter participation, legislative malapportionment, interparty competition, and degree of party control of the state government. Dye's outputs were the commonly used state expenditures for education, highways, welfare, etc. His conclusions were much the same as Dawson and Robinson's--that economic and social characteristics of the state are more influential than political system characteristics in shaping public policy in the states.[34] While Dye has been criticized for selecting weak indicators of the political structure (Dye admitted that they were "crude at best"), nonetheless his study stands as a landmark in policy analysis as it provided the basic framework for the plethora of studies to follow.

The systems approach along with Dye's model have been widely accepted as providing a conceptual framework for analysis at the local as well as the state level. Any number of reasons can be cited for using the systems approach in the search for understanding urban political behavior. For one thing, it forces the researcher to separate political activity from other activities. It also forces attention on the specific components of the political system. In years past, government research emphasized the formal, or structural, aspects of the system. The systems approach forces a look at all of the components of the allocative system--not merely the structural. And finally, systems analysis is highly compatible with empirical research. The systems framework provides a useful model for the statistical and mathematical techniques in common use today.[35] Brett Hawkins is more pragmatic--he advocates systems analysis simply because he finds thinking in terms of systems useful.[36] Figure 1.4 presents a model of a political system with its environment and output, which presents a clear frame of reference for continued discussion of federal grants to local government. The only concept not adequately portrayed in the model is the concept of feedback.[37] Feedback connotes a continuous process. By adding a feedback loop connecting output to the environment, we can think in terms of a complete pattern of interrelationships between environment, the political system, and outputs.

The systems approach thus provides a useful framework for the analysis of federal grants to local government. Accepting federal grants is unquestionably a local policy decision. The systems approach thus presents one useful way of examining grant utilization and impact.

GRANT USE

Little has been done in the analysis of public policy that indicates which cities utilize federal grants and why; the effects attributed to grants are much more commonly discussed. In 1969 Morley Segal, Lee Fritschler, and Douglas Harman conducted a survey of all cities over 10,000 population concerning many aspects of intergovernmental relations.[38] One area of some interest was the result of their findings concerning distribution of federal grants. According to their data, all cities received an average of $52.25 in federal grants for every man, woman, and child residing within the city. Within this average, however, were many disparities in terms of size, geography, and city type.

Cities between 50,000 and 100,000 and those between 250,000 and 500,000 seem to benefit least from federal grants with grants per capita of only $39.95 and $38.74 respectively. The smaller communities appeared to do quite well--those in the 25,000 to 50,000 category received slightly more than $13.00 above the average for all cities. As Table 1.1 illustrates, cities under 250,000 seem to do quite well as far as grant receipts are concerned--they appear to

FIGURE 1.4

A Political System, Its Environment and Output

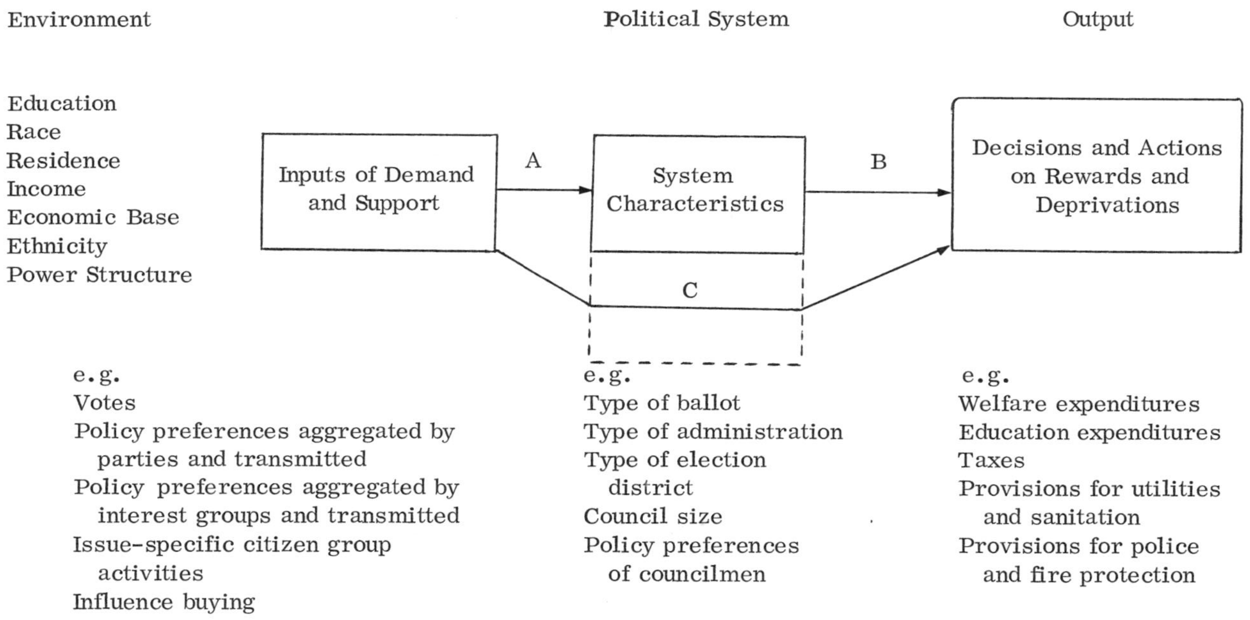

Environment   Political System   Output

Environment

Education
Race
Residence
Income
Economic Base
Ethnicity
Power Structure

e.g.

Votes
Policy preferences aggregated by
   parties and transmitted
Policy preferences aggregated by
   interest groups and transmitted
Issue-specific citizen group
   activities
Influence buying

Inputs of Demand and Support

System Characteristics

Decisions and Actions on Rewards and Deprivations

e.g.

Type of ballot
Type of administration
Type of election
   district
Council size
Policy preferences
   of councilmen

e.g.

Welfare expenditures
Education expenditures
Taxes
Provisions for utilities
   and sanitation
Provisions for police
   and fire protection

Note: Line C shows a direct impact of inputs on outputs, independent of the characteristics of the political system. Lines A and B show a set of relationships in which inputs shape system characteristics, which in turn shape the policy decisions that are made.

Source: Brett W. Hawkins, Politics and Urban Policies (Indianapolis: Bobbs-Merrill, 1971), p. 12.

TABLE 1.1

Federal Grants to Cities

Classification	Number of Cities Reporting	Total Population (in thousands)	Number of Grants	Total Dollars (in thousands)	Grants per Capita
Total, all cities	642	34,935	3,247	$1,825,490	$52.25
Population group					
Over 500,000	7	6,281	269	350,894	55.87
250,000-500,000	18	6,096	400	236,147	38.74
100,000-250,000	41	5,950	801	334,172	56.16
50,000-100,000	84	5,731	419	228,934	39.95
25,000- 50,000	160	5,626	566	367,179	65.26
10,000- 25,000	332	5,251	792	308,164	58.64
Geographic division					
New England	54	1,752	271	162,516	92.76
Mid-Atlantic	68	2,843	183	206,797	72.74
East North-Central	114	5,702	467	305,008	53.49
West North-Central	79	3,244	362	192,898	59.46
South Atlantic	90	5,379	496	298,500	55.49
East South-Central	27	2,221	189	147,315	66.33
West South-Central	59	3,669	527	94,679	25.80
Mountain	36	1,562	166	94,110	60.25
Pacific Coast	115	8,563	586	323,667	37.80
City type					
Central	118	21,026	1,680	1,065,547	50.68
Suburban	272	8,293	809	308,228	37.17
Independent	252	5,616	758	451,715	80.43

*These figures are based on information from the chief administrative officer of responding cities.

Source: Morley Segal and A. Lee Fritschler, "Emerging Patterns of Intergovernmental Relations," in The Municipal Year Book 1970 (Washington, D.C.: International City Management Association, 1970), p. 15.

be doing better on a per capita basis than are the large cities. These figures contradict the claim by many of the smaller cities that they are losing out to the larger cities in the battle for federal aid.[39]

Independent cities (those outside of Standard Metropolitan Statistical Areas (SMSAs) received a much higher per capita amount than did cities within SMSAs--central cities and their suburbs. Suburban communities average a very low $37.17 in per capita grants as compared to the $80.43 received by the independent cities.

Table 1.1 also shows the geographic distribution of grants. New England cities received a whopping $92.76 in per capita grants followed by Mid-Atlantic cities with $72.74. West South-Central cities appeared to be low in the scramble for federal aid with only $25.80 in grants per capita. It is impossible to determine the independent effects of city size, city type, and geographic region as statistical controls were not used to consider the independent contribution of each variable. It is possible (though unlikely), for example, that there is no real difference in per capita grant receipts due to region--that the variation is explained by the differences in average city size within the regions.

Organizing to deal with the sources of assistance from Washington has increasingly become a major activity of local governments. The most visible form that this organization takes is an office created to initiate and coordinate federal grants. Segal and Fritschler term this a "federal liaison office."[40] Table 1.2 shows the relationship between federal grants per capita and the existence of and attitude toward federal liaison offices (FLO). Cities are classified by population and city type as successful believers, unsuccessful believers, successful nonbelievers, and unsuccessful nonbelievers, depending on per capita grants and the percent of cities having a federal liaison office. The authors note that the successful believers are the large cities that receive a large amount of grant money and also attempt to tie into the intergovernmental system (as indicated by the percent with a federal liaison office). The unsuccessful believers are the cities with populations of 250,000 to 500,000. A high percent of these cities have established federal liaison offices but they receive a low level of per capita aid. Segal and Fritschler have similarly categorized the smaller cities (under 250,000) and found them to be either successful nonbelievers or unsuccessful nonbelievers.[41] A different description might be appropriate, however, if the number of grants per city from Table 1.1 is compared with the percent of cities having a federal liaison office (Table 1.2). This comparison is shown in Table 1.3. Note that the number of grants per city rises both as population and the percent of cities with a federal liaison office increases. Thus cities that are unsuccessful when considering per capita grants only are quite

TABLE 1.2

Grants Per Capita and the Existence of and Attitude Toward Federal Liaison Offices[a]

Classification	Per Capita Grants	Percent Who Have a FLO	Percent Who Do Not Have a FLO but Believe Having One Would Help Obtain Grants	Percent Who Have Attempted to Establish a FLO
		"Successful Believers"[b]		
Over 500,000	$55.87	62	80	40
Central cities	50.68	54	63	18
		"Unsuccessful Believers"[b]		
250,000 to 500,000	38.74	60	100	25
		"Successful Nonbelievers"[b]		
100,000 to 250,000	56.16	47	46	19
25,000 to 50,000	65.26	21	52	6
10,000 to 25,000	58.64	6	47	7
Independent cities	80.43	33	57	9
		"Unsuccessful Nonbelievers"[b]		
50,000 to 100,000	39.95	21	47	11
Suburban cities	37.17	45	34	5

[a]Information is taken from "Federal, State, Local Relationships," Urban Data Service, ICMA 1, no. 12 (December 1969), Tables 10-12.

[b]"Successful" and "Unsuccessful" refer to those jurisdictions above and below the average grant per capita of $52.25. "Believers" and "Nonbelievers" refer to those jurisdictions that seem to support the idea of having a federal liaison office and those that do not.

Source: Morley Segal and A. Lee Fritschler, "Emerging Patterns of Intergovernmental Relations," in The Municipal Year Book 1970 (Washington, D.C.: International City Management Association, 1970), p. 18.

successful when considering number of grants. It is possible that both criteria are valid. Perhaps economies of scale contribute to the fluctuations in per capita grants. In any event, Table 1.3 shows the relationship between city size, percent of cities with a federal liaison office, and number of grants per city. A causal relationship cannot be established. It is noted, however, that there is a positive relationship between city size and both percent of cities having a federal liaison office and grant success as measured by number of grants per city. It is also noted that a linear relationship does not exist between any of the three aforementioned variables and grant success as measured by per capita grants. Table 1.3 also shows the average total dollars per city for each of the population categories. This financial measure indicates a relationship between city size and total grant-in-aid dollars received. Thus while grants per capita does not increase as city size increases, total dollars in grant money does appear to be related to city size.

TABLE 1.3

Grants Per City as Compared to the Percent of Cities
with a Federal Liaison Office

Population Group Classification	Number of Grants Per City[a]	Percent of Cities with a Federal Liaison Office[b]	Average Dollars Per City[a] (in thousands)
Over 500,000	38.4	62	50,127
250,000 to 500,000	22.2	60	13,119
100,000 to 250,000	19.5	47	8,150
50,000 to 100,000	5.0	21	2,725
25,000 to 50,000	4.5	21	2,294
10,000 to 25,000	2.4	6	928

[a]Computed from information in Table 1.2.

[b]From Table 1.2.

The Advisory Commission on Intergovernmental Relations, while presenting no empirical evidence, also related grants to city size. They believe that the present grant system has led to confusion and uncertainty as to what grants are available, how to apply for them, what the requirements are, etc. This, they say, gives an advantage to the larger and better organized states and cities in getting federal money.[42]

A study somewhat similar to Segal and Fritschler's examined some of the influences on city managers' knowledge of grant-in-aid programs in four states.[43] Ted Hebert and Richard Bingham initially examined the relationship between the city managers' knowledge of grants with congressional obligations and found a low, but significant, relationship. Managers showed a greater knowledge of those programs with the most money available. They also noted a substantial difference in knowledge depending upon the federal department or agency managing or operating the program. The programs sponsored by the Department of Housing and Urban Development were clearly the best known. The authors found a positive relationship between knowledge of grants and managers' education but noted little relationship between knowledge and managers' experience in terms of number of years as a city manager.

The strongest relationship of the study was shown when city size was correlated with the manager's knowledge. Managers in the larger cities were clearly more knowledgeable of grant programs than were their counterparts in smaller cities. When the authors reexamined the relationship between knowledge and education while controlling for size, they found that the importance of education was substantially reduced. Education was only significantly related to the manager's knowledge in the large cities. The relationship between city size and knowledge held, however, when education was controlled. The study also confirmed the Segal and Fritschler findings relating city size to the use of a grantsman (or federal liaison office). The probability that a city utilizes the services of a grantsman increases as city size increases. The fact that a city utilized a grantsman apparently has little relationship to the manager's knowledge of grants. It was only in very small cities (less than 5,000 population) where managers having either a full- or part-time grantsman on their staff indicated a level of knowledge higher than those managers without grantsmen.

The Segal and Fritschler and Hebert and Bingham studies complement each other. Both emphasize the importance of city size when examining federal grant-in-aid programs, specifically concerning the apparent relationships between size, number of grants used, and knowledge. The relationship between size and use of a grantsman or federal liaison office was also confirmed. Obviously weaker relationships were shown when grants were examined in dollar terms. No relationship was shown between city size and grants on a per capita basis and the relationship between manager's grant knowledge and grant obligations was shown to be weak. About all that can be confirmed is the obvious premise that large cities receive more grant money than small cities. The sparse literature clearly shows the relationship between one environmental variable, city size, and the political variable, grant use.

GRANT EFFECTS

Referring again to Figure 1.4, it is necessary to examine the output side of the model. Once a city decides to use federal grants, what difference does it make? What effect do grants have? Far and away, the effects of grants have been a dominant concern of economists with the National Tax Journal acting as the primary vehicle for continuing debate. Obviously, each grant is designed for a specific purpose and should have an effect that is at least slightly different from any other grant. Chapter 2 will examine in depth the past studies dealing with public housing and urban renewal--the specific grants that form the basis of this study. The purpose here will be to examine the general effects of grants, primarily from a fiscal perspective.

A common complaint about federal grants concerns their effect upon state and local expenditures. Grants are often accused of causing a "skewing" of state and local budgets. These governments are induced to change their expenditure patterns away from what they would otherwise prefer and to budget money that will allow them to spend more of their resources on programs with high federal matching.[44] To some degree, of course, this is exactly what federal grants are designed to do--encourage participation in programs that foster national goals. If lower units of government can be persuaded fiscally to change policies that conflict with national goals (maintaining separate segregated schools, for example), skewing is the desired result.

Federal grants to local governments may be said to have three effects: they are either additive, stimulative, or substitutive.[45] Actually, most grants are probably some combination of all three. An additive effect might be achieved when a fiscal grant is provided, generally conditionally, that "adds to" funds available for a given objective (or objectives). In pure form an additive effect is almost unknown for it causes no change in normal fiscal behavior of the receiving unit. A stimulative effect occurs when the budgetary unit increases its revenue beyond what it would normally raise to provide funds to meet the matching requirements of the grant. A perfect stimulative effect would occur if the budgetary unit's increased revenue was at least equal to its matching share. A perfect substitutive effect occurs when the budgetary unit does not increase revenue to provide funds for matching but instead transfers the required funds from another function. The new function is thus substituted for the old.

Mushkin and Cotton provides a schematic display of stimulative and substitutive effects (Figure 1.5).[46] The vertical axis measures the level of expenditures of a function for which a federal grant is not provided (Y) while the horizontal axis measures the level of expenditures of a function for which a grant is intended (X). Line AB represents the budget constraint applied to programs X and Y prior to the grant, with point C representing the chosen expenditure package that the unit would adopt in the absence of grants.

FIGURE 1.5

Stimulative and Substitutive Effects
of Grant-in-Aid Programs

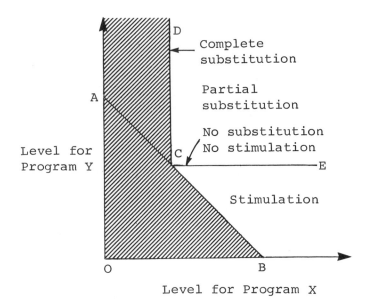

Source: Selma J. Mushkin and John F. Cotton, <u>Sharing Federal Funds for State and Local Needs</u> (New York: Praeger, 1969), p. 95.

If the unit were to move to any point along line CD when offered the grant, the grant would have a perfect substitutive effect since it would produce no increase in the level of X. Adopting a program of expenditures that fell in the area bounded by line DCE would give the grant a partial substitutive effect. A portion of the added revenues would be diverted to programs for which the grant was not intended. Points on line CE are illustrative of a perfect additive effect. In this case the grant is neither substitutive for other programs nor stimulative of increased expenditures for the grant program by the unit concerned. And finally, perfect stimulation occurs if the program distribution were to fall into the area bounded by ECB and the X axis. All additional revenue raised by the unit is earmarked for the grant program, program X.

Thus far, the fiscal effects of grants have been examined in a theoretical vein--no attempt has been made to look at studies in a practical light. The discussion will turn to a review of recent literature concerning general grant effects to see if grants actually have the substitutive and/or stimulative effects often attributed to them. Studies covered in this examination generally utilize empirical methods on the effects of grants on state and/or local governments. Since many of these studies draw on the work of predecessors, this short review will present the major findings ordered by date rather than conclusion. The final paragraphs will attempt to summarize the findings.

In a case study of Philadelphia published in 1961, W. H. Brown and C. E. Gilbert noted the "skewing" effect later publicized by the Advisory Commission on Intergovernmental Relations.[47] They found that federally (and state) funded projects were given a preference in Philadelphia's capital programming. They concluded that revenue type, in this case "free" money, may bias a city's resource allocations.

Seymour Sacks and Robert Harris empirically examined the effects of grants.[48] They viewed the theoretical effect of federal grants as stimulative of state expenditures. Their research, in fact, confirmed their a priori assumption. They noted the fact that a high intergovernmental flow of funds is related to a high level of expenditures for state and local governments combined. They also noted that in areas where federal aid is substantial, for example in welfare and highway expenditures, "federal aid is by far the most important determinant of expenditures as measured by the beta weights."[49]

George Bishop found education grants more substitutive than stimulative.[50] In a study of state aid to education in New England, he measured the effect of state aid to local schools and found that the primary effect was to substitute state aid for the local tax burden.

Roy Bahl and Robert Saunders were more interested in the determinants of changes in state and local expenditures, a la Fabricant, than in the effects of grants per se.[51] They used multiple regression analysis and found that, of their five variables, per capita federal grants to states was the only factor that significantly affected changes in state and local per capita spending. They concluded that "the generally diminished ability of Fabricant's three standard variables to explain variations in the level of per capita state and local expenditures is primarily due to the increasing importance of federal aid as a determinant of state and local spending."[52]

Bernard Booms studied the effects of state aid on cities with populations between 25,000 and 100,000 in Ohio and Michigan and reached some surprising conclusions.[53] He noted that the effect of state aid in Ohio is substantially different from the effect in Michigan. In Ohio he found aid to be both stimulative and substitutive while in Michigan it appeared that state aid was purely stimulative.

Jack Osman used two classes of federal aid variables--per capita aid to the function under study and per capita aid to all other functions when examining the impact of federal grants on lower units of government.[54] He concluded that federal aid was stimulative of those functions to which it was directed and was not merely substitutive. He attempted to measure the stimulatory effects of federal aid to six common functions (that is, highways, health and hospitals, local schools, etc.) and found that per capita expenditures for a given function would rise with both increases in per capita federal aid to the particular function under study and with increases in per capita aid to all other functions.[55] Wallace Oates, however, is critical of Osman's study on methodological grounds--"the econometric problems inherent in Osman's study are such that we cannot place much credibility in his results."[56]

L. R. Gabler and Joel Brest raise a serious methodological question.[57] They note a tendency to "double-count" the aid money. Since federal grant programs require matching funds, every dollar of federal aid will represent a fixed fraction of the resultant expenditure. Thus some portion of total state and local expenditure for a given function will correlate perfectly with federal matching funds. This is likely to exaggerate the overall statistical association between the expenditures for the given function and federal grants for that function.

Edward Gramlich developed a time series statistical model designed to compare the effects of several alternative policies that might influence total state and local expenditures.[58] Table 1.4 shows his computed responses to a hypothetical billion dollar federal policy action. He finds that there is little doubt that matching grants, even though accompanied by a substitution effect, are an effective means of stimulating state and local expenditures. The performance of the block grants in the model, especially the unconditional block grant, was rather disappointing. If block grants were offered with no federal strings attached, they increased expenditures by less than 30 percent of the grant.

TABLE 1.4

State and Local Expenditure Response to a Hypothetical
Billion Dollar Policy Action, Ranked by Potency

Policy Action		Expenditure Response (billions)
1. Open market purchase (monetary policy)		1.36
2. Matching grant-in-aid		1.21
3. Block grant that has to be spent		1.00
4. Income tax credit	tie	.55
5. Block grant with tax effort formula		.55
6. Unconditional block grant		.28
7. Federal income tax cut		.05

Source: Edward M. Gramlich, "Alternative Federal Policies for Stimulating State and Local Expenditures: A Comparison of Their Effects," National Tax Journal 21 (June 1968): 128.

In a later article Gramlich affirmed his earlier findings.[59] He notes the weakness of unconditional grants as stimulators of state spending. He thus speculates that the various conditions that may be attached to federal grants, matching requirements or effort formulas, appear to be most essential in insuring that grants are stimulative of state and local spending.

David Smith examined the "skewing" or distortion issue.[60] Smith demonstrated that the distortion thesis is based upon the assumption that demand for the aided function is price elastic and that skewing could not occur where the demand for the aided function or service is price inelastic. He found that lower-level governments respond to grants with increased spending. Spending increases cover not only the aided functions but also the unaided. Grants, then, subsidize a wide range of government activities--well beyond the aided function. Smith's conclusions are substantially the same as Osman's.

James Wilde substantiated the work of Gramlich.[61] He developed a basic model designed to analyze how grant-in-aid programs might be expected to influence the expenditure level of the recipient governments. He concluded that only specific matching grants can be expected to increase expenditures by more than the amount of aid given.

Finally, Thomas O'Brien found that federal grants are stimulative of the function being aided but that expenditures for unaided functions are reduced.[62] The overall effect, however, has been stimulative when examining total state and local expenditures. O'Brien used a simultaneous equation approach to test the relationship between grants and state and local expenditures and concluded that grants and expenditures are not simultaneously determined. Grants then, he concludes, are exogenous variables in the determination of expenditures. His estimates "show that federal grants have stimulated state-local government expenditures from own funds on aided categories and have caused a reallocation of expenditures on other categories."[63]

Thus the literature concerned with the aggregate analysis of grant effects is mixed. It is difficult to draw any definite conclusions from a review of the literature, but it is possible to note certain trends. First, the literature does suggest some skewing of budgets, but this does not appear to be either substantial or significant. As in Philadelphia, federal grants to cities are probably far more likely to effect capital accounts and bonded debt rather than a city's operating budget.

Second, most studies attribute some stimulative effect to federal matching grants. The only question here appears to be one of degree. Unconditional block grants are not considered stimulative to any substantial degree, but such is not the case with the matching grant. Matching grants, either project or formula, are found to be highly stimulative--especially with regard to the aided function. The literature is not clear concerning the unaided functions. Some studies empirically show that grants have a stimulative effect on unaided as well as aided functions while others show that there is no stimulative effect on the unaided functions.

Closely tied to the issue of stimulation toward unaided functions is the issue of substitution. Again, findings are mixed. Some studies report a clear substitution effect while others report that substitution does not occur, or that the effect is so small as to be negligible. Some substitution undoubtedly does occur but it is extremely difficult to determine empirically. Such studies must be done over time and probably by a combined mathematician/seer. Not only quantitative analysis is needed but the researcher must predict what a unit's expenditure pattern would have been like had the unit not used the grant--a highly improbable task.

NOTES

1. Sophie R. Dales, "Federal Grants to State and Local Governments, 1967-68," Social Security Bulletin 32, no. 8 (August 1969): 21.
2. Ibid., pp. 21-22.
3. James A. Maxwell, Financing State and Local Governments, rev. ed. (Washington, D.C.: Brookings Institution, 1969), p. 52.
4. Advisory Commission on Intergovernmental Relations, Fiscal Balance in the American Federal System, vol. 1 (2 vols.; Washington, D.C.: Government Printing Office, 1967), p. 138.
5. Ibid., p. 139. See also Maxwell, Financing State and Local Governments, p. 52.
6. Advisory Commission, Fiscal Balance, p. 139.
7. Maxwell, Financing State and Local Governments, p. 54.
8. Advisory Commission, Fiscal Balance, p. 139.
9. Deil S. Wright, Federal Grants-In-Aid: Perspectives and Alternatives (Washington, D.C.: American Enterprise Institute for Public Policy Research, 1968), pp. 64-65; and F. Ted Hebert and Richard D. Bingham, Personal and Environmental Influences upon the City Manager's Knowledge of Federal Grant-In-Aid Programs (Norman: Bureau of Government Research, University of Oklahoma, 1972), p. 1.
10. John Kenneth Galbraith, The Affluent Society (New York: New American Library, 1958), pp. 206-7.
11. Advisory Commission, Fiscal Balance, p. 150.
12. U.S. Office of Economic Opportunity, Catalog of Federal Domestic Assistance (Washington, D.C.: Government Printing Office, 1970).
13. Advisory Commission, Fiscal Balance, pp. 164-65.
14. Ibid., p. 165.
15. Maxwell, Financing State and Local Governments, pp. 55-56.
16. Richard H. Leach, American Federalism (New York: Norton, 1970), pp. 135 and 150.
17. Terry Sanford, Storm Over the States (New York: McGraw-Hill, 1967), p. 24.
18. Maxwell, Financing State and Local Governments, p. 56.
19. Advisory Commission, Fiscal Balance, pp. 153-54.
20. Ibid., p. 138.
21. As of 1972, all states had passed the necessary enabling legislation so that their local governments could participate in the housing program.
22. Advisory Commission, Fiscal Balance, p. 138.
23. Ibid.
24. Selma J. Mushkin and John F. Cotton, Sharing Federal Funds for State and Local Needs (New York: Praeger, 1969), p. 33.
25. Ibid., pp. 34-35.

26. Ibid., pp. 24-30.

27. Ibid., p. 25.

28. Solomon Fabricant, The Trend of Government Activity in the United States Since 1900 (New York: National Bureau of Economic Research, 1952).

29. Richard E. Dawson and James A. Robinson, "Inter-Party Competition, Economic Variables, and Welfare Policies in the American States," Journal of Politics 25 (May 1963): 265-89.

30. David R. Morgan, Handbook of State Policy Indicators (Norman: Bureau of Government Research, University of Oklahoma, 1971), p. 2.

31. Ibid.

32. David Easton, A Framework for Political Analysis (Englewood Cliffs, N.J.: Prentice-Hall, 1965); and David Easton, A Systems Analysis of Political Life (New York: John Wiley, 1965).

33. Thomas R. Dye, Politics, Economics, and the Public: Policy Outcomes in the American States (Chicago: Rand McNally, 1966).

34. Ibid., p. 296.

35. David R. Morgan and Samuel A. Kirkpatrick, eds., Urban Political Analysis: A Systems Approach (New York: The Free Press, 1972), pp. 9-11.

36. Brett W. Hawkins, Politics and Urban Policies (Indianapolis: Bobbs-Merrill, 1971), p. 11.

37. For a discussion of feedback, see Edmund P. Fowler and Robert L. Lineberry, "Patterns of Feedback in City Politics," in Morgan and Kirkpatrick, Urban Political Analysis, pp. 361-367.

38. Morley Segal and A. Lee Fritschler, "Emerging Patterns of Intergovernmental Relations," in The Municipal Year Book 1970 (Washington, D.C.: International City Management Association, 1970), pp. 13-38.

39. Advisory Commission, Fiscal Balance, p. 12.

40. Segal and Fritschler, "Emerging Patterns," p. 17.

41. Ibid., pp. 17-18.

42. Advisory Commission, Fiscal Balance, p. 12.

43. F. Ted Hebert and Richard D. Bingham, "The City Manager's Knowledge of Grants-In-Aid: Some Personal and Environmental Influences," Urban Affairs Quarterly 7 (March 1972): 303-6; and Hebert and Bingham, Personal and Environmental Influences.

44. Advisory Commission, Fiscal Balance, p. 160.

45. A good background discussion of the three financial effects may be found in Deil S. Wright, "The States and Intergovernmental Relations," Publius 1 (Winter 1972): 15-18.

46. Mushkin and Cotton, Sharing Federal Funds, pp. 94-95.

47. W. H. Brown, Jr. and C. E. Gilbert, Planning Municipal Investment: A Case Study of Philadelphia (Philadelphia: University of Pennsylvania Press, 1961), p. 270.

48. Seymour Sacks and Robert Harris, "The Determinants of State and Local Government Expenditures and Intergovernmental Flow of Funds," National Tax Journal 17 (March 1964): 75-85.

49. Ibid., p. 85.

50. George A. Bishop, "Stimulative Versus Substitutive Effects of State School Aid in New England," National Tax Journal 17 (June 1964): 133-43.

51. Roy W. Bahl, Jr. and Robert J. Saunders, "Determinants of Changes in State and Local Government Expenditures," National Tax Journal 18 (March 1965): 50-57.

52. Ibid.

53. Bernard H. Booms, "City Governmental Form and Public Expenditure Levels," National Tax Journal 19 (June 1966): 187-99.

54. Jack W. Osman, "The Dual Impact of Federal Aid on State and Local Government Expenditures," National Tax Journal 19 (December 1966): 362-73.

55. Ibid.

56. Wallace E. Oates, "The Dual Impact of Federal Aid on State and Local Government Expenditures: A Comment," National Tax Journal 21 (June 1968): 220-23.

57. L. R. Gabler and Joel I. Brest, "Interstate Variations in Per Capita Highway Expenditures," National Tax Journal 20 (March 1967): 78-85.

58. Edward M. Gramlich, "Alternative Federal Policies for Stimulating State and Local Expenditures: A Comparison of Their Effects," National Tax Journal 21 (June 1968): 119-29.

59. Edward M. Gramlich, "A Clarification and A Correction," National Tax Journal 22 (June 1969): 286-90.

60. David L. Smith, "The Response of State and Local Governments to Federal Grants," National Tax Journal 21 (September 1968): 349-57.

61. James A. Wilde, "The Expenditure Effects of Grant-In-Aid Programs," National Tax Journal 21 (September 1968): 340-47.

62. Thomas O'Brien, "Grants-In-Aid: Some Further Answers," National Tax Journal 24 (March 1971): 65-77.

63. Ibid., p. 70.

2

Although the studies reviewed earlier provide a basis for the analysis of federal grants to local governments, the limitations of aggregative analysis are readily apparent. This approach has not been helpful in determining patterns of grant use or in attempting to identify characteristics that might stimulate a local government to take advantage of federal offerings. Furthermore, the aggregative approach only scratches the surface of the entire area of grant effects since the approach is primarily concerned with the fiscal effects of grants on recipient government units. Economist David Smith, author of a number of such aggregative studies, recognizes the need to change approaches:

> In the end, it may be that the usefulness of aggregative studies of state and local spending has been maximized or even pushed to the point of diminishing returns, and the time has come for disaggregative studies of state-local behavior. In particular, I think that attention should be devoted to detailed analysis of the relative valuation of various public goods and to the response of state and local governments to specific grant programs.[1]

Unfortunately, most of the analyses of grant programs have taken the form of case studies. Brett Hawkins notes the plentiful supply of descriptive studies of state and federal grants to local governments and the laws governing their use.[2] He complains that a major weakness in the available literature is the lack of attempts to assess the impact of grants on local governments. Hawkins finds that little of the research is guided by a theoretical perspective, almost none involves systematic comparison of one community with another, and very few are quantitative in nature.

Lee Fritschler and Morley Segal note the movement to apply advanced methodological and analytical techniques to most of the subfields of political science.[3] They lament, however, the lack of professional attention given to intergovernmental relations. They refer to intergovernmental relations as "a kind of methodological Cinderella after midnight."[4]

This study will utilize a disaggregative approach to explore two fundamental questions pertaining to federal grants to local governments. First, why do some cities make extensive use of federal grants while other cities virtually ignore them? Second, what impact have these grants actually had on cities?

SELECTION OF THE GRANT PROGRAMS

The first task in developing the analytic framework for grant study was the selection of the specific grant programs to be analyzed. A number of criteria were used in the selection process. The first might be considered obvious: Since this study is concerned with "direct federalism" or federal-local relations, only grants made directly to local units of government with a minimum of state interference were considered. Secondly, and closely related, only project grants requiring application were considered. In order to study patterns of grant use, grants distributed automatically on a formula basis have not been included. Thirdly, grant history was considered in selection. The grant programs had to have been in existence long enough (theoretically at least) to have had a measurable impact. Closely related is the fourth criterion: The grants must have a history of appropriations that are large enough over time to have been capable of producing change and to have been utilized by a reasonable number of cities. The grants were also limited to those with a physical impact. Many of today's grants can only be judged on a "cases treated" basis--people seen, workers trained, etc., but the actual effects of the grants are never known. Leonard Goodwin, for example, makes a good case against the federal government's Work Incentive Program when he examines the job success of the graduates rather than figures concerning "people trained."[5] Thus, the programs selected for analysis here are those with a measurable physical impact. The sixth criterion relates closely to the fourth: Programs selected must be well known and they must present a real alternative to city governments. If it is unlikely that city officials are aware of the grants under study, findings concerning patterns of use might be unreliable or misleading. The final criterion is one of very

practical consideration--data availability. It would be foolish to select grant programs for analysis only to discover that data were not
available on a city-by-city basis. Data compiled only by SMSAs, for
example, would have little practical use in this study. Since the
study deals with effects and changes over time (insofar as possible),
data must also be available for the entire period under study, not
just a portion of it. Recordkeeping in some reasonably accessible
format is a new development with many federal agencies--a development that may be the only lasting contribution of planning-programming-
budgeting system (PPBS).[6]

Only two programs were found to satisfy adequately all of the
aforementioned criteria: public housing and urban renewal. Even
these programs will be limited. The study of public housing is confined only to the construction and occupation of low-income public
housing units by local housing authorities. Not included are programs
such as the 202 and 221(d)(3) Below Market Interest Rate programs,
Rent Supplement programs, or FHA 235 or 236 subsidy programs.
A wide range of urban renewal programs have been selected for analysis. The programs included are: (1) community renewal programs,
(2) urban renewal projects, (3) code enforcement projects, (4) demolition projects, (5) neighborhood development programs, (6) interim
assistance programs, (7) certified area programs, and (8) demonstration programs. The nature of each of these programs will be
examined later in this chapter.

HISTORY

Low-income public housing was born in the depression of the
1930s. In 1933 the Public Works Administration (PWA), established
by the National Industrial Recovery Act to administer public works
projects, constructed some 21,600 units of housing. The PWA Housing Division was authorized to lend money to limited-dividend corpo-
rations involved in slum clearance or construction of low-income
housing and to buy, condemn, sell, or lease property while developing new projects itself. The PWA program met with limited success. The limited-dividend projects succeeded primarily as a
vehicle by which real estate agents unloaded property at excessive
valuation on the government. A 1935 federal court ruling deprived
the Housing Division of condemnation power, which severely weak-
ened the program. And finally, many of the projects that were constructed under the act were too expensive for the poor or the working class to afford. Despite the failures, the PWA projects set a
precedent for future policy.[7]

Low-rent public housing as we know it today began with the
United States Housing Act of 1937.[8]

An act to provide financial assistance to the states
and political subdivisions thereof for the elimination of unsafe and unsanitary housing conditions,
for the eradication of slums, for the provision of
decent, safe, and sanitary dwellings for families
of low income, and for the reduction of unemployment and the stimulation of business activity,
to create a United States Housing Authority, and
for other purposes.[9]

Public housing, then, was a program of multiple goals. Not
only designed to provide "decent, safe, and sanitary dwellings" for
low-income families, the public housing program was designed to
aid unemployment and to stimulate business.

The public housing program places the responsibility for design, development, and project management on local government.
These functions are generally performed by an independent local
government agency called a housing authority. The governing officers are usually appointed by the chief elective officer of the city;
however, the city countil may, and sometimes does, appoint itself
as the local housing authority. To receive federal assistance, the
local authority must have the approval of both the local government
and the Department of Housing and Urban Development (HUD). A
wide variety of state laws lay down even more stringent require-
ments--some, for example, require local government approval of
specific sites. The cost of housing authority project development is
financed by issuance and sale of long-term, tax-exempt bonds while
rents in public housing are lowered through a number of subsidies.
The federal government annually contributes an amount equal to the
debt retirement costs. Over and above this, the government pays a
subsidy to the local authority for each of the elderly, disabled, and
poor that it houses. Finally, authority property is tax-exempt--in-
stead of the normal real estate taxes on real property, authorities
pay a much lower payment in lieu of taxes.[10] Operating expenses
for the authority are paid by rental income plus the applicable subsidies mentioned above.

The next major change in the housing program was contained
in the Housing Act of 1949, some twelve years after the original act;
but the public housing sections of the act were little changed. The
provisions for loans and subsidies remained the same as in the 1937
act but with 135,000 new housing structures authorized per year for
the next six years. The president was also empowered to increase
or reduce this figure (within specified limits) upon the recommendations of his Council of Economic Advisors. The unique feature of
the 1949 act was Title I.[11] Title I provided for slum clearance and

a redevelopment program that has since evolved into the present-day
urban renewal program. It became the responsibility of local governments to clear slums and blighted areas and to provide land for
private enterprise to construct residential, commercial, or industrial facilities on the renewed land. Title I authorized loans to cities
to plan for the redevelopment of blighted areas. A city would complete the planning for the redevelopment of an area and submit the
plans to the federal government for approval. Once the project was
approved, the city would purchase the land, clear it, develop it according to the approved plan (that is, streets, etc.), and sell the
land to a private developer--at a price usually substantially less than
acquisition and clearance costs. Two-thirds of the difference between
what the city paid the the price received for the land was paid for by
a federal grant with the remaining one-third of the cost being borne
by the city. Bellush and Hausknecht note that

> there is apparent in the law a not-too-subtle shift
> to concern with private enterprise rather than the
> very real housing need of the society. Thus,
> Title I helps clear slums by helping private en-
> trepreneurs, but Title I does nothing about the
> reverse side of the coin--standard housing for
> the displaced slum dweller. In 1937, public hous-
> ing was seen, in part at least, as a means of allevi-
> ating the distress of the slum dweller. In 1949
> such housing is seen as a prerequisite for private
> redevelopment projects; that is, public housing
> is justified to a larger extent for those displaced
> by private projects who cannot find housing at
> rents they can afford. In sum, the emphasis
> shifts from the social and economic situation
> of the slum resident to the needs of private
> enterprise. [12]

The Housing Act of 1954 added a new dimension to both public
housing and urban renewal. It required that communities develop
a "workable program" before they could become eligible for assistance under the public housing, urban renewal, and later the 221(d)(3)
programs. [13]

> The workable program shall include an official
> plan of action, as it exists from time to time,
> for effectively dealing with the problem of urban
> slums and blight within the community and for
> the establishment and preservation of a well-

planned community with well-organized residential neighborhoods of decent homes and suitable living environment for adequate family life.[14]

The workable program requirement thus forced the community to plan, and to integrate renewal and public housing into the plan, for community development. The workable programs required master planning, zoning, fire standards, and the adoption of building codes and ordinances.

The Housing Act of 1959 foretold another major trend in low-income housing. Section 202 of the act authorized direct loans from the federal government to nonprofit sponsors of rental housing for the elderly and the handicapped.[15] These loans were originally at a rate based on the interest on outstanding federal debt, but this rate was later limited to a maximum of 3 percent. The significance of Section 202 was the fact that it recognized the need for a housing program for those families whose incomes were marginally above the eligibility for public housing. Secondly, this was the first housing program where Congress authorized direct loans at a below market interest rate to a private corporation--albeit a nonprofit private corporation; thus, the stage was set for the next major change in housing policy--the Housing Act of 1961.

The Act of 1961 provided for a program commonly referred to as 221(d)(3), after the applicable section of the 1961 act. Section 221 was "designed to assist private industry in providing housing for low- and moderate-income families and families displaced from urban renewal areas or as a result of governmental action."[16]

The 221(d)(3) Below Market Interest Rate (BMIR) program greatly increased the opportunity for private development and investment in low-income housing. The program authorized the FNMA (Federal National Mortgage Association--commonly referred to as Fannie May) to purchase mortgage loans made to limited-dividend profit-making organizations as well as to nonprofit organizations. Calculation of the interest rate was based on the interest rates on outstanding federal debt as with Section 202 housing. By 1965 the interest on the federal debt had risen to over 4 percent. The Housing Act of 1965 therefore pegged the below market interest rate at a maximum of 3 percent. This rate applied to both 202 and 221(d)(3) housing. Both programs, then, enjoyed a direct federal subsidy since the Treasury ultimately made up the difference between the federal borrowing rate and the 3 percent ceiling.[17] The Act of 1965 also introduced several other innovations into low-income housing, one of which, the rent supplements program, was extremely controversial.[18] The supplement program provided direct payment to private nonprofit or limited-dividend organizations housing low-income tenants. Under the law, the tenant was required to pay one-fourth of his income as rent, and the federal government made up the difference between this amount and the actual unit rental. Eligibility for the program was restricted to the elderly, the handicapped, families displaced by urban renewal, other government action or natural disaster, and occupants of substandard housing. The program had several substantial advantages. First, the amount of the subsidy was related to a tenant's need; and second, housing costs to the federal government were spread over a lengthy period of time. The implications of this program were clear--it fostered economic as well as racial integration. The program, however, was given congressional approval only by a slim margin and has since been restricted in a number of ways. First, appropriations have been limited. Second, congressional pressure forced HUD to impose regulations on the program that have made its use increasingly limited. Limits on construction costs and maximum rents, for example, have almost restricted application of the program to the South and certain areas of the Southwest. Limitations on amenities allowed in rent supplement projects have been so severe that developers find it difficult to rent to nonsupplement tenants. Builders now assume that 90 percent or more of the supplement project tenants will receive supplements. These pressures have essentially destroyed the original goal of the program--economic integration within projects as well as cities. [19]

The other new technique provided by the 1965 Act was the Section 23 Leased Housing program. [20] Under this section, public housing agencies were encouraged to the maximum extent possible to take advantage of vacancies in the private housing market by leasing privately owned housing and then utilizing these dwellings for public housing. This program also served to foster both economic and racial integration in the community but did not meet with the congressional resistance that the rent supplement program received. The major limitation to Section 23 housing is the restriction that the annual contribution for housing under the act cannot exceed the amount of the contribution that would have been established had the authority constructed a new project of the same number of units. In effect, this forces the authority to absorb the higher maintenance costs connected with scattered sites. This has been one of the limiting factors in application of the Section 23 program.

The Housing Act of 1968 continued the movement toward subsidized housing. Section 235 provides a subsidy to allow low-income families to purchase their own homes, and Section 236 provides for a new rental program for those just above public housing incomes. [21] Under the home ownership program (235), the federal government pays part of the buyer's mortgage payment. The government subsidy may reduce the purchaser's payment to that which he would pay if his mortgage loan were financed at a 1 percent interest rate. There are restrictions, however. Each family must devote a minimum of 20 percent of its income to paying off the mortgage. As family income rises, the family assumes a larger share of the payment, and the subsidy payment is reduced. This may continue until family income reaches a level where there is no longer a subsidy payment. This program provides modest but adequate housing for those families with incomes of approximately $3,000 to $7,000 (depending on family size). Downpayments are very low--in no case more than 3 percent of the value of the house.[22]

The Section 236 program was designed to replace the 202 and 221(d)(3) programs. In many respects it is similar to the rent supplement program in that it relies on private developers and provides subsidy payments. A tenant in a 236 project will pay 25 percent of his income toward rent, and the federal government will make up the difference. The maximum federal payment on a unit is the difference between the actual payment on the project mortgage and the figure that would have been paid had the project been financed with a 1 percent mortgage. The maximum subsidy for a family will run about $50 to $60. To be eligible for 236 housing, a family's income must not exceed 135 percent of the limits for admission to public housing. The 236 program thus fails to reach very poor families, but it does provide a deeper subsidy than those available under either Section 202 or Section 221(d)(3).[23]

Urban renewal goals are not as easy to identify as are the goals of the housing provisions. The effects of renewal are complex and varied, with many effects being unintended. Since the Housing Act does not deliniate specific goals for renewal, goals are thus implicit in the intended consequences. Jerome Rothenberg lists three goals that he finds important in the case of residential redevelopment: (1) elimination of slums, (2) enhancement of the economic viability of the central city, and (3) subsidization of central city financial resources.[24]

The program that is commonly known as the Urban Renewal program, or Title 1 of the Housing Act of 1949, permitted land cleared with the aid of federal funds to be sold or leased to private developers for residential development.[25] The Housing Act of 1954, besides requiring the workable program, established the concept of rehabilitation by recognizing the need to retain and improve existing sound structures within the urban framework. In addition, the act broadened the program by recognizing the need to attack decay and blight in commercial and industrial areas as well as in residential districts. Initially, 10 percent of all renewal funds could be used for nonresidential renewal; but that figure has subsequently been increased to 35 percent. A research orientation was also added with the Act of 1954 with a provision for a demonstration grant program.

The Housing Act of 1959 created the Community Renewal Program. This program provides federal financial assistance for a comprehensive long-range program for the community's renewal, both public and private.

The 1965 Act extended federal aid for concentrated code enforcement projects to reverse the deterioration process and provided grants for the demolition of buildings determined to be a public hazard.

And finally, the Housing Act of 1968 authorized grants for neighborhood development programs--urban renewal projects of various types that are carried out on the basis of annual increments. Financing is thus on a year-by-year basis. The act also set up an interim assistance program to provide interim assistance for slums or blighted areas scheduled for renewal but where some immediate public action was necessary. The other significant feature of the act was the initiation of the certified area program to rehabilitate residential structures within areas planned for future urban renewal or concentrated code enforcement projects.[26]

For cities with a population of 50,000 or more, federal renewal grants covered up to two-thirds of the net project costs for urban renewal projects, neighborhood development programs, code enforcement projects, demolition projects, interim assistance, and community renewal programs. Grants could also cover up to nine-tenths of the cost of demonstration projects; they also covered the full cost of writing and publishing the reports of the findings. In addition, relocation payments to businesses and families dislocated by any of the above renewal programs were covered by 100 percent grants. This included payment for moving, property loss, certain relocation adjustment payments, and grants to owner-occupants of residences to assist in the purchase of replacement homes. The full amount of rehabilitation grants to individual property owners to cover the cost of repairs and improvements to structures in renewal areas was also borne by the federal government.[27]

Progress in the housing and renewal areas ground to a slow halt with the election of Richard M. Nixon in 1968. No major housing or renewal legislation was enacted until President Ford signed S8066, the Omnibus Housing Bill (the Housing and Community Development Act of 1974), into law in August 1974.[28] The bill was largely a compromise between the Nixon administration and the Democratically controlled Congress. President Nixon was concerned about two aspects of the low-income housing program--a concern that led him to clamp a moratorium on the construction of public housing units. First, he was concerned about the physical aspects of public housing projects: "I have seen a number of our public housing projects. Some of them are impressive, but too many are monstrous, depressing places--run down, overcrowded, crime-ridden, falling apart."[29] Using the Pruitt-Igoe project in St. Louis as an example, Nixon declared that "the Federal Government has become the biggest slumlord in history."[30]

Nixon's second concern was with rapidly increasing subsidy payments for low-income housing. He complained that it cost the government between 15 and 40 percent more to provide housing for people than for people to acquire the same quality housing themselves on the private market.[31] Thus the Nixon plan proposed a new approach--that of direct cash assistance. Under this approach, instead of providing housing directly, the federal government would provide qualified recipients with an appropriate housing payment and would allow them to choose their homes based upon the housing available in the private market.

The Omnibus Housing Bill did not achieve all of the Nixon objectives in either housing or renewal but it did provide a sharp shift from the categorical grant mechanism through which activities such as urban renewal were dispensed.[32] The new approach relies heavily on the block grant with $8.6 billion authorized for community development programs consolidating 10 categorical urban development programs. Entitlement is automatic--determined by a formula reflecting a community's population, poverty, and extent of housing overcrowding. Communities may use their grants for

> (1) general acquisition of land for public purposes, (2) construction or improvement of public works facilities, neighborhood facilities, senior centers, water and sewer facilities, parks and recreation facilities, flood and drainage facilities, street lights, parking facilities, solid waste disposal facilities and fire protection facilities, (3) housing code enforcement, (4) slum clearance and renewal, (5) historic preservation, (6) relocation payments to individuals displaced by slum, (7) planning and other activities. . . .[33]

In addition, the bill expanded the Section 23 rental leasing subsidy program to provide an additional 400,000 units of subsidized housing and it provided funds for the development of about 40,000 new units of conventional public housing. The bill also provided new commitments for the Section 235 and Section 236 programs.[34] Nowhere in the bill, however, was the direct cash assistance program proposed by the Administration.

ANALYTIC FRAMEWORK

A review of the literature dealing with public housing and urban renewal suggests the theoretical model presented in Figure 2.1. The model hypothesizes that certain city characteristics (physical, socio-economic, etc.) generate pressures that operate on a given political environment (the intervening variables) to produce decisions concerning the use of federal low-income housing and urban renewal programs. The results of these decisions concerning program use substantially alter the environment, which, in turn, alters the character of the city profile and the political environment. The model thus assumes a continuous process over time whereby the effects of political decisions are continually modifying the profile and the political environment that produces the decisions. The analysis of housing and renewal presented in this study covers a time frame of 10 years, from 1960 to 1970. The city profiles were constructed from 1960 data (t_1). The political environment includes variables that existed in 1960 as well as indicators (for example, voting) between 1960 and 1970 (t_2). In the aggregate, then, the exact time frame for t_2 is not certain; t_2 represents some average time between 1960 and 1970. Housing and renewal decisions are summarized for the entire period 1960 through 1970 and are represented by the total t_1 through t_3 ($t_1 - t_3$). The decisional effects are thus measured at 1970 and are represented by t_3. While this representation is simplistic at best and attempts to put artificial time constraints on what is really an ongoing process, the model should provide the time differential for the required temporal ordering.

DETERMINANTS OF GRANT USE

The first task of grant analysis is an investigation into the patterns of use of urban renewal grants and public housing construction. The study attempts to isolate the variables within the community that are significantly related to the use of the public housing and urban renewal programs. The Segal-Fritschler study of grant use discussed in Chapter 1 found that grant use was related to city size.[35] There is no reason to believe that urban renewal and public housing grants do not fit this general pattern.

Amos Hawley investigated the relationship between highly centralized city power structures and urban renewal expenditures.[36] He hypothesized that cities with a high concentration of the power function (as measured by a ratio of managers, proprietors, and officials to the employed labor force) would show a greater success in urban renewal endeavors than those with a diffuse power structure.

FIGURE 2.1

A Model of the Urban Political System

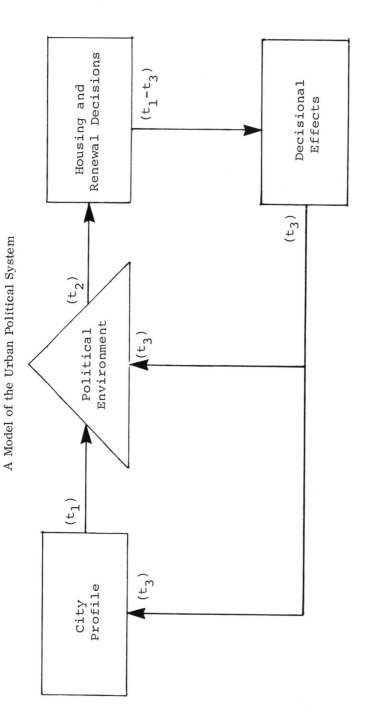

He found that his hypothesis was essentially correct--that power was highly concentrated in execution-stage cities and was most diffuse in those cities not attempting renewal. Hawley introduced extensive controls for such factors as metropolitan status, type of government, region, and a number of socioeconomic measures and found that power was related to urban renewal success under virtually all conditions of control.

Terry Clark's study of 51 U.S. communities produced findings that were substantially at odds with Hawley's results.[37] He found that a zero order correlation of .35 existed between his measure of decentralized decision-making structure and urban renewal expenditures. Clark, however, does not necessarily consider his work to be in conflict with Hawley's. He defines urban renewal as a "fragile issue," or a new issue. Hawley studied renewal during the 1950s when the program was new and subject to the stresses of new programs. Clark believes that the issue has matured since Hawley's investigation, and thus the relationship between renewal and power changed from centralized to diffuse. In any event, he found that urban renewal expenditures were positively related to a decentralized decision-making structure.

Michael Aiken and Robert Alford analyzed urban renewal programs in the 582 U.S. cities with 1960 populations over 25,000.[38] They used measures of urban renewal as indicators of community innovation. The presence of innovation was measured by the presence of an urban renewal program, the speed of innovation by the number of years after 1949 before entering the urban renewal program, and by the number of years it took to establish a local agency after state enabling legislation was present, and the level of output by the number of dollars reserved per capita. Aiken and Alford correlated a variety of community characteristics with these variables and found a substantial but negative correlation between renewal expenditures and family income and measures commonly associated with government reform. They also found a positive relationship with unemployment, city size, substandard housing, and non-white population. They noted that middle-class cities have less urban renewal than do highly ethnic larger cities. The authors concluded that older and larger cities, those with high unemployment, low levels of education and income, and a slow growth rate are the most innovative. Also of interest was the use of an electoral variable--percent voting Democratic in the 1964 presidential election--as an attempt to isolate the presence of a population holding private-regarding values.[39] A low positive correlation (.08) was noted between this variable and the number of dollars reserved per capita for urban renewal.

Aiken and Alford conducted a comparable study concerning public housing.[40] Using a methodology similar to their renewal study, they measured the presence of innovation by the presence of a public housing program, the speed of innovation by the number of years after 1933 before construction began on the first housing project as well as the number of years it took after state enabling legislation was present, and the level of output by the number of public housing units constructed per 100,000 population. The same independent variables were used to represent political culture, community power, and community differentiation as were used in the renewal study. The findings were also very similar--that is, there was the substantial and negative correlation between housing construction and family income and with government reform measures. Again, as with renewal, a significant and positive relationship was noted between housing and unemployment, city size, substandard housing, and nonwhite population. One might thus suspect that there is a positive relationship between housing construction and renewal expenditures.

The aforementioned quantitative studies have been in a distinct minority when examining renewal and housing literature. Most studies of urban renewal have utilized the case studies approach,[41] while housing has been approached from a sociological perspective.[42]

Many of the case studies emphasize the role of the executive director of the renewal agency as a new breed of "entrepreneur."[43] The role of the renewal entrepreneur is characterized by three elements: First, he supplies the money (through grants); second, he manages the organization; and third, he provides the necessary link between the public and private sectors.[44] Louis Danzig of Newark, Edward Logue of New Haven and Boston, and Robert Moses of New York are oft-cited examples of successful renewal entrepreneurs.[45]

A number of case studies also underscore the important role citizen organizations have had in the urban renewal process. Renewal in Pittsburgh provides an excellent illustration of the impact and influence of citizen organizations.[46] The impetus to the redevelopment in Pittsburgh, as well as the character of that redevelopment, was substantially different from cities with the spark for development provided by renewal entrepreneurs. The power behind renewal in Pittsburgh was a coalition between the Mellon-sponsored Allegheny Conference on Community Development, a group of industrial and business leaders, and the Democratic administration of Mayor David L. Lawrence. The redevelopment brought about by this coalition had a distinct flavor--an orientation toward slum clearance for downtown commercial revitalization and land assembly for industrial expansion. Lacking was any substantial program to deal with slum housing or programs to halt the spread of blight in residential areas. Since the orientation of the powers behind Pittsburgh's renewal was to the business world, it comes as no surprise to find that the city's renewal efforts reflected this orientation. The decay and stagnation of the business climate in Pittsburgh shaped the redevelopment efforts of the city. While commercial expansion and renewal undoubtedly helped the city, the orientation of the power structure guided redevelopment along a narrow plane and tended to ignore many pressing city problems.

The force behind the renewal efforts in Philadelphia was strikingly similar to Pittsburgh but on a much broader basis.[47] Philadelphia borrowed Pittsburgh's formula--the combination of public and private powers--but in Philadelphia

> the combination is more intricately orchestrated
> and multilayered, more democratic and diverse.
> The new direction was not imposed from the top;
> it emerged from many sources, and progress
> has been infused with the critical viewpoints and
> talents of middle-class civic leaders, university
> professors, urban designers, political adminis-
> trators, as well as the dynamic leadership of
> city hall and top business.[48]

The best-known political folk hero of the renewal process is undoubtedly Richard C. Lee of New Haven.[49] He was one of the first mayors in the country to make urban renewal the cornerstone of his administration. New Haven's program is often cited as a model for renewal for the rest of the nation. Lee strongly identified himself with urban renewal, spent countless hours interpreting the program to the people and basing his election campaigns on the redevelopment program.

A review of the urban renewal case studies has shown the importance of some diverse political elements affecting the scope and character of the local urban renewal programs. The case studies seem to show the emergence of three distinct groups or bodies that are influential in the renewal process: (1) renewal entrepreneurs, (2) civic groups (generally business-oriented), and (3) political leaders. Apparently one or some combination of one or more of these characters is necessary for large-scale programs.

The Oakland Task Force found the location of federal offices to be an important variable in a city's grant success.[50] They noted that cities that are located close to an agency's regional headquarters have fewer problems with intergovernmental communications than do cities not as favorably situated. They also found that agencies located in Oakland itself seemed to have a clearer view of the city's problems and appeared to give the city a higher priority for grants.

Finally, community attitudes appear to play a major part in determining the community's pattern of grant uses.[51] Warren,

Michigan, a Detroit suburb, recently conducted a referendum that
would repeal the city's urban renewal program--a program designed
to refurbish older residential areas. The issue was somewhat mud-
dled with concerns over federal "strings" that were perceived as
threats to Warren's way of life. One of these strings was

> a demonstration of "affirmative" action toward
> integration, and thus, one vote here is often
> interpreted as a clear-cut referendum on the
> white workingman's feelings about integration.
> Indeed, 17 percent of the voters here cast their
> ballots for George Wallace in the 1968 Presi-
> dential election, which suggests that there is
> some racism here.[52]

When HUD Secretary Romney visited Warren to talk to Warren
officials, he was hooted and jeered by 300 to 400 angry demonstrators. These same demonstrators then cheered the avowed segrega-
tionist mayor of Dearborn who was also present for the meeting.
It thus appears that the political and social attitudes of a city's population may play a significant part in shaping housing and renewal developments.

ANALYZING GRANT USE

The literature examining the examples of patterns of grant use
summarized above suggests two complementary modes of analysis
designed to answer the first major research question: Why do some
cities make extensive use of federal grants while other cities virtually ignore them? Thus, both quantitative and qualitative analyses
were used in the investigation of grant use. Initially, a quantitative
explanation of renewal and housing will be posited, followed by more
qualitative data that will be used to add insight to the variance explained by the quantitative analysis and to suggest explanations for
the remaining unexplained variance.

QUANTITATIVE ANALYSIS

Before analysis of grant use was possible, it was first necessary to develop procedures that might identify characteristics of
cities that might determine or predict such use. Thus the initial
task of the methodological design became the development of the
city profiles.

City Profiles

Several alternatives were available in the development of the profiles. The most common approach would be to select a substantial number of demographic and socioeconomic variables from census data and similar sources, group these variables to represent certain city characteristics such as socioeconomic status, suburban characteristics, etc., and let the variables stand by themselves as city indicators. An alternative approach would be to utilize a mathematical technique such as factor analysis or cluster analysis to group the variables.

There are serious drawbacks to the first approach. In the first place, it takes a very large number of census-type variables to do even the most superficial job of coming to grips with city characteristics. If an adequate number of variables are finally selected, description of relationships becomes extremely complex simply because of the large number of variables involved. Factor analysis provides a viable method for identifying the underlying dimensions of a large number of variables that might accurately describe a city in quantitative terms.[53] As C. F. Schmid noted, factor analysis possesses two special advantages: the first is parsimony or data reduction. Factor analysis can reduce a large number of interrelated variables to a manageable number of factors. Secondly, factor analysis is an excellent technique for identifying underlying unities.[54]

The use of both cluster analysis and factor analysis as techniques to identify the underlying dimensions of U.S. cities is not new.[55] Schmid, and later Schmid, MacCannell, and Van Arsdol examined some 40 census variables for 1940 and 1950 and concluded that there was a major socioeconomic dimension underlying the structure of cities.[56] One of the most complete factor analytic studies of U.S. cities was published in 1965 by Jeffrey Hadden and Edgar Borgatta.[57] They employed principal components factor analysis with a varimax rotation and analyzed some 65 variables of 1960 census data for cities over 25,000 population. They developed 16 factors that they believe are crucial for the analysis of urban structures. In their initial analysis they noted an overwhelming dominance of a total population or size factor.[58] They attempted to "control" for this domination by examining factors within constructed categories such as large, medium, and small cities, and central, suburban, and independent cities. They found substantial parallelism between the categories. Using the Hadden-Borgatta correlation matrices, John Tropman reanalyzed the data and found four major dimensions.[59] They were size, socioeconomic class, racial composition, and maturity/growth.

Richard Forstall grouped U.S. cities based on a multivariate factor analysis of 97 variables for 1,761 cities.[60] He found some

14 factors or underlying dimensions describing cities: factors that were very similar to the Hadden-Borgatta dimensions. Forstall used only five of his factors (size, socioeconomic status, stage in family cycle, percent nonwhite, and percent in manufacturing) in his classification scheme.

This study also utilized factor analytic procedures to identify the underlying dimensions of U.S. cities. Some 24 variables were selected from 1960 census data.[61] These variables were carefully selected in an attempt to identify those variables that might provide the most comprehensive description of the cities. A listing of the variables is found in Table 2.1. Variables 18 and 19 were then used to compute a new variable, percent housing owner occupied (V18/19). Similarly, variables 21 and 22 were combined ([100 - V21] + V22) to form a dependency variable made up of the percent of the population under age 21 and over 64. Variables 23 and 24 were also combined (V23 + V24) to form an ethnic index. Thus a total of 21 variables were finally subjected to factor analysis. Both orthogonal and oblique rotations were performed on the data using principal component factor analysis with the number of factors produced being limited by Kaiser's criterion (eigenvalues greater than unity). Since the factors will ultimately be used in a "causal" explanation along with a number of other variables, factor scores for each city were obtained from the orthogonal factor matrix. Orthogonal rotation was selected for a number of reasons: simplicity, conceptual clarity, and amenability to further analysis. In orthogonal rotation the factors are by definition uncorrelated as the axes are 90 degrees from each other. Thus an orthogonal restriction ensures that the factors were statistically independent of one another.[62]

Cities having missing data for any of the variables did not have factor scores computed for them. Although it was possible to assign the mean value for a given variable to a city to replace missing data in the computation of the factor score, it was felt that since the city profile was to be used to "predict" renewal expenditures and housing construction, a greater accuracy might be obtained without this distortion--no matter how minor it might be.[63]

Political Environment

The next step in the analysis was to attempt to identify and account for the areas making up the political/government environment at all levels--federal, state, and local.

Federal, State, and Local Government

For the purpose of this study, variables representing each level of the federal structure were examined separately. The

TABLE 2.1

Selected 1960 Census Variables

---

1. Total population
2. Population per square mile
3. Population increase or decrease, 1950 to 1960 (percent)
4. Percent population nonwhite
5. Percent population living in group quarters
6. Median family income (dollars)
7. Percent of families with income under $3,000
8. Percent of families with income $10,000 and over
9. Median school years completed for population 25 years and older
10. Percent college graduates for population 25 years and older
11. Percent of population residing in the same house in 1960 that they were living in five years prior
12. Percent of the population living in a different county in 1960 from the one in which they lived five years prior
13. Percent of civilian labor force unemployed
14. Percent of employed persons in white-collar occupations
15. Percent of employed persons working outside of county of residence
16. Percent of housing units in one-unit structures
17. Percent of housing units sound with all plumbing facilities
18. Number of owner occupied housing units
19. Total number of occupied housing units
20. Number of manufacturing establishments with 20 or more employees
21. Percent of population 21 years and over
22. Percent of population 65 years and over
23. Percent foreign born
24. Percent native of foreign or mixed parentage

Source: U.S. Department of Commerce, Bureau of the Census, County and City Data Book 1961 (Washington, D.C.: Government Printing Office, 1961), pp. 476-575.

investigation at the federal level concerned distances of cities from HUD regional offices; major state variables concerned degree of difficulty imposed upon cities attempting to use housing and renewal grants by state laws and enabling legislation; and city variables were the commonly used government reform measures. Measures of city government reform--specifically the council-manager government, at-large representation, and nonpartisan election--have often been linked to policy outputs.[64] Robert Lineberry and Edmund Fowler developed a simple reformism scale by adding the number of these reform characteristics in each city.[65] While emphasizing the crudity of their index, their findings strongly suggested that reformism may be a continuous variable. Table 2.2 presents a listing of the operational definitions representing government influence on grant use. A detailed discussion of the definitions will be given in the appropriate evaluative chapters to follow.

Local Political Values

Several variables were selected to represent local political attitudes of the community: percent voting for Goldwater in 1964, percent voting for Wallace in 1968, a scale score representing political culture, and a regional variable. Voting statistics on a city-by-city basis were not available, therefore the 1964 and 1968 voting percentages are figures for the county in which the city is located.[66] There are a number of studies that tie the Goldwater and Wallace votes to conservative political attitudes[67]--especially to attitudes that might be expected to influence grant use. While the county vote obviously will not conform to the city vote in most cases, it is assumed that the general differentials in voting between counties will provide a rough measure of these attitudes.

Daniel Elazar's concepts of American political culture were operationalized to provide the scale representing political culture. Elazar identified three dominant political cultures in American life: individualistic, moralistic, and traditionalistic.[68] The individualistic political culture emphasizes government instituted for strictly utilitarian reasons; an ideological concern for a "businesslike" operation of government, and a belief that government need not have any direct concern with questions of a "good society." The moralistic culture emphasizes democratic participation; politics is considered one of the great activities of man. Consequently, the moralistic culture sees politics as an activity concerned with the public good and the advancement of the public interest. The traditionalistic political culture exhibits a paternalistic and elitist concept of government. This culture accepts the idea of a hierarchical society and expects those at the top to take an active part in government.

TABLE 2.2

Variables Used to Operationalize Concepts of the
Political Environment, Housing and Renewal
Decisions, and Decisional Effects

Political Environment
    Federal effects
            Designation as model city
            Location of HUD regional offices
    State effects
            Renewal difficulty scale
                Years since 1949 to local renewal agency
                Years since 1960 to state renewal enabling legislation
            Housing difficulty scale
                Years since 1937 to local housing authority
                Years since 1960 to state housing enabling legislation
    Local effects
            Form of government
            Representation
            Type election
    Local political culture
            Wallace vote in 1968
            Goldwater vote in 1964
            Elazar's political cultures
            Metropolitan status
Housing and Renewal Decisions
    Urban renewal receipts
    Public housing construction/leasing
Decisional Effects
    Business and economics
            Percent unemployed 1970
            Housing permits 1960-70
    Politics and government
            Size of city planning staff
            Number of park and recreation employees
            Number of employees in common functions
            Number of employees in variable functions
            Intergovernmental revenue received
            Change in general revenue
            Change in city taxes
            Change in property tax
            Change in general expenditures
            Change in total debt
            Number of mayors 1960-70
    Physical city
            Percent of land privately owned
            Change in school recreation land
            Change in city park and recreation land
    Social effects
            Change in percent housing lacking plumbing
            Change in number rental units under $60
            Change in percent rental units under $60

Political functions are thus relegated to a rather small elite who almost inherit their "right" to govern. Parties here are of minimal importance. Maintenance of the traditional order is a dominant characteristic. Elazar traced the origins of these dominant cultures and their migration across the United States. Each of the cities in this study was assigned a classification based on the location of the city in comparison to Elazar's cultural distribution. Elazar's cultures were then operationalized as follows:

MT	M	MI	IM	I	IT	TI	T	TM
0	1	2	3	4	5	6	7	8

A similar operationalization of Elazar's cultures was used at the state level by Ira Sharkansky.[69] His operationalization (below) was only slightly different from the one designed for grant analysis.

M	MT	MI	IM	I	IT	TI	TM	T
1	2	3	4	5	6	7	8	9

Elazar's original scale had omitted the MT (moralistic-traditionalistic) classification as is shown below:

M	MI	IM	I	IT	TI	T	TM

Sharkansky added the MT category and assumed that the M (moralistic) and T (traditionalistic) classifications were considered as opposites. This study, on the other hand, operationalizes Elazar's concept merely by adding the MT classification at the beginning of Elazar's original scale rather than changing the order of the classifications since the interest in this study is in Elazar's conceptualizations rather than for comparison with Sharkansky's findings. The basic scales, however, are very much the same. As Sharkansky notes, "Because of the small number of states that are primarily 'MT' or 'TM,' however, there is little substantive differences between the positions of most states on our revised scale, and Elazar's scale."[70] Sharkansky's analysis generally supported Elazar's designations of political culture. He reported that

> the resulting scale of political culture shows important relationships with several traits of state politics and public service. Many of these relationships are independent of both the social-economic characteristics of personal income and urbanism, and other features of

each state's regional history and traditions. The findings indicate that Elazar is a perceptive--if sometimes abtruse--observer of state cultures.[71]

Simple regression was used to identify the relationships between the independent variables and dependent variables, while stepwise multiple regression was used to explain the variation in the dependent variables accounted for by variation in the independent variables. Stepwise regression introduces the independent variables one by one beginning with the variable that yields the largest reduction in the unexplained variance of the dependent variable. The remaining independent variables are then added in the same manner (for example, the second variable added yields the next largest reduction in the unexplained variance) until all variables are included or until the contribution of the remaining variables falls below a given threshold.
Partial correlation coefficients were also computed to evaluate the independent contribution of the variables within the model.

GRANT EFFECTS

A major purpose of grants is to effect change, and public housing and urban renewal grants are no exception. This section will examine the housing and renewal literature dealing with the effects of these grant programs in four broad areas: effects on the physical city itself, on local business, on city government and politics, and the social effects. The methodology used to examine these effects will also be discussed.
A recent feasibility study of cost-benefit applications in urban renewal groups the explicit and implicit goals of the renewal program into three categories: (1) elimination of blight and slums, (2) enhancement of the competitive position of the central city with respect to the suburbs, and (3) strengthening of the fiscal capacity of the central cities.[72] A more detailed breakdown of these goals as enunciated in legislation from official HUD statements and implicit program objectives deduced from actual operation of the programs themselves is found in Table 2.3. While these goals are quite explicit and straightforward, total effects are not so clear-cut. Students of renewal programs have documented a variety of benefit spillover effects--both positive and negative. Public housing goals are equally straightforward--a decent home for every American and business and economic stimulation. But again, like renewal, there are both positive and negative spillover effects.

TABLE 2.3

Urban Renewal Goals

I. Elimination of Blight and Slum-Living Conditions
    1. Improvement in life opportunities for slum dwellers (employment, education, health, etc.)
    2. Increase in supply of low-cost housing
    3. Removal of physical blight (increase in productivity of land use)
    4. Inducement of private investment into renewal
    5. Decrease in social costs of slum living
II. Enhancement of the Central City vis-a-vis the Suburbs
    1. Enticement of moderate-income households into central city
    2. Attraction of "clean" industry into central city and job creation
    3. Revitalization of commercial core (CBD)
    4. Expansion and support of central-city institutions (for example, universities and hospitals)
    5. Increase in efficiency (for example, reduced cost) of public-renewal investments
III. Strengthening of Fiscal Capacity of the Central City
    1. Increase in central-city tax base and fiscal capacity
    2. Decrease in social costs of slum living
    3. Increase in efficiency (that is, reduced cost) of public-renewal investments

---

Source: Philip H. Friedly et al., Benefit-Cost Applications in Urban Renewal: Summary of the Feasibility Study (Washington, D.C.: Government Printing Office, 1968), p. 6.

Effects on Business

There is little question but that public housing and renewal activities are of benefit to local business. Scott Greer contends that renewal occurs not where it might benefit the community, but where it will benefit business. Any benefit to the general public, he believes, is indirect.[73]

Jerome Rothenberg used Chicago as a laboratory for an economic evaluation of urban renewal. He reported three main slum

51

removal benefits. Initially he found an increase in the productivity
of land made possible by urban renewal. Secondly he noted that re-
moving slums and replacing them with higher-quality uses improves
the neighborhood for nearby property and generally enhances its quality. Increases in property value were noted several blocks from the
renewal site. The third benefit derives from the physical destruction of slums themselves. Slum occupancy is decreased, although
the benefit is partially offset by the creation of new slums.[74]

Housing and renewal programs were ostensibly developed to
provide decent housing for the poor and to remove slums. However,
the fact that the program relies on the private sector changes the
underlying motivation from social conscience to a profit motivation.
This generally surfaces in development of middle-income housing,
central-city office buildings, industrial expansion, and the like.
"Though not cynical in intent, the program operated in the name of
housing the poor to unhouse the poor and the black and to rehouse
banks and other downtown businesses."[75] Even with the business
orientation of the housing and renewal programs, Norton Long believes that the programs have done little to focus concern on the
overall economic problems of the city. Renewal, as an economic
tool, is too "bound up in brick and mortar" to be effective.[76]

Robert Lineberry and Ira Sharkansky note an adverse effect
of renewal on small business. Small businessmen have been shown
to be particularly vulnerable to relocation with renewal forcing some
30 to 40 percent of the evicted enterprises out of business.[77]

A detailed analysis designed to evaluate the assertion that the
liquidation rate of small businesses dislocated by urban renewal is
excessive was undertaken in Chicago.[78] The authors studied business relocations in the Hyde Park-Kenwood area of Chicago and
found that, in the aggregate, the liquidation rate was not excessive.
They conclude that

> it was not as high as it might have become if re-
> newal had not taken place and Hyde Park had ex-
> perienced the same transition as Woodlawn.
> Secondly, the substantial decline in the number
> of businesses operating in the community was
> accomplished by clearance of land that effec-
> tively reduced the entry rate of new businesses
> rather than the exit of old. Viewed dispassion-
> ately, dislocation at worst hastened the inev-
> itable for a few.[79]

This is not to say that there were no adverse effects on the individual businessmen involved; there obviously were. From the view-

point of the individual businessman, renewal did introduce a number of costs, even though the costs did not alter the liquidation rate in the aggregate.

The Oakland Task Force attempted to assess the economic impact of a number of grant programs on the city of Oakland.[80] Table 2.4 presents an impact summary indicating the income-generating effects of a variety of federal programs. The table dramatically illustrates the difference in income generation capabilities between "hardware" programs such as urban renewal and "software" programs like job-training. In the short run the hardware programs generate a much smaller dollar impact than do the software programs. The Task Force does caution, however, that their model neglects the secondary effects of hardware programs--effects that would probably place these programs in a more favorable light. In the Acorn renewal project, only 16 percent of the federal money spent could be said to have contributed to local income. An important factor here was the fact that 71 percent of the people working for the Redevelopment Agency lived outside the city and, consequently, spent the major part of their wages outside the city. The impact of the project through sales-tax generation was considered negligible. Of far more importance was the effect of the program on land value in and around the project area.

The Task Force also assessed the economic impact of the construction of a 105-unit public housing project in Oakland--the Tassafaronga Housing Project.[81] Local income generated by this project was estimated at 34.2 percent of the total development cost. In terms of total income-generating effect, the sum increased to 45.5 percent of the project cost. These figures seem to suggest that federal projects that require federally funded (development) and controlled construction have a greater income-generating effect than do programs involving only site preparation.

Nevertheless, the aggregate effects of public housing on total construction appear to be very small indeed. Public programs are often accused of suffering from a "hardening of the arteries." Robert Weaver notes that in recent years the better financed and more sophisticated limited-dividend sponsors can build more units more quickly than can a public sponsor. The limited-dividend sponsor is by far the most effective and efficient.[82]

As a major sponsor of the Housing Act of 1949, Senator Robert Taft expected public housing to account for 10 percent of the homes built each year. This, of course, would have had a substantial effect on the construction industry. In essence, public housing appears to have had a negligible effect on business, accounting for only 1 percent of the total housing construction.[83]

TABLE 2.4

Impact of Federal Grant Programs on the City of Oakland

Agency	Program	Federal Expenditures in Oakland	Man-Years of Work Generated	Total Sales Taxes to Oakland	Total Federal Assistance	Local Income Generation of One Federal Dollar
HUD	Title I Urban Renewal	$1,255,559	54.00	$8,461	$10,039,116	$0.221
EDA	Public Works Grant and Loan–Block B	258,142	9.00	1,790	1,704,113	0.267
OEO	Legal Services–CAP	43,116	1.85	290	194,067	0.38
HUD	Public Housing	200,587	17.60	2,721	1,518,705	0.45
HEW	Mental Retardation Clinic & Services	28,066	1.20	189	98,621	0.491
OEO	Family Planning–CAP	12,623	.50	85	40,604	0.510
DOL	Job Training–MDTA	199,958	8.60	1,346	635,246	0.543
HEW	Title I, ESEA Compensatory Education	917,553	34.90	6,185	2,508,484	0.611
DOL	Job Training–NYC	304,765	13.00	1,833	472,673	1.105

Source: Oakland Task Force, Federal Decision–Making and Impact in Urban Areas (New York: Praeger, 1970), pp. 137–38.

Effects on the Physical City

There is no question but that urban renewal, and to some extent public housing, dramatically changes the physical face of the city. One of the foremost urban renewal critics, economist Martin Anderson, recognizes the dramatic effect of the construction of new buildings on former slum areas. He also notes the changes in land use as measured by total construction in renewal areas. For example, 24 percent of the total construction was devoted to public works (parks, schools, libraries, roads, and other public facilities), 6 percent to publicly subsidized housing, and 56 percent to private residential housing.[84] Thus, while the overall destructive and damaging effects of renewal programs are difficult to get at, some effects on the physical city can probably be detected and measured.

City size is considered by some to be a major factor influencing the impact urban renewal will have on a city. Some New York City officials, for example, dismiss New Haven's dramatic achievements as irrelevant to large cities. The problems of race, poverty, and slums were not nearly as extensive in New Haven as they were in most larger cities.[85] Renewal and housing, then, may have a greater impact on cities where problems are more manageable.

One factor noted in renewal studies has been the change in the balance between public and privately owned land in urban renewal areas. Urban renewal appears to result in an increase in the proportion of tax-exempt land (parks, playgrounds, etc.) in the redeveloped areas.[86]

The belief that public housing projects generally degenerate into slums is apparently widespread. Former President Nixon attacked several federal public housing and urban renewal projects as "wasteful" in an attempt to end these programs.[87] Concerning the housing issue, he said, "We must stop programs that have been turning the Federal Government into a nationwide slumlord."[88]

Alvin Schorr emphasizes the relationship between public housing and urban renewal. He noted that public housing historically finds its sites chiefly on land cleared for renewal. He also found that growing suburbs have successfully resisted public housing, and thus these facilities are largely confined to the central city.[89]

Changing patterns of land use is the obvious result of urban renewal projects. Because of the profit factor necessitated by private rather than public development, the net effect on the face of the city is to redistribute land to higher and higher cost uses.[90]

Effects on Politics and Government

The case studies mentioned earlier concerned with renewal politics (New Haven, Pittsburgh) indicate a trend in some big cities for mayors to bet their political futures on the renewal issue. In the studies cited, renewal seems to have been a factor in the mayors' longevity in office. Renewal is essentially a political issue. While a renewal agency may be autonomous, it is politically and fiscally responsible to city hall.[91]

A positive effect of urban renewal programs commonly conceded by friend and foe alike is the effect on the tax base. There is unquestionably a great deal of variation in the amount of tax benefit from city to city depending upon the size and type of project. One fact is clear, however: An increase in the tax base is one of the major effects of the urban renewal program. William Slayton, for example, examined 403 projects in which redevelopment was started or had been completed. He noted that assessed valuations increased by 427 percent when comparing valuations before urban renewal with valuations after renewal.[92]

Rothenberg noted that subsidization of the central city through urban renewal is important chiefly for its redistributional effect. Thus, the intergovernmental subsidization of the central city might produce an improvement in overall resource use that might be a real income gain. This, however, must be determined on a case-by-case basis.[93]

Lineberry and Sharkansky also believe that the most valid claim for urban renewal is that it has expanded the tax base and improved the economic vitality of the city.[94]

Housing and renewal grants are thought to be stimulatory toward other grant use. Urban renewal has forced cities to examine slums and blight realistically and to look at their social and racial problems although they may have lacked the means or desires to solve them. It has long been recognized that extensive government assistance and further subsidy is necessary for renewal to help slum dwellers or improve housing in low-income neighborhoods.[95]

Social Effects

The major criticisms of urban renewal and public housing programs usually cover the social costs or social effects of the programs. Jane Jacobs, an early critic of the renewal program, believes that the program is a failure because, at best, it merely shifts slums from one place to another; at worst, it destroys viable neighborhoods.[96] She claims that renewal officials worry about high density when they should really be concerned with overcrowding (1.5 or more persons per room). She maintains that high densities are required to produce city liveliness, safety, convenience, and interest.[97]

A well–documented effect of renewal programs has been the issue of "Negro removal." Typically, renewal has meant the displacement of blacks by whites or by economic symbols of the white world. [98] Segregation has forced minority groups into areas that are prime targets for renewal. In 1961, for example, of the almost 100,000 families living in renewal areas, over two-thirds were black. Even where renewal is fostered as an aid to integration, over half of the families relocated move into predominantly minority areas.

In some respects, however, renewal does foster integration. In five case studies of urban renewal in Detroit, Eleanor Wolf and Charles Lebeaux confirmed earlier findings by Chester Rapkin and William Grigsby concerning racial mixture in renewal areas. [99] Contrary to many discussions concerning "white flight," they found little reluctance on the part of white households to rent in predominantly black areas. Such reluctance was only exhibited in areas concerning home ownership.

> The most stable interracial housing thus far appears to be new, fairly large-scale developments often brought into existence through urban renewal programs . . . a key element in their stability may be the centralized marketing and the high prices of dwellings. Whether these areas would continue to remain racially stable if built for somewhat lower-income groups in cities with large Negro populations has not yet been determined. [100]

Probably the most frequent criticism of the urban renewal program concerns a change in the structure of the housing market. Many students of housing mention a discrepancy between program goals and performance. While the goal of housing and renewal programs is to provide a decent home for every American, renewal is often blamed for reducing the amount of low-rent housing available to city dwellers. [101]

One of the principal objectives of urban renewal is to attract more middle–class families back to the central city. Toward this objective, renewal has wrought a major change in the cost of housing. Development activities by private enterprise on renewal land has generally produced higher-cost housing. [102]

Rothenberg, in his economic analysis, noted a regressive income redistribution attributed to urban renewal. As expected, the lower-income groups consuming at the bottom end of the housing stock suffer the most. [103]

Chester Hartman examined the relocation pattern of a Boston renewal project and found that the families were spread rather evenly throughout the city of Boston and in the inner-core suburbs.[104] In other words, the neighborhood or community (taken in a social sense) was not relocated, it was destroyed. He also noted an increase in the living space of the relocated families as well as an increase in private outdoor space and an improvement in the overall physical quality of the houses to which they moved. Relocation also resulted in a marked increase in housing costs. The median rent rose from $41 to $71 per month--a 73 percent increase. The rent/income ratio rose from 13.6 percent before relocation to 18.6 percent after relocation. Hartman also examined and summarized relocation data from 33 U.S. relocation studies between 1933 and 1963. Of the nine studies covering the 1960s, the majority show an increase in housing quality accompanied by an increase in housing costs. In the aggregate, however, Hartman concludes that

> given the premise that one of the cardinal aims
> of renewal and rehousing should be the improved
> housing welfare of those living in substandard
> conditions, it is questionable whether the lim-
> ited and inconsistent gains reported in most
> studies represent an acceptable level of
> achievement.[105]

Public housing projects have frequently been considered massive slums. Harrison Salisbury refers to them as "human cesspools . . . massive barracks for the destitute . . . a $20,000,000 slum."[106] Public housing has become synonomous with welfare, unemployment, illegitimacy, crime, drugs, etc. Gilbert Steiner reports on a study conducted by Austin Hollingshead and L. H. Rogler matching two groups of families in San Juan, Puerto Rico.[107] All of the families lived either in a slum or in public housing. The families living in public housing had superior living conditions--were housed more adequately, paid less rent, and were less crowded. When queried about their environment, 65 percent of the men and woman who lived in slum homes liked the slums, while some 85 percent of the men and 71 percent of the women living in public housing disliked public housing. When asked about the neighborhood as a place to raise children, 38 percent of the slum-dwelling husbands and 15 percent of the wives pronounced the slum a good place to raise children. On the other hand, only 7 percent of the husbands and none of the wives in public housing found the environment good for children.

These studies, while perhaps more interesting than most, are not really representative. In general, public housing performs at least acceptably well for a large number of poor families.

When they are asked, the majority of families
who live in public housing say that they like it.
They appreciate its facilities; their general
morale is higher than it was in substandard
housing . . . for those who take up tenancy,
public housing represents a considerable improvement in physical surroundings.[108]

Wolf and Lebeaux, in a participant observation study, examined the extent to which the slum clearance phase of urban renewal
uprooted and destroyed a satisfactory neighborhood social matrix
and compared the results with studies conducted in Boston's West
End.[109] In contrast to the extensive feelings of positive sentiments
about their Italian West End neighborhood, only about one-fourth of
the predominantly black residents of the Detroit area under study expressed any positive sentiment concerning their neighborhood. In
addition, the less-liked poor black neighborhood was less crowded,
had a higher rate of owner-occupied dwellings, and was probably of
about the same physical quality as the West End. People remained
in the West End on the basis of personal preferences, while most
residents of the Detroit study did not.[110]

Concerning the consequences of relocation on Boston's North
End families, psychologist Marc Fried found that the loss of the
feeling of community was readily visible for more than two years
after relocation. Far from adjusting to their new neighborhoods,
26 percent of the women remained sad or depressed even after two
years in the new neighborhoods.[111]

And yet, perhaps the consequences are not always that bleak.
Wolf and Lebeaux note that

the changes that come into the lives of these
people as a consequence of relocation were about
what one would expect if a block of substandard
homes had been destroyed in a fire and the families living there had insurance enough to cover
moving costs. Many would miss old neighbors
(as people often do when they move); the houses
to which they moved probably were structurally
superior simply because not much housing remained as substandard as that on the burned-
down block; on the other hand, the new housing
was somewhat more expensive and meant borrowing funds from other kinds of expenditures.
Some (usually elderly people) who owned their
homes would be glad to get some compensation

for a house no one wanted to buy; others, attached to dwelling or ownership, knew they had
scant chances of buying elsewhere and were ac-
cordingly resentful. [112]

Housing and Renewal Decisions and Effects

The literature thus suggests that housing and renewal decisions
will have certain measurable effects on the environment that will, in
turn, modify the city's physical, social, and political profile. The
hypothesized effects are in the four broad areas discussed: effects
on economics and business, the physical structure of the city, government and politics, and effects on the social community. Again,
operational definitions are presented later in Table 3.2 with a detailed discussion of the definitions in the evaluative chapters. Simple
and partial correlation will again be used to examine pertinent relationships between grant use and grant effects.

QUALITATIVE ANALYSIS

The quantitative analysis outlined earlier will account for the
bulk of the analysis presented in this study. However, quantitative
methods in social science generally leave large amounts of unexplained variance. To examine qualitative factors that might explain
additional variance in patterns of grant use and the effects of grants,
six cities were subjected to investigation through the use of field
study and observation. In a broad operational sense, field studies
include a blend of methods and techniques involving social and other
interaction in the field between the researcher and the subjects under
study. The end product is

> an analytic description of a complex social or
> political organization. . . . An analytic de-
> scription (1) employs the concepts, proposi-
> tions, and empirical generalizations of a body
> of scientific theory as the basic guides in analy-
> sis and reporting of facts, (2) employs thorough
> and systematic collection, classification, and
> reporting of facts, and (3) generates new em-
> pirical generalizations (and perhaps concepts
> and propositions as well) based on these data. [113]

The author spent approximately one week in each city examining
public records, interviewing elites, and generally trying to get a

"feel" for housing and renewal issues and applications within each community.

The difficulty with the application of observation to this study was not a methodological problem, but was the more realistic difficulty of selecting the cities that would be subjected to qualitative analysis. Ideally, of course, the researcher should visit all in the population, or at least a representative random sample, to be able to generalize about the findings with any degree of certainty. Only six cities were selected for detailed analysis here because of the realistic constraints imposed by limited funds and lack of time.

City Selection Procedures

Selection of the six cities was nevertheless accomplished in as "scientific" a framework as possible. Certain criteria were therefore adopted for city selection: (1) two large cities, two medium-sized cities, and two small cities would be visited; (2) at least two of the cities would be suburban and two would be central cities; (3) cities would be selected in pairs (at least two per state) so that comparisons could be made within the framework of given state laws; (4) the pairs of cities would be geographically diverse to avoid a regional bias; and finally (5) three cities would be high grant users and three would deviate to the low end of the national pattern with regard to grant use.

The actual city selection was accomplished through the use of residuals generated through stepwise multiple regression. The factor scores obtained from the 21 selected variables were the initial independent variables used. In addition, factors were obtained to represent political values of the community. The factors are composed of the loadings of four variables: percent voting for Goldwater in 1964, percent voting for Wallace in 1968, the scale score representing Elazar's political cultures, and a regional variable. The regional variable is a simple South-non-South dichotomous variable. This, again, was based upon research at the state level by Sharkansky and others.[114] The final variable utilized in city selection was Lineberry and Fowler's reformism scale score for each city.

Generation of Residuals

The factor scores representing the city profile, the political culture factor scores, and the reformism scale scores were taken as the independent variables, and urban renewal expenditures and public housing occupancy were the dependent variables for each city.

61

Stepwise multiple regression was performed to obtain a multiple correlation coefficient and constant values for the regression equation. The regression equation was then used to predict a value for the dependent variables for each city. Residuals for each city were then computed by subtracting the actual value of the dependent variables from the predicted values. Thus a positive residual of $5.0 million for a given city, for example, indicates that the city received $5.0 million more in renewal funds than its physical and political patterns predicted based upon an equation for all cities. Complete details of city selection are presented in Chapter 3.

ORGANIZATION OF THE VOLUME

In summary, then, the ensuing pages will encompass both a quantitative and qualitative examination of public housing and urban renewal. The basic thrust of the study is quantitative--both in determining the patterns of grant use and in examining grant effects. The data generated through the participant observation are used basically to "explain" the unexplained variance of the quantitative work. The greatest reliance on qualitative data will be in the second half of the study--determining the effects of grants. Many effects are not quantifiable and thus the study must rely heavily on much more impressionistic data. This is especially noted in the unintended effects of grants (for example, destruction of "sense of community").

Chapter 3 will examine the patterns of use of the grants under investigation. Since both quantitative and qualitative data are needed to explain grant use, the first part of Chapter 3 will present a detailed discussion of the city selection procedure. This will be followed by the quantitative explanation of renewal expenditures and housing construction; and finally the results of the six field experiences will be used to posit explanation for the unexplained variance and to add insight to the variance explained by the quantitative analysis. Chapters 4 through 7 will deal exclusively with grant effects, while Chapter 8 will present a summary of the study and some concluding remarks.

NOTES

1. David L. Smith, "Federal Grant Elasticity and Distortion: A Reply," National Tax Journal 21 (December 1969): 553.
2. Brett W. Hawkins, Politics and Urban Policies (Indianapolis: Bobbs-Merrill, 1971), pp. 102-3.

3. A. Lee Fritschler and Morley Segal, "Intergovernmental Relations and Contemporary Political Science: Developing an Integrative Typology," Publius 1 (Winter 1972): 95-122.

4. Ibid., pp. 94-95.

5. Leonard Goodwin, Do the Poor Want to Work? (Washington, D.C.: Brookings Institution, 1972).

6. Leonard Merewitz and Stephen H. Soznick, The Budget's New Clothes (Chicago: Markham, 1971).

7. Jewel Bellush and Murray Hausknecht, "Urban Renewal: An Historical Overview," in Urban Renewal: People, Politics and Planning, ed. Jewel Bellush and Murray Hausknecht (Garden City, N.Y.: Doubleday, 1967), pp. 6-9.

8. Public Law 412, 75th Congress, 50 Stat. 888, 42 U.S.C. 1401 et seq.

9. Quoted in U.S. Congress, House, Committee on Banking and Currency, Basic Laws and Authorities on Housing and Urban Development (Washington, D.C.: Government Printing Office, 1969), p. 225.

10. The President's Committee on Urban Housing, The Report of the President's Committee on Urban Housing: A Decent Home (Washington, D.C.: Government Printing Office, 1968), pp. 59-61.

11. Public Law 171, 81st Congress, 63 Stat. 413-414, 42 U.S.C. 1450.

12. Bellush and Hausknecht, "Urban Renewal: An Historical Overview," p. 13.

13. The President's Committee, A Decent Home, p. 57.

14. Quoted in Committee on Banking, Basic Laws, pp. 357-58.

15. Public Law 86-372, 73 Stat. 654, 667, 12 U.S.C. 1701q. Excerpts may be found in Committee on Banking, Basic Laws, pp. 283-87.

16. Committee on Banking, Basic Laws, p. 60.

17. The President's Committee, A Decent Home, pp. 58-59. See also pp. 61-64 for a more detailed description of 202 and 221 (d)(3) programs.

18. Public Law 89-117, 79 Stat. 451, 12 U.S.C. 1701s. Excerpts may be found in Committee on Banking, Basic Laws, pp. 262-66.

19. The President's Committee, A Decent Home, pp. 64-65.

20. Committee on Banking, Basic Laws, pp. 252-55.

21. Ibid., pp. 98-108.

22. The President's Committee, A Decent Home, p. 66.

23. Ibid., pp. 65-66.

24. Jerome Rothenberg, Economic Evaluation of Urban Renewal (Washington, D.C.: Brookings Institution, 1967), p. 13.

25. Public Law 171, 81st Congress, Stat. 413, 414, 42 U.S.C. 1450.

26. Carl G. Lindbloom and Morton Farrah, The Citizen's Guide to Urban Renewal, rev. ed. (West Trenton, N.J.: Chandler-Davis, 1968), pp. 179-83.

27. U.S. Department of Housing and Urban Development, Urban Renewal Directory: As of December 31, 1970 (Washington, D.C.: Government Printing Office, 1971), pp. 147-48.

28. "First Major Housing Bill Since 1968 Enacted," Congressional Quarterly Weekly Report 34 (August 24, 1974): 2319.

29. U.S. President, Weekly Compilation of Presidential Documents (Washington, D.C.: Office of the Federal Register, 1973), Richard M. Nixon, 1973, p. 1147.

30. Ibid.

31. Ibid., p. 1148.

32. "Urban Experiment." New York Times, August 23, 1974, p. 28.

33. "First Major Housing Bill," pp. 2319-20.

34. Ibid., p. 2321.

35. Morley Segal and A. Lee Fritschler, "Emerging Patterns of Intergovernmental Relations," in The Municipal Year Book 1970 (Washington, D.C.: International City Management Association, 1970), pp. 13-38.

36. Amos H. Hawley, "Community Power and Urban Renewal Success," in Community Structure and Decision-Making: Comparative Analyses, ed. Terry N. Clark (San Francisco: Chandler, 1968), pp. 393-405.

37. Terry N. Clark, "Community Structure, Decision-Making, Budget Expenditures, and Urban Renewal in 51 American Communities," American Sociological Review 33 (August 1968): 576-93.

38. Michael Aiken and Robert R. Alford, "Community Structure and Innovation: The Case of Urban Renewal," American Sociological Review 35 (August 1970): 650-65.

39. Ibid., p. 653.

40. Michael Aiken and Robert R. Alford, "Community Structure and Innovation: The Case of Public Housing," American Political Science Review 64 (September 1970): 843-64.

41. For example, Robert A. Dahl, Who Governs? (New Haven, Conn.: Yale University Press, 1961); Harold Kaplan, Urban Renewal Politics (New York: Columbia University Press, 1963); and James Clarence Davies III, Neighborhood Groups and Urban Renewal (New York: Columbia University Press, 1966).

42. For example, Lee Rainwater, Behind Ghetto Walls: Black Family Life in a Federal Slum (Chicago: Aldine, 1970).

43. Jewel Bellush and Murray Hausknecht, "Entrepreneurs and Urban Renewal: The New Men of Power," in Bellush and

Hausknecht, Urban Renewal, pp. 209-24; and also contained in Journal of the American Institute of Planners 32 (September 1966), 289-97.

44. Bellush and Hausknecht, "Entrepreneurs and Urban Renewal," p. 211.

45. Robert L. Lineberry and Ira Sharkansky, Urban Politics and Public Policy (New York: Harper and Row, 1971), p. 332.

46. Jeanne R. Lowe, Cities in a Race With Time (New York: Random House, 1967), pp. 110-63.

47. Ibid., pp. 313-404.

48. Ibid., p. 314.

49. Ibid., pp. 405-554; and Dahl, Who Governs?

50. Oakland Task Force, Federal Decision-Making and Impact in Urban Areas (New York: Praeger, 1970), p. 17.

51. Walter S. Mossberg, "A Blue-Collar Town Fears Urban Renewal Perils Its Way of Life," Wall Street Journal, November 2, 1970, pp. 1, 13.

52. Ibid., p. 1.

53. R. J. Rummel, Applied Factor Analysis (Evanston, Ill.: Northwestern University Press, 1970); and Harry H. Harman, Modern Factor Analysis, 2d ed. (Chicago: University of Chicago Press, 1967).

54. C. F. Schmid, "Urban Crime Areas: Part 1," American Sociological Review 25 (August 1960): 535.

55. A fine review of this literature is found in Desmond S. Cartwright, "Ecological Variables," in Sociological Methodology 1969, ed. Edgar F. Borgatta (San Francisco: Jossey-Bass, 1969), pp. 155-218.

56. C. F. Schmid, "Generalizations Concerning the Ecology of the American City," American Sociological Review 15 (April 1950): 264-81; and C. F. Schmid, E. H. MacCannell, and M. D. Van Arsdol, "The Ecology of the American City: Further Comparison and Validation of Generalizations," American Sociological Review 23 (August 1958): 392-401.

57. Jeffrey K. Hadden and Edgar F. Borgatta, American Cities: Their Social Characteristics (Chicago: Rand McNally, 1965).

58. Ibid., p. 39.

59. John E. Tropman, "Critical Dimensions of Community Structure: A Reexamination of the Hadden-Borgatta Findings," Urban Affairs Quarterly 5 (December 1969): 215-32.

60. Richard L. Forstall, "A New Social and Economic Grouping of Cities," The Municipal Year Book 1970 (Washington, D.C.: International City Management Association, 1970), pp. 102-59.

61. U.S. Department of Commerce, Bureau of the Census, County and City Data Book 1962 (Washington, D.C.: Government Printing Office, 1962), pp. 476-575. The data utilized in this computation were made available by the Inter-university Consortium for

Political Research. The data were supplied in partially proofed form and the Consortium bears no responsibility for either the analyses or interpretations presented here.

62. Rummel, Applied Factor Analysis, pp. 384-89.

63. Seven cities had missing data.

64. Edward C. Banfield and James Q. Wilson, City Politics (New York: Random House, 1963); Amos H. Hawley, "Community Power and Urban Renewal Success," in Clark, Community Structure and Decision-Making, pp. 393-405; and Bernard H. Booms, "City Governmental Form and Public Expenditure Levels," National Tax Journal 19 (June 1966): 187-99.

65. Robert L. Lineberry and Edmund P. Fowler, "Reformism and Public Policies in American Cities," American Political Science Review 61 (September 1967): 701-16.

66. Richard M. Scammon, ed., America Votes 7 (Washington, D.C.: Governmental Affairs Institute, 1968); and Richard M. Scammon, ed., America Votes 8 (Washington, D.C.: Governmental Affairs Institute, 1970).

67. Robert A. Schoenberger, ed., The American Right Wing: Readings in Political Behavior (New York: Holt, Rinehart, 1969); and Philip E. Converse et al., "Continuity and Change in American Politics: Parties and Issues in the 1968 Election," American Political Science Review 63 (December 1969): 1083-1105.

68. Daniel J. Elazar, American Federalism: A View from the States, 2d ed. (New York: Crowell, 1972), pp. 93-139.

69. Ira Sharkansky, "The Utility of Elazar's Political Culture," Polity 2 (Fall 1969): 66-83.

70. Ibid., p. 71.

71. Ibid., p. 83.

72. Philip H. Friedly et al., Benefit-Cost Applications in Urban Renewal: Summary of the Feasibility Study (Washington, D.C.: Government Printing Office, 1968), p. 5.

73. Scott Greer, The Urbane View: Life and Politics in Metropolitan America (New York: Oxford University Press, 1972), p. 215.

74. Rothenberg, Economic Evaluation, pp. 13-18.

75. Norton Long, The Unwalled City (New York: Basic Books, 1972), p. 134.

76. Ibid., p. 173.

77. Lineberry and Sharkansky, Urban Politics, p. 341.

78. Brian J. L. Berry, Sandra J. Parsons, Rutherford H. Platt, The Impact of Urban Renewal on Small Business (Chicago: Center for Urban Studies, The University of Chicago, 1968).

79. Ibid., p. xv.

80. Oakland Task Force, Federal Decision-Making, pp. 132-49.

81. Ibid., pp. 146-49.

82. Robert C. Weaver, "The Role of Government in Improving the Urban Environment," in The Urban Environment: How It Can Be Improved, William E. Zisch, Paul H. Douglas, and Robert C. Weaver (New York: New York University Press, 1969), pp. 82-83.

83. Lowe, Cities in a Race, p. 253.

84. Martin Anderson, The Federal Bulldozer (Cambridge, Mass.: MIT Press, 1964), pp. 90-110.

85. Lowe, Cities in a Race, p. 548.

86. William L. Slayton, "Report on Urban Renewal," in Bellush and Hausknecht, Urban Renewal, p. 386.

87. "Nixon Says Crisis in Cities Is Over; Cities Dip in Crime," New York Times, March 5, 1973, pp. 1, 20.

88. Ibid., p. 20.

89. Alvin Schorr, "Slums and Social Security," in Bellush and Hausknecht, Urban Renewal, pp. 415-17.

90. Lineberry and Sharkansky, Urban Politics, p. 337.

91. Greer, Urbane View, p. 215.

92. Slayton, "Report on Urban Renewal," p. 385.

93. Rothenberg, Economic Evaluation, p. 16.

94. Lineberry and Sharkansky, Urban Politics, p. 336.

95. Lowe, Cities in a Race, p. 560.

96. Jane Jacobs, The Death and Life of Great American Cities (New York: Random House, 1961), p. 271.

97. Ibid., pp. 205-10.

98. Jewel Bellush and Murray Hausknecht, "Relocation and Managed Mobility," in Bellush and Hausknecht, Urban Renewal, pp. 366-77.

99. Chester Rapkin and William G. Grigsby, The Demand for Housing in Racially Mixed Areas (Berkeley: University of California Press, 1960), pp. 54-55.

100. Eleanor Paperno Wolf and Charles N. Lebeaux, Change and Renewal in an Urban Community (New York: Praeger, 1969), p. 509.

101. Roland L. Warren, "Politics and the Ghetto System," in Politics and the Ghettos, ed. Roland L. Warren (New York: Atherton, 1969), p. 12.

102. Robert C. Weaver, The Urban Complex (Garden City, N.Y.: Doubleday, 1964), p. 37.

103. Rothenberg, Economic Evaluation, p. 15.

104. Chester W. Hartman, "The Housing of Relocated Families," in Bellush and Hausknecht, Urban Renewal, pp. 315-53.

105. Ibid., p. 330.

106. Harrison Salisbury, The Shook-Up Generation (New York: Harper, 1958), p. 74.

107. Gilbert Y. Steiner, "Trends in Welfare Assistance for Low-Income Families--Their Significance for Housing Assistance Programs," in Critical Urban Housing Issues: 1967, ed. National Association of Housing and Redevelopment Officials (Washington, D.C.: National Association of Housing and Redevelopment Officials, 1967), pp. 36-44.

108. Alvin Schorr, "Slums and Social Security," in Bellush and Hausknecht, Urban Renewal, p. 418.

109. Herbert Gans, The Urban Villagers (Glencoe, Ill.: Free Press, 1962); Marc Fried and Peggy Gleicher, "Some Sources of Residential Satisfaction in an Urban Slum," Journal of the American Institute of Planners 27 (November 1961): 305-15; Chester Hartman, "Social Values and Housing Orientations," Journal of Social Issues 19 (April 1963): 113-31.

110. Wolf and Lebeaux, Change and Renewal, pp. 530-37.

111. Summarized in Herbert J. Gans, "The Failure of Urban Renewal: A Critique and Some Proposals," in Bellush and Hausknecht Urban Renewal, p. 469.

112. Wolf and Lebeaux, Change and Renewal, p. 529.

113. George J. McCall and J. L. Simmons, eds., Issues in Participant Observation: A Text and Reader (Reading, Mass.: Addison Wesley, 1969), p. 1. See also Norman K. Denzin, ed., Sociological Methods (Chicago: Aldine, 1970), and William J. Filstead, ed., Qualitative Methodology (Chicago: Markham, 1970).

114. Ira Sharkansky, "Economic Development, Regionalism and State Political Systems," Midwest Journal of Political Science 12 (February 1968): 41-61, and Sharkansky, "Regional Patterns in the Expenditures of American States," Western Political Quarterly 20 (December 1967): 955-71.

CHAPTER
3
PATTERNS OF USE

The preceding chapters have presented a background for this study in some detail, developed a framework for analysis, and outlined the methodology used in the analysis. This chapter is devoted to the determinants of grant use--that is, the chapter will attempt to answer the first major research question: Why do some cities make extensive use of federal grants while other cities virtually ignore them? As mentioned previously, examination of patterns of use will be accomplished through the use of both quantitative and qualitative methods. The first part of this chapter, then, will be devoted to the selection of the six cities that were subjected to field study. The second area for discussion will be the quantitative analysis of grant use; and finally, findings from the field observations will be posited as explanatory factors for the remaining unexplained variance of the quantitative analysis and to provide additional insight into the quantitative results.

Two areas were common to both the city selection procedure and the quantitative analysis. First was the development of the factors representing the city profiles and second was the operational definition of the dependent variables--housing and renewal grants. Urban renewal grants included in this study are defined by federal dollars actually disbursed to cities (as opposed to program approval used by some authors) between January 1, 1960, and December 31, 1970, for a variety of renewal activities.[1] Disbursals for urban renewal projects, neighborhood development programs, demonstration programs, code enforcement projects, interim assistance programs, demolition projects, community renewal programs, and certified area programs make up the total renewal grants. Public housing construction is operationally defined by the total number of low-rent public housing units having a date of occupancy for the first unit occupied in the project between January 1, 1960, and June 30, 1970.[2] In other words, a public housing project must have construction (or leasing) completed and at least one housing unit of the project occupied between 1960 and 1970 to merit inclusion in the study.

CITY PROFILE

The city profile was developed through the use of principal components factor analysis of the 21 variables listed in Table 3.1. The factor matrix for the unrotated principal components analysis is presented in Table 3.2. The number of factors was limited by Kaiser's criterion--all have eigenvalues greater than unity. Factor 1 explained 27.75 percent of the total variance; Factor 2, 19.27 percent; Factor 3, 11.67 percent; Factor 4, 8.22 percent. and Factor 5, 6.15 percent of the total variance.

Both orthogonal and oblique rotations were performed on the data. The orthogonal solution is presented in Table 3.3. Most of the variables loaded rather clearly on one, or at the most two, of the factors. Both Factor 1 and Factor 2 contain primary loadings of variables designed to measure socioeconomic status. Eight variables load highly on Factor 1--most in a negative direction. That is, the extreme end of this underlying dimension denotes high unemployment, residential stability, low levels of education, and low income. The factor was thus termed Status, Wealth, and Education.

Factor 2 also contains significant loadings of variables that are also measures of socioeconomic status. It is characterized by low income, a high percent nonwhite, low quality, renter occupied, multifamily housing, and a low level of ethnicity. Since this factor contains high loadings of variables usually associated with core or central cities, the factor was named Central City.

Urban Density was the name given to Factor 3. Characterized by a high ethnic population, multifamily rental housing, high density population concentration, and a low dependency ratio, the factor is highly descriptive of densely populated central city ethnic neighborhoods.

Only two variables loaded highly on Factor 4. This factor was clearly a measure of Size/Manufacturing and was so named.

And finally, Factor 5 was termed Commuting/Growth. Three variables loaded heavily on this--measures of population growth, migration, and commuting.

The selected census variables have thus been used to clearly identify five underlying dimensions of U.S. cities. However, a few of the variables loaded highly on more than one factor (see Table 3.3).

70

TABLE 3.1

Variables Included in City Profile Factors

---

1. Percent of the population living in a different county in 1960 from the one in which they lived five years prior

2. Percent of the civilian labor force unemployed

3. Percent of employed persons in white collar occupations

4. Percent of population residing in the same house in 1960 that they were living in five years prior

5. Percent college graduates for population 25 years and older

6. Median school years completed for population 25 years and older

7. Percent of families with income $10,000 and over

8. Median family income (dollars)

9. Percent of population living in group quarters

10. Percent of families with income under $3,000

11. Percent population nonwhite

12. Percent of housing units sound with all plumbing facilities

13. Percent housing units owner occupied

14. Ethnic index

15. Population per square mile

16. Percent of housing units in one-unit structures

17. Dependency ratio

18. Total population

19. Number of manufacturing establishments with 20 or more employees

20. Population increase or decrease, 1950-60 (percent)

21. Percent of employed persons working outside of county of residence

---

Source: U.S. Department of Commerce, Bureau of the Census, County and City Data Book 1962 (Washington, D.C.: Government Printing Office, 1962), pp. 476-575.

TABLE 3.2

Principal Components Unrotated Factor Matrix

	1	2	3	4	5
Total population	0.15163	0.36915	-0.45981	0.75633	-0.16211
Pop per sq mile	0.20425	0.71827	-0.18172	0.01029	0.14945
Pop chg 50-60	-0.13005	-0.07143	0.20200	0.24578	0.69859
Percent nonwhite	0.48865	-0.27862	-0.45912	0.02060	0.03104
Pct in grp quarters	0.05816	-0.16702	-0.52120	-0.35927	0.07114
Med family income	-0.85029	0.39451	0.14378	0.03012	-0.07416
Pct income -3,000	0.71553	-0.47133	-0.30852	-0.06500	0.03344
Pct income +10,000	-0.83809	0.30485	-0.13340	-0.05433	-0.07893
Med school complete	-0.84825	-0.20975	-0.21825	0.00265	-0.05842
Pct college grad	-0.66955	-0.13724	-0.53937	-0.20491	-0.04059
Pct same house	0.36164	0.58720	0.39448	-0.15615	-0.23865
Pct diff county	-0.48340	-0.54866	-0.30939	0.13622	0.43144
Pct unemployed	0.56578	-0.02163	0.21826	0.18666	0.18813
Pct white-collar	-0.78876	-0.04933	-0.35574	-0.09143	-0.10467
Pct commuting work	-0.17301	0.35425	0.08227	0.11463	0.59296
Single family house	-0.31356	-0.73706	0.31329	0.32777	-0.12907
Sound housing	-0.80383	0.29283	0.18249	0.11270	0.04164
Owner occupied	-0.52683	-0.40443	0.57788	0.31671	-0.15360
Manufacturing	0.15628	0.40802	-0.43701	0.74009	-0.16975
Dependency rate	0.08147	-0.59539	0.30181	0.15298	-0.10153
Ethnic index	-0.09180	0.81423	0.17720	-0.15437	0.09733
Pct total variance	27.75	19.27	11.67	8.22	6.15 73.07

TABLE 3.3

Varimax Rotated Factor Matrix (normalized solution)

	Status, Wealth and Education (low)	Central City	Urban Density	Size/ Manufacturing	Commuting/ Growth
Pct diff county	-0.60190	0.18341	-0.40907	-0.02885	0.52011
Pct unemployed	0.59455	0.22933	-0.02578	0.07185	0.16294
Pct white-collar	-0.83782	-0.25508	-0.04824	0.01158	-0.03102
Pct same house	0.57126	-0.29464	0.43809	-0.05987	-0.32229
Pct college grad	-0.89414	-0.00354	0.01315	-0.03731	-0.02465
Med school complete	-0.80454	-0.30716	-0.26225	-0.02061	0.06124
Pct income +10,000	-0.67450	-0.58403	-0.15716	0.03863	0.00833
Med family income	-0.48327	-0.81066	0.11010	0.02037	0.04942
Pct in group qtrs	-0.36689	0.49134	0.18775	-0.14851	-0.06110
Pct income -3,000	0.26112	0.86019	-0.13905	-0.00645	-0.08464
Pct nonwhite 60	0.04408	0.70599	-0.00360	0.16098	-0.04785
Pct sound housing	-0.42221	-0.75326	0.01193	0.02852	0.18169
Pct owner occupied	-0.04963	-0.55581	-0.75931	-0.08321	0.06389
Ethnic index	0.14358	-0.50036	0.68075	-0.01228	0.03946
Pop per sq mile	0.16056	-0.07753	0.71272	0.25987	0.07621
Pct 1 family house	-0.10251	-0.11030	-0.91419	-0.04363	0.05909
Dependency ratio	0.17796	0.10726	-0.65327	-0.12405	-0.02469
Total population	0.02069	0.05093	0.15780	0.97005	-0.00911
Manufacturing	0.04118	0.02364	0.18835	0.95928	-0.02179
Pop chg 50-60	0.08103	-0.10001	-0.10670	-0.04033	0.76268
Pct commuting work	0.01521	-0.24806	0.30693	0.02754	0.60844
Pct total variance	20.77	19.25	16.67	9.61	6.78

73.08

While the factor scores will be generated through the orthogonal factor matrix for reasons of statistical independence, conceptual clarity, amd amenability to further analysis, an oblique rotation was performed to attempt to isolate variables loading on more than one factor. Two matrices were obtained for the oblique solution--the matrices containing the primary structure and primary pattern loadings. Since it was important that the underlying dimensions of the city be identified as clearly as possible, the primary pattern loadings were examined in some detail.[3]

While oblique rotation attempts to best identify the underlying dimensions of the variables, there is no restriction on the correlation between the dimensions. Thus while the oblique solution also identified five major dimensions, it was possible that some of the dimensions may be so highly correlated as to measure the same thing. Table 3.4 presents two correlation matrices--correlations between reference factors and correlations between primary factors. Multicollinearity between factors does not appear to be a major problem, although some relationship between factors is noted. The highest correlation coefficient was $r = .19$ between Factors 1 and 2 on the reference factor matrix.

TABLE 3.4

Correlations between Reference Factors and Correlations
between Primary Factors for Oblique Solution

	1	2	3	4	5
Correlations between reference factors					
1	1.00000				
2	0.19151*	1.00000			
3	-0.04098	-0.03965	1.00000		
4	0.04059	0.07183	0.07186	1.00000	
5	-0.17744*	-0.14086*	-0.15560*	-0.06948	1.00000
Correlations between primary factors					
1	1.00000				
2	-0.16545*	1.00000			
3	0.06217	0.05577	1.00000		
4	-0.02247	-0.06233	-0.06742	1.00000	
5	0.16146	0.11459*	0.16681*	0.04441	1.00000

*Significant at the .05 level.

With the apparent independence of factors generated through the use of oblique rotation, it was logical to predict that the loadings on the primary pattern matrix would be quite similar to the matrix generated through orthogonal rotation. Indeed, this was the case. The similarity between the oblique and orthogonal matrices was striking. There were virtually no differences in variable loadings on Factors 4 and 5. Only two variables of the 21 showed any substantial change in loadings depending on solutions—both of the mobility variables, variable 1 and variable 4 (Table 3.1). Variable 1, the percent of the population living in a different county in 1960 from the one in which they lived five years prior, loaded quite evenly on Factors 1, 2, 3, and 5 of the oblique matrix. On the orthogonal matrix, however, this variable loaded clearly on Factors 1 and 5. Variable 4, the percent of population residing in the same house in 1960 that they were living in five years prior, loaded evenly on Factors 1, 2, and 3 of the oblique matrix. Utilizing the orthogonal solution, however, the variable clearly loaded on Factor 1.

The differences between solutions thus proved to be minor. Without question, the underlying descriptive dimensions remained the same. The descriptive names given the five factors based upon loadings on the orthogonal matrix are equally valid for the oblique factors. As Rummel notes, "the spatial configuration of variables defined by the preliminary solution is not altered by rotation. Rotation changes only the perspective, not the interrelationship between the variables."[4]

The orthogonal factor matrix was thus deemed suitable for generation of the factor scores. Factor scores for the five factors were computed for most of the 310 cities--the exception being those cities with missing data for any of the 21 input variables.[5] Cities having missing data did not have factor scores computed for them to avoid possible distortion of the results of the quantitative analysis and to avoid selection of cities for detailed study based upon erroneous data.

POLITICAL CULTURE

A factor attempting to describe community political culture was developed through the use of principal components factor analysis of the four variables listed in Table 3.5. Only one factor was created as only the eigenvalue (lambda) of the first factor satisfied Kaiser's criterion. This factor explained 61.94 percent of the total variance. Table 3.6 presents the factor matrix for this one factor. With only a single factor, there is obviously no distinction between types of rotation so only the one matrix is presented. The factor was named Local Culture. As with the profile factors, factor scores for each of the 310 cities were computed. Again, cities having missing data for any of the four input variables did not receive factor scores.[6]

TABLE 3.5

Variables Descriptive of Community Political Culture

1. Percent voting for Wallace in 1968
2. Percent voting for Goldwater in 1964
3. Scale score for Elazar's political culture
4. Geographic region (South/non-South)

TABLE 3.6

Factor Matrix (Local Culture)

	Local Culture	
Wallace vote	0.87909	
Goldwater vote	0.77441	
Elazar's cultures	0.78512	
South/non-South	-0.69911	
Percent total variance	61.94	61.94

REFORMISM

The final independent variable designated for use in the city selection process was Lineberry and Fowler's simple scale of reformism in city government.[7] Reformism here encompassed the usual three reform measures often adopted by city governments: the council-manager government, at-large representation, and nonpartisan elections. Reformism scores were assigned as follows:

0   City has adopted no reform measures
1   City has adopted one reform measure
2   City has adopted two reform measures
3   City has adopted all three reform measures.

These structural measures of the city conform to the time period of the city profile. They, too, were city characteristics as of 1960.

CITY SELECTION

The seven variables identified thus far in this chapter were used to select the six cities subjected to field study analysis. The housing and renewal variables were the dependent variables and were treated separately. The independent variables were the same for both housing and renewal regressions and correlations. The seven independent variables included the five city profile factors, the political attitude factor, and the reformism scale score. Stepwise multiple regression was initially computed with renewal receipts as the dependent variable and the factor scores and reformism score as independent variables. All results were included in the stepwise regression regardless of statistical significance. Stepwise regression was selected so that the multiple correlation coefficient, the b values, and constant terms for the regression equation could be obtained. Table 3.7 presents the results of this regression. Seven steps of regression were performed. The computations were highly successful with the independent variables explaining 65.5 percent of the variation in the renewal variable. The computation also confirms the expected importance of the Size/Manufacturing variable with an initial correlation coefficient of $r = .75$ between Size/Manufacturing and urban renewal. Constant terms and b values were also obtained for use in a regression equation that would ultimately be used to predict urban renewal receipts for each of the 310 cities.

In a similar manner, stepwise multiple regression was computed with public housing occupancy as the dependent variable and the factor scores and reformism scores as independent variables. Again, all steps of the regression were used regardless of statistical significance. Table 3.8 presents the results of this regression. The housing computations were even more successful than the renewal results. In this case, the seven independent variables explained 81.9 percent of the housing variation. Once again, Size/ Manufacturing proved dominant with a correlation coefficient of $r = .89$. Constant terms and b values for the housing regression equation were also obtained.

TABLE 3.7

Results of Stepwise Multiple Regression Explaining Urban Renewal Funds Received

Step Number	Variable Added	Cumulative R	Cumulative R^2
1	Size/Manufacturing	0.745*	0.555
2	Urban Density	0.791*	0.625
3	Central City	0.798*	0.638
4	Status, Wealth, and Education (low)	0.805*	0.648
5	Commuting/Growth	0.807	0.651
6	Reformism	0.808	0.653
7	Local Culture	0.809	0.655

*Significant at the .05 level.

TABLE 3.8

Results of Stepwise Multiple Regression Explaining Public Housing Construction/Leasing

Step Number	Variable Added	Cumulative R	Cumulative R^2
1	Size/Manufacturing	0.887*	0.769
2	Urban Density	0.898*	0.806
3	Central City	0.903*	0.815
4	Commuting/Growth	0.904*	0.818
5	Reformism	0.905	0.818
6	Status, Wealth, and Education (low)	0.905	0.819
7	Local Culture	0.905	0.819

*Significant at the .05 level.

The constant terms and b values obtained for both renewal and housing equations were then used in separate equations to predict renewal receipts and housing construction for each of the cities.[8] Residuals for each city were computed by subtracting the predicted value of the dependent variables from the actual values.

The cities with large positive residuals were cities receiving more urban renewal funds/constructing more public housing units than predicted on the basis of the values of the independent variables. Conversely, cities with negative residuals received fewer renewal funds/constructed less public housing than was expected. The list of residuals was carefully examined to select six cities also meeting the criteria discussed in Chapter 2: specifically, (1) two large cities, two medium-sized cities, and two small cities; (2) at least two of the cities would be suburban and two would be central cities; (3) cities would be selected in pairs (at least two per state); (4) the pairs of cities would be geographically diverse; and (5) three cities would be high grant users and three would be low grant users.

Six of the cities meeting the criteria were then selected for further qualitative analysis through participant observation techniques. They were Austin and Beaumont, Texas; Alhambra and Vallejo, California; and Buffalo and Syracuse, New York. Table 3.9 compares the cities in relation to some of the criteria for city selection. The findings from the participant observation studies will be presented following the quantitative analysis in each chapter.

URBAN RENEWAL GRANT USE

Simple, partial, and multiple regression and correlation was then used to quantitatively determine patterns of urban renewal grant use. The independent variables identified as representing the city profile are the factor scores for the same five factors developed for the city selection procedure: Status, Wealth, and Education; Central City; Urban Density; Size/Manufacturing; and Commuting/Growth. Orthogonal rotation was utilized to insure the independence of the factors and to reduce problems of multicollinearity. To insure that the factors were indeed independent, Pearson's product moment correlation coefficients were computed showing the relationship between the factor scores. Table 3.10 shows these relationships. The matrix again confirms the relative independence of the factors with only the scores of Factor 1 and Factor 5 significantly related at the .05 level ($r = -.14$). This same relationship existed between the reference factors ($r = -.16$) utilizing oblique rotation. The other significant relationships between the reference factors did not prove to be statistically significant when factor scores were computed from

TABLE 3.9

Cities Selected for Qualitative Study

	State	Size and Population[a] (1960)		Metro Status [b]	Renewal Residual	Housing Residual
Austin	Texas	Medium	186,545	Central City	+5,868,895	+32
Beaumont	Texas	Medium	119,175	Central City	-7,722,403	-456
Alhambra	California	Small	54,807	Suburb	-6,196,166	-278
Vallejo	California	Small	60,877	Suburb	+2,914,423	+300
Buffalo	New York	Large	532,759	Central City	-9,801,040	-1,968
Syracuse	New York	Large	216,038	Central City	+19,264,128	+513

[a]U.S. Department of Commerce, Bureau of the Census, County and City Data Book 1962 (Washington, D.C.: Government Printing Office, 1962), pp. 476-575.

[b]The Municipal Year Book 1960 (Chicago: International City Managers' Association, 1960), pp. 89-117.

the orthogonal matrix. In spite of the data manipulations, then, the factor scores for the cities on the five factors are relatively independent of each other.

TABLE 3.10

Zero Order Product Moment Correlation Coefficients
between City Profile Factor Scores

	Status	Central City	Urban Density	Size/ Manufac- turing	Commuting/ Growth
Status, Wealth, Education (low)	1.000				
Central City	0.010	1.000			
Urban Density	0.006	-0.005	1.000		
Size/Manufacturing	0.007	-0.004	-0.002	1.000	
Commuting/Growth	-0.235*	0.086	0.060	0.040	1.000

*Significant at the .05 level.

Product moment correlation coefficients were then computed to show the relationship between urban renewal and each of the five factors. These coefficients are shown in Table 3.11. Two relationships immediately stand out. Size/Manufacturing is significantly and substantially related to grant use with r = .75. This one factor "explains" approximately 56 percent of the variation in urban renewal funds received by the cities. The Urban Density factor was also substantially related to the dependent variable with r = .26. Central City and Status, Wealth, and Education (low) were also positively related to renewal grants with r = .11 in both cases (not statistically significant at the .05 level). Only the Commuting/Growth factor did not show a substantial relationship with the dependent variable.

Effects of Federal Environment

Two variables were selected for analysis as indicators of federal influence on grant use. First was the designation of a city as a "model city" under the Demonstration Cities and Metropolitan Development Act of 1966.[9] Designation as a model city would presumably give a city priority in obtaining renewal funds although the relationship might be expected to be weak since the model cities concept was not developed until the mid-1960s. The second federal variable was the location of HUD regional offices.[10] It was expected that cities located in the same states with a HUD regional office would have a greater degree of grant success than cities in states without such offices. The location of the HUD regional offices changed in the late 1960s with a change in federal service concepts; however, the location used in this analysis was the early location covering the period up to 1968 (approximate). Both federal-level independent variables were dichotomous.

TABLE 3.11

Zero Order Product Moment Correlation Coefficients
between City Profile and Urban Renewal

	Urban Renewal
Status, Wealth, and Education (low)	0.109
Central City	0.108
Urban Density	0.263*
Size/Manufacturing	0.745*
Commuting/Growth	−0.018

*Significant at the .05 level.

Pearson's product moment correlation coefficients were computed between these independent variables and the dependent variable. Only one, however, was found to be significantly related to urban renewal use as Table 3.12 shows. A significant correlation coefficient of $r = .36$ was found to exist between model cities and urban renewal. The surprising relationship--or better, lack of relationship--was the low coefficient of $r = .04$ between the location of the regional HUD office and urban renewal funds. Nor was HUD office location substantially related to model cities--the coefficient here was only $r = -.09$. It is apparent then that this hypothesis will be rejected. Cities located in the same state with HUD regional offices do not appear to be any more successful in obtaining urban renewal funds than do cities in states without such offices.

State Environmental Effects

State laws were also hypothesized to have a substantial effect on grant use. Some state legislatures have made participation in federal-local grant programs quite easy. These states passed enabling legislation quickly and insured that the legislation did not place substantial prerequisites in the way of city participation. On the other hand, a few states were extremely slow to pass enabling legislation and/or placed impediments (for example, requiring a local referendum to establish a renewal authority) in the way of use of the grant programs by city government. These differences in state laws and enabling legislation are obviously important and are therefore included in the model.

TABLE 3.12

Zero Order Product Moment Correlation Coefficients
between Federal Variables and Urban Renewal

	Urban Renewal
Model city	0.357*
HUD office in state	0.042

*Significant at the .05 level.

The Department of Housing and Urban Development was able to provide a listing of the years each state passed enabling legislation for both public housing and urban renewal programs.[11] HUD was not, however, able to furnish any estimate of the difficulty cities might have in establishing these programs based upon requirements in the various state laws. To obtain this information, the legislative council in each state was surveyed by mailed questionnaire. All states having cities with populations over 50,000 with the exception of Michigan and Nebraska responded to the survey. States were asked when housing and renewal enabling legislation was first passed, whether a local referendum is required to establish renewal and/or housing authorities, and whether a local referendum is required for approval of each individual project. A simple difficulty scale was then constructed ranging from 0 to 2. Cities were scored 0 if no referendum was required, 1 if referendum was required either to establish a renewal authority or to approve individual projects, and a 2 if referendum was required for both authority and project approval.

In order to discover what difficulties, if any, cities had in establishing urban renewal authorities, two variables were selected as indicators of a city's difficulty: the number of years from 1949 until cities established renewal agencies, and the number of years from the date of the state enabling legislation until cities established renewal agencies. In attempting to assess this difficulty the number of years from 1949 to the time it took states to pass enabling legislation and the renewal difficulty scale were treated as independent variables and were correlated with the difficulty indicators. Table 3.13 shows the relationships between these variables. Neither of the independent variables was significantly related to the length of time since 1949 that it took cities to establish urban renewal agencies. Both of the independent variables, however, were significantly related to the length of time between state enabling legislation and the establishment of local urban renewal agencies. The peculiar nature of the relationship is its direction--both coefficients were negative. Apparently cities in states that delayed passage of enabling legislation were quick to establish renewal agencies once the states allowed them to do so. While this idea of cities trying to play "catch-up" in the competition for federal grants is logical, there is no direct explanation for the other negative coefficient. Cities located in states having a high degree of difficulty attached to urban renewal success through restrictive state laws were quicker to establish renewal agencies than those located in states without such restrictions. One explanation for this relationship is the possible interrelationship of the independent variables. If states that delay passage of renewal enabling legislation also make use of renewal grants more difficult, the obvious explanation for the relationship between difficulty and speedy agency establishment makes good sense. This was indeed the case. There was a significant positive relationship ($r = .31$) between the length of time a state took before passing enabling legislation and the difficulty scale. This suggests, then, that cities in slower states established renewal agencies rapidly in spite of a higher degree of difficulty.

TABLE 3.13

Zero Order Product Moment Correlation Coefficients between State Enabling Legislation and Establishment of Local Urban Renewal Authorities

	Years Since 1949	Years Since Enabling Legislation
Time to state enabling legislation	0.024	−0.772*
Renewal difficulty scale	−0.124	−0.275*

*Significant at the .05 level.

Is there then any relationship between renewal difficulty and success in obtaining urban renewal funds? Apparently not. Table 3.14 presents the correlation coefficients between several measures of renewal difficulty and urban renewal funds received. None of the coefficients were significant at the .05 level. There was no apparent relationship between renewal difficulty, or enabling legislation, and the amount of money a city received from 1960 to 1970. There was also no relationship between the length of time since 1949 that it took for cities to establish renewal authorities and funds received. Since urban renewal funds in this study were only measured between 1960 and 1970, it was possible that the date states passed enabling legislation might be important if 1960 were taken as the base year-- that is, all cities in states with enabling legislation passed in 1960 or prior would be coded 0; with legislation passed in 1961, coded 1, etc. Even this scale did not prove to be significantly related to renewal receipts. Analysis of the state variables, then, proved to be disappointing. While there was a definite relationship between a number of variables and the date local renewal authorities were established, there was no significant relationship between the state level independent variables and local urban renewal receipts.

TABLE 3.14

Zero Order Product Moment Correlation Coefficients
between Measures of Renewal Difficulty
and Urban Renewal

	Urban Renewal
Renewal difficulty scale	−0.050
Years since 1949 to local agency	−0.083
Legislation since 1960	0.111

Local Effects

Certain measures of city government were also hypothesized to effect grant use. They included the three measures of reformism commonly considered: council-manager form of government, at-large representation, and nonpartisan elections.[12] The three variables were considered both independently and collectively. To indicate strength of reformism, the Lineberry and Fowler scale was also included in the evaluation.

The relationship between the individual reform measures and the reformism scale was initially examined. Table 3.15 presents a correlation matrix showing these relationships. All individual measures of reformism were found to be substantially interrelated with the highest relationship between form of government and representation ($r = .49$). The lowest, but still significant, relationship was between representation and type of election with a coefficient of $r = .24$. Of course, all three measures correlated highly with the reformism scale score with coefficients of $r = .78$, $r = .78$, and $r = .67$ respectively.

TABLE 3.15

Zero Order Product Moment Correlation Coefficients
between Measures of Local Government Reform

	Government	Representation	Election	Score
Form of government	1.000			
Representation	0.487*	1.000		
Type of election	0.299*	0.240*	1.000	
Reformism score	0.780*	0.779*	0.669*	1.000

*Significant at the .05 level.

The relationship between these four variables and urban renewal receipts was then considered. The results are shown in Table 3.16. In each case the coefficients were negative, ranging from $r = .23$ between form of government and renewal and $r = -.12$ between type election and renewal. The coefficient showing the relationship between renewal and the reformism score was -0.20, a figure slightly below the relationship renewal and form of government. The use of the reformism scale will be examined again later in this chapter, but indications thus far do not substantiate the claim that reformism is additive--at least not concerning urban renewal funds.

Local Political Culture

The final political variables included in this analysis were measures designed to indicate the dominant political attitudes of local citizens. A number of measures were selected as possible indicators of community attitudes toward "liberal" federal programs. These measures included the variables discussed earlier in the construction of the Local Culture factor and a simple dichotomous variable, metropolitan status, which divided cities between central or independent cities and suburbs. The interrelationships between these variables can be found in Table 3.17. All relationships were relatively straightforward and in the direction one might expect (that is, the Wallace and Goldwater votes were interrelated, etc.). One problem did appear with the inclusion of the metropolitan status variable. This variable was included as an attempt to measure differences in attitude concerning grant use between central city and suburban residents.[13] One might expect, however, that this distinction was captured by the city profile factors. To test this possibility, metropolitan status was correlated with the five factors making up the profile (Table 3.18). As expected, the status variable was significantly related to all five factors. Thus while this variable may measure differences in attitudes, the five factors probably also measure most of the same thing.

TABLE 3.16

Zero Order Product Moment Correlation Coefficients
between Measures of Local Government Reform
and Urban Renewal

	Urban Renewal
Form of Government	−0.233*
Representation	−0.128*
Type of election	−0.117*
Reformism score	−0.203*

*Significant at the .05 level.

The five attitudinal variables were then correlated with the dependent variable with very disappointing results. Of the five variables, only two (the Goldwater vote and metropolitan status) were significantly related to urban renewal grants with correlations of $r = -.23$ and $r = -.19$ respectively.(Table 3.19). The type of political conservatism represented by the Goldwater vote appears to be the only attitudinal variable presented here that either encourages or discourages grant use. The Goldwater vote thus appears to represent a cultural value that discourages the use of federal grants by local government, while the metro status variable merely indicates the obvious: that central cities receive more urban renewal funds than do suburbs.

In summary then, of the 17 independent variables hypothesized to be related to urban renewal, 8 were found to be statistically significant at the .05 level. On the other hand, when the individual government reform measures were combined into a reformism score and when the Local Culture factor was substituted for the Elazar scale and Goldwater and Wallace votes, only 5 of the 13 variables were significant at the .05 level when zero order correlation coefficients were computed.

TABLE 3.17

Zero Order Product Moment Correlation Coefficients
between Measures of Local Political Attitude

	Wallace Vote	Goldwater Vote	Elazar Scale	Local Culture Factor	Metro Status
Wallace vote	1.000				
Goldwater vote	0.632*	1.000			
Elazar scale	0.602*	0.432*	1.000		
Local culture factor	-0.718*	-0.308*	-0.520*	1.000	
Metro status	-0.254*	-0.192*	-0.270*	0.279*	1.000

*Significant at the .05 level.

TABLE 3.18

Zero Order Product Moment Correlation Coefficients
between Measures of City Profile
and Metropolitan Status

	Metro Status
Status, Wealth, and Education (low)	-0.137*
Central City	-0.501*
Urban Density	0.261*
Size/Manufacturing	-0.128*
Commuting/Growth	0.250*

*Significant at the .05 level.

TABLE 3.19

Zero Order Product Moment Correlation Coefficients
between Measures of Local Political Attitudes
and Urban Renewal

	Urban Renewal
Wallace vote	-0.084
Goldwater vote	-0.232*
Elazar scale	-0.021
Local culture	0.068
Metro status	-0.189*

*Significant at the .05 level.

Multivariate Relationships

Once the zero order relationships between the independent variables and urban renewal were examined in some detail, stepwise multiple regression and correlation was utilized to compute the overall explanatory power of the independent variables. The multiple correlation coefficients are shown in Table 3.20. The 17 variables explain 71.9 percent of the variation in urban renewal funds received with one variable, Size/Manufacturing, accounting for the initial 55.5 percent of the variance explained. The variables added during the first nine steps were significant at the .05 level and accounted for almost all of the explained variance (71.6 percent) in renewal receipts. The first five variables added had previously been found to be significantly related to urban renewal when zero order relationships were computed. The variables added at steps 6 through 9 were not, however. The three variables added at steps 6 through 8 were all of the variables selected as indicators of the effect of state government on the use of urban renewal by local governments. None of the state variables were significantly related to renewal at the zero order level, but when considered along with all of the other independent variables, all three make a significant contribution to the variance explained. The final variable to make a significant contribution to renewal explanation, the Central City factor, had not been significant in zero order relationship with renewal (r = .11).

It was interesting to note that the three variables representing local reformism had been significantly related to urban renewal at the zero order level. Within the framework of multivariate relationships, however, all three were unable to make a significant contribution to the explanation of variation in urban renewal receipts. These variables are probably too interrelated to make a unique contribution. They lose their explanatory power when considered along with measures of the city profile and federal and state political variables. This finding adds support to Richard Cole's conclusion concerning local political structure: "by itself, political structure is an inadequate predictor of urban policy."[14]

TABLE 3.20

Results of Stepwise Multiple Regression (with individual political variables) Explaining Urban Renewal Funds Received

Step Number	Variable Added	Cumulative R	Cumulative R^2
1	Size/Manufacturing	0.745*	0.555
2	Urban Density	0.791*	0.625
3	Model City	0.810*	0.657
4	Metro status	0.820*	0.672
5	Goldwater vote	0.829*	0.687
6	Years since 1949 for URA	0.837*	0.700
7	Years since 1960 for legislation	0.840*	0.706
8	Renewal difficulty	0.843*	0.711
9	Central City	0.846*	0.716
10	Form of government	0.847	0.718
11	Elazar scale	0.848	0.719
12	Status, Wealth, and Education (low)	0.848	0.719
13	Wallace vote	0.848	0.719
14	Type of election	0.848	0.719
15	HUD office in state	0.848	0.719
16	Representation	0.848	0.719
17	Commuting/Growth	0.848	0.719

*Significant at the .05 level.

A second attempt to measure the combined effect of the independent variables on the dependent variable utilizing multiple regression and correlation was computed, but this time using a more parsimonious approach. The reformism scores were substituted for the three reform measures at the local level, and the Local Culture factor scores were substituted for the Wallace vote, Goldwater vote, and Elazar's political cultures. The result of the stepwise computations are found in Table 3.21. Neither the reformism score nor Local Culture made a significant contribution to the R^2. The reformism score made no significant contribution to the explained variance just as the three measures taken individually made no significant contribution. More interesting perhaps was the effect of Local Culture. This factor also made no significant contribution to the explained variance--in fact, use of the factor hid the influence of local conservative attitudes as expressed by the vote for Goldwater. Thus, while the use of this factor might add parsimony to the model, it also hides what might be an important attitudinal constraint to the use of grants.

TABLE 3.21

Results of Stepwise Multiple Regression (with combined
political variables) Explaining Urban Renewal
Funds Received

Step Number	Variable Added	Cumulative R	Cumulative R^2
1	Size/Manufacturing	0.745*	0.555
2	Urban Density	0.791*	0.625
3	Model city	0.810*	0.657
4	Metro status	0.820*	0.672
5	Years since 1960 for legislation	0.825*	0.680
6	Years since 1949 for URA	0.829*	0.687
7	Renewal difficulty	0.833*	0.694
8	Reformism score	0.835	0.696
9	Central City	0.835	0.697
10	HUD office in state	0.835	0.697
11	Local culture	0.835	0.697
12	Status, Wealth, and Education (low)	0.835	0.698
13	Commuting/Growth	0.835	0.698

*Significant at the .05 level.

Partial correlation coefficients were then computed between each of the independent variables and urban renewal while controlling for all other independent variables. Partials were used to identify the independent relationships between the independent variables and renewal that could be hidden in stepwise regression where all variables are not controlled at each step. The partial coefficients are shown in Table 3.22. There were no surprises. Of the 17 independent variables, 9 were found to be significantly and independently related to renewal. These were the same 9 variables making a significant contribution to the explained variance in the stepwise computation. Again, as with the stepwise regression and correlation, the reformism score and Local Culture were substituted for the three reform measures and the individual measures of political attitude. Once again, no surprising relationships appeared. Of the 13 independent variables, 7 were significantly and independently related to renewal (Table 3.23). Once again, these 7 variables were the same 7 making a significant contribution to the explained variance in the multiple correlation computation.

The model in Chapter 2 suggested that the political variables acted as intervening variables between the city profile factors and urban renewal funds received. By this it is suggested that the influence of the city profile is carried through, or modified by the political variables. With 17 independent variables to work with, causal modeling would be impractical, as it would add more confusion than conceptual clarity. It might be appropriate, however, to present a model of urban renewal grant use based upon partial correlation coefficients. Even though avoiding causal modeling techniques, an attempt to portray the relationships discovered thus far is difficult at best. To simplify matters somewhat, certain intervening variables have been eliminated from consideration--specifically, all intervening variables have been eliminated that were not significantly related to urban renewal when controlling for all other variables in the model. Likewise, connecting links between the variables are not shown where the relationship was not statistically significant.[15] The city factors are by definition (orthogonal) independent of each other (actually there is the small but statistically significant relationship between Commuting/Growth and Status, Wealth, and Education discussed earlier). Directional lines were drawn showing all significant relationships discovered. Partial correlation coefficients were then computed between urban renewal and all of the independent variables and between the intervening variables while controlling for the remaining variables in the model (only the relationship between model city and the Goldwater vote was significant, r = -.20). Again, directional lines were drawn and numerical values assigned to the lines. All relationships not reaching the .05 level of significance were then deleted from the model. The rather complex model presented in Figure 3.1 shows the remaining relationships.

TABLE 3.22

Partial Correlation Coefficients (with individual political
variables) between Independent Variables and Urban
Renewal Funds Received

City profile factors	
Status, Wealth, and Education (low)	−0.038
Central City	0.138*
Urban Density	0.265*
Size/Manufacturing	0.782*
Commuting/Growth	−0.009
Political variables	
Federal level	
Model city	0.143*
HUD office in state	−0.017
State level	
Renewal difficulty	−0.132*
Years since 1949 for URA	−0.190*
Years since 1960 for legislation	0.184*
Local level	
Form of government	−0.052
Representation	−0.010
Type of election	−0.031
Local political attitudes	
Wallace vote	0.031
Goldwater vote	−0.234*
Elazar scale	−0.051
Metro status	−0.114*

*Significant at the .05 level.

All of the city factors appeared to contribute to the explanation of urban renewal grant use. Three, Central City, Urban Density, and Size/Manufacturing, are related both independently and through the intervening political variables, while Status, Wealth, and Education, and Commuting/Growth are related only through the intervening variables. Size/Manufacturing was significantly related to four of the intervening variables when controlling for all others. Central City, Commuting/Growth, and Status, Wealth, and Education were significantly related to three, and Urban Density to two intervening variables. Only one of the factors correlated significantly with the federal-level variable. Three factors were related to at least one of the state political variables, and all five of the city factors were independently related to at least one of the indicators of local political attitude. All five factors of the community profile apparently made a substantial contribution to the use of urban renewal grants. While Commuting/Growth and Status, Wealth, and Education showed no significant independent relationship with urban renewal, both are significantly related to three of the intervening variables—two state variables and one cultural variable. Size/Manufacturing was undoubtedly the most important determinant of renewal grant use. It was not only highly related to grant use directly ($r = .78$), but it was significantly and independently related to four of the six intervening variables.

TABLE 3.23

Partial Correlation Coefficients (with combined political variables) between Independent Variables and Urban Renewal Funds Received

City profile factors	
Status, Wealth, and Education (low)	0.025
Central City	0.046
Urban Density	0.367*
Size/Manufacturing	0.771*
Commuting/Growth	0.013
Political variables	
Federal level	
Model city	0.202*
HUD office in state	−0.037
State level	
Renewal difficulty	−0.130*
Years since 1949 for URA	−0.160*
Years since 1960 for legislation	0.182*
Local level	
Reformism score	−0.079
Local political attitudes	
Local culture	0.030
Metro status	−0.133*

*Significant at the .05 level.

FIGURE 5.1

Model of Urban Renewal Grant Use

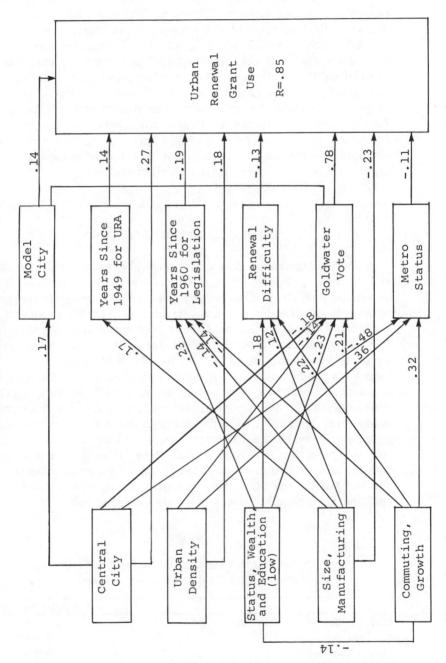

The quantitative analysis presented thus far substantiates the general model with some modification. The city profile measures operate both independently and through intervening political variables to predict urban renewal receipts. Political variables measuring federal and state influence appear to act as intervening variables as do local political attitudes. The surprising finding thus far was the lack of influence that government reform measures appear to have on grant use--either independently or as intervening variables. This discovery will be discussed at length later in this chapter. Since both housing and renewal grants serve as the operational definitions of local grant use, conclusions with regard to the specific hypotheses will be delayed until a detailed analysis of public housing grant use has been completed.

LOW-INCOME PUBLIC HOUSING

As with the analysis of urban renewal grants, simple, partial, and multiple regression and correlation were used quantitatively to determine patterns of construction and leasing of low-income public housing units. The independent variables used in this section of the study were almost the same as those examined with urban renewal. The city profile was once again represented by the factor scores for the same five factors developed for the city selection procedure. Pearson's product moment correlation coefficients were computed to show the zero order relationship between public housing and the factors (Table 3.24). Again, Size/Manufacturing is the dominant independent variable $(r = .88)$ with Urban Density also proving to be significant $(r = .19)$. Size/Manufacturing is more closely related to public housing than to urban renewal while Urban Density explains less of the variation in housing than it did for renewal. Central City, Status, Wealth, and Education, as well as Commuting/Growth were again not significantly related to the dependent variable.

TABLE 3.24

Zero Order Product Moment Correlation Coefficients
between City Profile and Public Housing

	Public Housing
Status, Wealth, and Education (low)	0.036
Central City	0.093
Urban Density	0.189*
Size/Manufacturing	0.877*
Commuting/Growth	0.005

*Significant at the .05 level.

Federal Effects

Three variables were selected to represent the influence of the federal government on public housing. The first two are the same variables used to explain variations in urban renewal receipts: designation as a model city and location of the HUD regional offices. The third variable is the previous dependent variable--urban renewal receipts. Two basic facts suggest this relationship. First, low-income public housing is heavily relied on to provide standard low-cost rental housing for families faced with relocation as a result of urban renewal.[16] And second, federal law requires that a majority of the total housing units provided in a community's urban renewal projects will be standard housing units for low- and moderate-income families (20 percent of the total must be for low-income).[17]

Pearson's product moment correlation coefficients were computed between the three federal-level independent variables and public housing. Two of the three were found to be statistically significant (Table 3.25). Model city was found to be significantly related to public housing with a coefficient of r = .33. As with renewal, the location of the HUD regional office was not a determining factor in grant use. Apparently, then, cities located in the same state with HUD regional offices did not receive the favored treatment this study hypothesized. The striking relationship of this section of the study is the extremely high correlation coefficient (r = .80) between urban renewal and public housing. In spite of some difficulty in trying to deal with problems of temporal ordering, urban renewal funds received explains almost 64 percent of the variance in public housing construction and leasing. While some relationship was certainly expected, a correlation coefficient of this magnitude was not. The independent effect of urban renewal will be discussed later in this chapter.

TABLE 3.25

Zero Order Product Moment Correlation Coefficients
between Federal Variables and Public Housing

	Public Housing
Model city	0.329*
HUD office in state	0.071
Urban renewal	0.796*

*Significant at the .05 level.

State Effects

Again, as with urban renewal, the state was expected to have some effect on public housing construction through state laws and enabling legislation. Table 3.26 presents zero order relationships between measures of public housing difficulty imposed by the state on the cities' ability to establish local housing authorities. Two variables were selected as indicators of difficulty for the city: number of years since 1937 until cities established housing authorities, and number of years since the state passed enabling legislation until cities established housing authorities. Both of the independent variables were significantly related to the length of time after 1937 before the state passed public housing enabling legislation. The first relationship was expected--using 1937 as a base; the longer it took states to pass enabling legislation, the longer it took for cities in those states to establish housing authorities. This type of relationship had not been found to be statistically significant within the urban renewal model. A partial explanation for this difference between housing and renewal might be found in the next relationship. Recall that the zero order correlation coefficient between the time (since 1949) a state took before passing renewal enabling legislation and the time between the date of this legislation and establishment of local renewal authorities was $r = -.77$. In the case of public housing, the relationship between enabling legislation and local housing authorities was only $r = -.32$. While this relationship is still statistically significant, it is not as strong as the relationship found in the case of urban renewal. With renewal, cities in those states lagging in the passage of enabling legislation appeared to establish renewal agencies as soon as they could after enabling legislation was passed. Not so with housing: While some cities did establish housing authorities as soon as they were able, the tendency to do so was not as strong as in the case of urban renewal--thus the significant positive relationship between the first two variables.

TABLE 3.26

Zero Order Product Moment Correlation Coefficients
between State Enabling Legislation and Establishment
of Local Public Housing Authorities

	Years Since 1937	Years Since Enabling Legislation
Time to state enabling legislation	0.233*	-0.324*
Housing difficulty scale	0.025	0.096

*Significant at the .05 level.

The housing difficulty scale was not significantly related to either the time since 1937 or the time since enabling legislation until establishment of local housing authorities. Apparently, a local referendum is not a significant factor that might serve to delay the establishment of public housing authorities.

Three variables were selected as independent variables measuring housing difficulty and were correlated with public housing construction/leasing. The independent variables were the housing difficulty scale, length of time since 1937 to establish a local housing authority, and a scale of state enabling legislation since 1960 (developed the same way as urban renewal since 1960). There was no statistically significant relationship between any of the independent variables and public housing (Table 3.27). As with renewal, then, measures of difficulty in state public housing legislation were not related to housing success. The highest relationship was between the years since 1937 to establish a local authority and public housing with $r = -.13$, but even this coefficient was not significant at the .05 level.

TABLE 3.27

Zero Order Product Moment Correlation Coefficients
between Measures of Housing Difficulty
and Public Housing

	Public Housing
Housing difficulty scale	-0.089
Years since 1937 to local authority	-0.125
Legislation since 1960	-0.025

Local Effects

City government reform measures were expected to be related to public housing success in much the same manner that these measures were related to urban renewal. This was indeed the case. Table 3.28 presents the zero order relationships between reform measures and public housing. Only one relationship was not statistically significant--the coefficient between type of election (partisan-nonpartisan) and public housing. The relationship between both form of government and type of representation and public housing was significant with coefficients of $r = -.20$ and $-.12$ respectively. The reformism scale score was also significantly related to public housing with r = -.16. Overall results were very similar to the relationships found between reformism and urban renewal. Measures of city reform were negatively related to public housing construction and leasing. Again, the reform measures do not appear to be additive as a higher correlation coefficient was found between form of government and housing than between the reformism scale score and public housing.

TABLE 3.28

Zero Order Product Moment Correlation Coefficients
between Measures of Local Government Reform
and Public Housing

	Public Housing
Form of government	−0.195*
Representation	−0.115*
Type of election	0.004
Reformism score	−0.163*

*Significant at the .05 level.

Local Political Culture

And finally, the political variables shown in Table 3.29 were correlated with public housing in an attempt to measure the relationship between local attitudes and public housing. Of the five variables, only the Goldwater vote was significantly related to housing with r = -.11. Once again, the type of political conservatism associated with the Goldwater vote appears to represent a value that discourages the use of low-income public housing programs.

Multivariate Relationships

Stepwise multiple regression and correlation was then utilized to test the overall explanatory power of the independent variables. The multiple correlation coefficients are shown in Table 3.30. Of the 18 independent variables, 9 made a significant contribution to the explained variance in housing (R = .93). The first nine steps of the regression accounted for virtually all of the explained variance with R = .92. Size/Manufacturing, the first variable added, accounted

100

for an explained variance of 76.9 percent. The first four variables added in the stepwise computation had previously been found to be related to low-income housing at the zero order level. Zero order computations between the state level housing difficulty measures and public housing showed no significant relationships. In the multiple relationship, however, two of the three state measures (steps 6 and 7) made a significant contribution to the explained variance in housing construction/leasing. Of the three individual measures of local reform, type of election was the only variable not significantly related to public housing at the zero order level. In the multiple relationship, however, type of election along with form of government makes a significant contribution. Representation, on the other hand, is not a major contributor. In the urban renewal computations presented earlier, the Goldwater vote was significantly related to urban renewal in both zero order computations and in the stepwise correlations. This variable behaves quite differently in the public housing model. While significantly related at the zero order level, the Goldwater vote makes no significant independent contribution to the explained variance in housing in a multiple relationship. A conservative political attitude (at least as measured in this study) may not be an important influence on the public housing program.

TABLE 3.29

Zero Order Product Moment Correlation Coefficients
between Measures of Local Political Attitudes
and Public Housing

	Public Housing
Wallace vote	−0.032
Goldwater vote	−0.112*
Elazar scale	0.005
Local culture	0.024
Metro status	−0.084

*Significant at the .05 level.

Table 3.31 presents the results of a second stepwise computation--this time adding the reformism score and Local Culture factor and deleting the individual variables making up these indices. The city profile factors and the federal-level intervening variables making a significant contribution to the explained variance in Table 3.30 also made a significant contribution here. Two major differences between the computations, however, were readily apparent. First, when the city reform measures were combined into the reformism score, the score failed to make a significant contribution to explained variance. In fact, the independent contribution of the score was so small that it was the last variable added in the stepwise computation. This finding substantiates the earlier discovery concerning the nature of the reformism scale--namely that reform measures are not additive as determinants of local grant use. The second unusual finding was the contribution made by Local Culture. None of the individual component measures of the Local Culture factor made a significant contribution to the explained variance in public housing (Table 3.30) and yet the factor, added at Step 5, was found to be significant. The contribution to the explained variance, however, was so limited as to be substantively insignificant.

TABLE 3.30

Results of Stepwise Multiple Regression (with individual political variables) Explaining Public Housing Construction/Leasing

Step Number	Variable Added	Cumulative R	Cumulative R^2
1	Size/Manufacturing	0.877*	0.769
2	Urban renewal	0.903*	0.815
3	Urban Density	0.910*	0.828
4	Model city	0.915*	0.838
5	Type of election	0.918*	0.842
6	Housing difficulty	0.919*	0.845
7	Years since 1937 for LHA	0.921*	0.848
8	Central City	0.923*	0.851
9	Form of government	0.924*	0.853
10	Years since 1960 for legislation	0.924	0.854
11	HUD office in state	0.925	0.855
12	Commuting/Growth	0.925	0.856
13	Wallace vote	0.925	0.856
14	Metro status	0.925	0.856
15	Elazar scale	0.925	0.856
16	Representation	0.925	0.856
17	Status, Wealth, and Education (low)	0.925	0.856
18	Goldwater vote	0.925	0.856

*Significant at the .05 level.

TABLE 3.31

Results of Stepwise Multiple Regression (with combined
political variables) Explaining Public Housing
Construction/Leasing

Step Number	Variable Added	Cumulative R	Cumulative R^2
1	Size/Manufacturing	0.877*	0.769
2	Urban renewal	0.903*	0.815
3	Urban Density	0.910*	0.828
4	Model city	0.915*	0.838
5	Local Culture	0.917*	0.842
6	Years since 1937 for LHA	0.919*	0.844
7	Central City	0.920*	0.846
8	Commuting/Growth	0.920	0.847
9	Years since 1960 for legislation	0.921	0.848
10	Housing difficulty	0.921	0.848
11	HUD office in state	0.921	0.848
12	Metro status	0.921	0.848
13	Status, Wealth, and Education (low)	0.921	0.849
14	Reformism score	0.921	0.849

*Significant at the .05 level.

Partial correlation coefficients were also computed between
each of the independent variables and public housing while controlling
for all other independent variables. These partials are shown in
Table 3.32. Of the 18 individual independent variables, 8 were significantly and independently related to housing. All 8 of these variables had previously made a significant contribution to the explained
variance in the stepwise computation. Only form of government had
been significant in the stepwise computation but was not found to be
independently related to public housing.

Once again, the reformism score and Local Culture were substituted for the three reform measures and the individual measures
of political attitude. Again, there were no surprises. Of the 14 independent variables, 6 were significantly and independently related
to public housing (Table 3.33). All 6 variables contributed significantly to the explained variance in the stepwise computations. Only
Local Culture had previously been significant but was now not found
to be independently related to public housing.

TABLE 3.32

Partial Correlation Coefficients (with individual political
variables) between Independent Variables and
Public Housing Construction/Leasing

City profile factors	
Status, Wealth, and Education (low)	0.004
Central City	0.142*
Urban Density	0.243*
Size/Manufacturing	0.751*
Commuting/Growth	−0.053
Political variables	
Federal level	
Model city	0.158*
Urban renewal	0.273*
HUD office in state	0.064
State level	
Housing difficulty	−0.117*
Years since 1937 for LHA	0.179*
Years since 1960 for legislation	0.098
Local level	
Form of government	−0.086
Representation	−0.012
Type of election	0.220*
Local political attitudes	
Wallace vote	−0.032
Goldwater vote	0.002
Elazar scale	0.015
Metro status	0.020

*Significant at the .05 level.

A model explaining public housing construction/leasing was
drawn in much the same manner that the urban renewal model had
been developed (see Figure 3.2). Again, the model is based upon
statistically significant partial correlation coefficients. All intervening variables not significantly and independently related to public
housing are not shown.

As with the urban renewal model, all of the city profile factors appear to contribute to the explanation of low-income public
housing construction and leasing. Three factors, Central City,
Urban Density, and Size/Manufacturing, contributed to the explained

104

FIGURE 3.2

Model of Public Housing Construction/Leasing

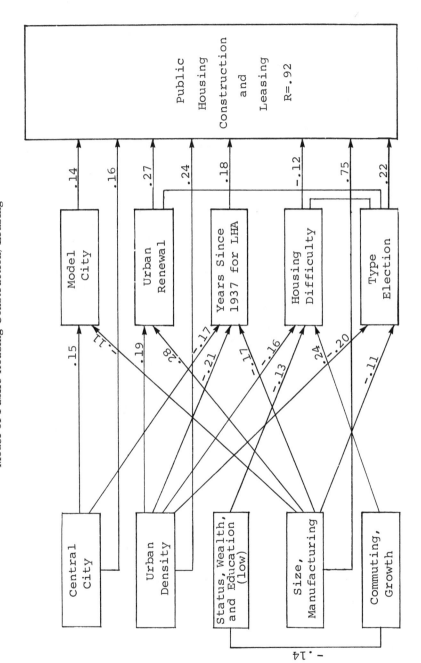

variance both directly and through the intervening variables, while the remaining two factors were related only through the intervening political variables. Once again, Size/Manufacturing was the dominant variable contributing to housing explanation directly as well as through four of the intervening variables. The apparent weakness of Commuting/Growth, and Status, Wealth, and Education was somewhat surprising. Both were only independently related to one intervening variable--housing difficulty. While neither variable had shown an independent linkage with urban renewal (Figure 3.1), both were significantly related to three intervening variables in the renewal model. In the case of public housing, however, their contribution was considerably reduced with an independent relationship between the factors and only one intervening variable.

TABLE 3.33

Partial Correlation Coefficients (with combined political variables) between Independent Variables and Public Housing Construction/Leasing

City profile factors	
Status, Wealth, and Education (low)	−0.028
Central City	0.130*
Urban Density	0.238*
Size/Manufacturing	0.754*
Commuting/Growth	−0.056
Political variables	
Federal level	
Model city	0.202*
Urban renewal	0.268*
HUD office in state	0.033
State level	
Housing difficulty	−0.060
Years since 1937 for LHA	0.157*
Years since 1960 for legislation	0.097
Local level	
Reformism score	−0.013
Local political attitudes	
Local culture	−0.060
Metro status	0.032

*Significant at the .05 level.

There is an obvious basic similarity between the two models--renewal and housing. The city profile measures have all been important contributors to the explained variance in the dependent variables--both independently and through the political system. Federal- and state-level intervening variables were also important in both models. The main difference between renewal and housing use appears to be determined at the local level. In the renewal model, city reform characteristics were only related to urban renewal at the zero order level. Reform characteristics did not contribute significantly to the explained variance in a multivariate setting--nor were reform characteristics independently related to renewal when controlling for the effects of the other independent variables. In the housing model, however, one of the reform measures, type of election, contributed to the explained variance in public housing and was also found to be independently related to housing when controlling for the other independent variables. Nonpartisan elections were, for some reason, associated with higher levels of public housing activity. One can only suggest that political parties emphasize the cleavages in an urban community and, as a strong issue area, public housing expansion is adversely affected by the cleavages. This possibility will be examined in more detail later in the chapter.

Local political attitudes, on the other hand, were much more important in the renewal model than they were in housing. Both metropolitan status and the Goldwater vote were important explanatory variables in the urban renewal model, while neither were significantly related to public housing. Suburban status is associated with low renewal grant use as is the Goldwater vote. This gives support to the contention that there is some kind of political culture, or significant local attitude, operating in opposition to certain types of grant use. It was interesting that this appeared only in the renewal issue and was not related to public housing construction. Again, this difference will be discussed in depth later in the chapter.

BACKGROUND FOR FIELD STUDIES

The author spent approximately one week in each of the cities selected for detailed study, examining public records and newspapers, interviewing administrators, elites, and past and present public officials, and recording impressions of factors in these cities as they related to grant use. Officials in each city were made aware of the author's impending visit and were advised of the purpose of the visit through letters of introduction. In addition, to secure the full cooperation of all of the individuals interviewed, anonymity was guaranteed to all of those persons consenting to the interviews. To respect this guarantee, this study will not name or give the job titles of any of the individuals interviewed. To place each community in an analytic perspective, a brief overview of each city is presented to serve as background material for the more detailed discussion of grant use to follow.

Alhambra

Alhambra, California, the smallest of the six cities visited, is a suburban city of some 62,147 population located adjacent to the City of Los Angeles in Los Angeles County, California. Alhambra is one of Southern California's oldest cities--incorporated in 1903. Small in area, only 7.6 square miles, the city is an attractive, balanced community of tree-lined streets, attractive homes and apartments, and fine commercial and industrial developments. Commercial activity, primarily in the form of retail specialty stores, is located along two East-West arteries--Main Street and Valley Boulevard. Alhambra serves as the gateway to the San Gabriel Valley, a former agricultural area now made up of numerous suburban communities. Multifamily housing has been an important recent trend in the city--so much so that by the end of the 1960s more than half of the city's population resided in multifamily structures.[18] The median family income is $11,004 with 5.4 percent of families with incomes below the poverty level. The population is 13 percent foreign born--primarily Mexican-American. Approximately 19 percent of the residents have Spanish surnames. There are only 114 black citizens of Alhambra (.2 percent).[19]

Alhambra is governed by a five-man city council elected for four-year terms under the council-manager plan. Representation is nonpartisan with at-large elections, although the councilmen are nominated from each of five geographic districts in which they reside. The city council elects one of its members to serve as mayor for a two-year term. Unlike many of the suburban communities of Los Angeles County, Alhambra provides local police and fire protection and maintains its own library rather than contracting with the county for such services.[20]

Vallejo

Vallejo, California, an independent suburb of some 66,209 population, is located in Solano County some 31 miles northeast of San Francisco on the eastern shores of San Pablo Bay. Vallejo's population is 16.8 percent black with another 9 percent of the population having Spanish surnames. Approximately 5 percent of Vallejo's population was foreign born. The median family income for the community is $10,596 with 8.4 percent of the families with incomes below the poverty level.[21] Vallejo was the site chosen for California's first permanent seat of government (1852), and it was incorporated in 1867. An attractive city of rolling hills overlooking the San Pablo Bay, Vallejo has been traditionally geared to a waterfront life. The local economy is dominated by the Mare Island Naval Shipyard (employing 8,488), one of the world's largest shipbuilding and repair stations. "Lower Georgia Street," the 26-square-block area of bars, gambling, and prostitution remembered by many World War II Navy personnel, is gone. The area has been rebuilt with high-rise and garden apartments as well as commercial and public buildings.

Vallejo provides a full range of urban services for its citizens. The city is governed through a council-manager form of government with nonpartisan representation and at-large elections. Six councilmen and the mayor are elected for four-year terms with elections staggered at two-year intervals.[22]

Beaumont

Beaumont, Texas, a city of 116,163 population established in 1838, is located in southeast Texas on the Neches River. It is 85 miles east of Houston and is the center of activity in a region containing over 10 percent of the world's oil refining capability. Only 1 percent of Beaumont's population is foreign born. Approximately 30 percent of the population is black and another 3 percent have Spanish surnames. The median family income is $8,925 with 14.1 percent of the city's families with income below the poverty level.[23] The city has been dominated by petroleum refining, petrochemical industries, and shipping-related activities during recent years, although most of the plants are not located within the Beaumont city limits. Lamar University, one of the universities in the Texas state system with an enrollment of approximately 11,000 students, is also located in Beaumont. Beaumont's population declined by 1.4 percent during the 1960s while the overall state population increased by about 14 percent. The city entered a period of economic stagnation during the 1960s and is now trying to combat the trend. The downtown area has a large number of vacant buildings and the three downtown hotels have been closed. A large percentage of the housing units within the city are substandard. Through its location on the Neches ship channel, Beaumont has an active port facility.[24]

Beaumont during the 1960s was also governed by a council-manager form of government with a mayor and four councilmen.

Elections were partisan and at-large with councilmen running for seats within wards but elected by the population at-large.

Austin

Austin, Texas, the fast-growing capital of the State of Texas with a population of 251,791, is located in central Texas about 200 miles south of Dallas and 160 miles northwest of Houston. The median family income for the city is $9,180 with 11 percent of the city families having incomes below the poverty level. The city has a large Mexican-American population with 15.7 percent of the citizens having Spanish surnames. About 12 percent of the population is black.[25]

Austin is the home of the University of Texas (the south's largest, with 35,500 students), a large number of state and federal offices, and Bergstrom Air Force Base (6,080 personnel). A city of hills, trees, lakes, and architectural beauty, Austin is one of the most attractive cities in the Southwest. The population of the city grew approximately 35 percent during the 1960s with much of the growth resulting from annexation.

Austin is governed by a council-manager form of government with a mayor and six councilmen elected for staggered terms. Elections are typical of council-manager cities with nonpartisan elections and at-large representation.[26]

Syracuse

Syracuse, New York, a city of 197,332 population in north central New York, was settled as the result of the economic potential of salt springs discovered near Syracuse, with commercial development of the springs beginning in 1793. Syracuse now has a median family income of $9,246 with 9.8 percent of the families below the poverty level. Some 8 percent of the residents of Syracuse are foreign born with a Spanish-speaking population of only 1 percent. Approximately 11 percent of the Syracuse residents are black.[27]

Like most large urban cities, Syracuse has been declining in total population while the lower-income population has been increasing relative to the total population. The city is noted for chemical production (originally because of the salt production) and electronics manufacturing. The city has large amounts of substandard housing with some areas (census tracts) having more than 50 percent substandard housing units. Syracuse University, a major private university with an enrollment of 23,000, is a dominant feature of the city.[28]

The city government of Syracuse is of the strong-mayor type administered by a mayor and common council. The mayor is elected on an at-large basis (partisan elections) for a four-year term. The Common Council is composed of ten councilmen--five members elected at-large (including the president) serve four-year terms, and five district councilmen serve two-year terms.[29]

Buffalo

Buffalo, New York, the largest of the cities selected for field study with a 1970 population of 462,781, is located on the St. Lawrence Seaway in northwestern New York. Median family income for Buffalo is $8,804 with 11.2 percent of the city families having incomes below the poverty level. Approximately 20 percent of the population is black while less than 2 percent have Spanish surnames. Almost 8 percent of the residents are foreign born.[30] Buffalo is a densely populated older industrial city whose total population is declining, housing stock is rapidly deteriorating, and whose lower income population is increasing relative to the total population.

Buffalo was incorporated in 1816 and developed into one of the largest industrial centers in the United States. The city's basic industries include chemical products, steel, flour milling, and shipping. The State University of New York at Buffalo is located on the outskirts of the city. The impact of the declining population, as well as its changing character, has been a declining tax base and increasing governmental costs. Buffalo has not significantly changed its boundaries since 1853 and is consequently faced with a shortage of undeveloped land. A critical housing situation exists in the city. During the 1960s Buffalo lost some 11,000 housing units, primarily as a result of urban renewal, highway construction, etc. On top of this loss, some sources estimate that another 17 percent of the housing stock requires immediate clearance.[31]

Buffalo has a strong-mayor form of government with three clear governmental divisions--the executive, legislative, and fiscal. Elections are partisan with a combination ward and at-large system. The mayor is elected for a four-year term to head the executive branch. The comptroller is the chief fiscal officer and is also elected for a four-year term. The Common Council is composed of 15 councilmen--6 members at-large (including the president) elected for staggered four-year terms, and 9 district members elected for two-year terms.[32]

QUALITATIVE ANALYSIS

Alhambra

Alhambra, California, is one of a number of cities in the United
States that uses neither public housing nor federal urban renewal
programs. There are a number of probable reasons for this based
upon both physical characteristics of the city and local community attitudes. Physically, Alhambra is a unique city in many respects:
It is extremely small (only 7.6 square miles) and has virtually no
vacant land (estimated less than ten acres of undeveloped land within
the city); and its physical appearance is one of a very homogeneous
middle-class community.

Physical Characteristics

Although no general plan existed for Alhambra until 1965, the
city experienced orderly, though somewhat peculiar, patterns of
growth within a framework of zoning laws. Zoning and development
in Alhambra date back to 1937. Thus a large number of commercial
buildings and residential dwellings are 30 to 40 years old. A large
part of the city is zoned for multifamily housing. In fact, Victor
Gruen Associates believes that Alhambra's present zoning would
accommodate a population of 170,000 (as compared to the 1970 actual
population of 62,147), in spite of the fact that there is virtually no
vacant land in the city. The general plan, however, favors the
eventual reduction of the amount of space presently zoned for high-
density residential use.[33] Of the 1,060 acres zoned for multifamily
dwellings, only 20 percent is currently used for this purpose. The
multifamily zoning is not new--it has been a characteristic of the
city for more than 30 years. Years ago people bought the multifamily zoned lots for long-term speculation and then built their
single-family homes on the lots. Thus the citizens had a nice home
as well as a long-term investment.

Recent years have brought pressure on Alhambra for increased
multifamily development, but developers have had some difficulty in
land assembly. With less than 10 acres of undeveloped land in the
city, developers have had to assemble the small lots (zoned multifamily) with the existing single-family homes. This is a slow and
expensive procedure, so multifamily developments have not increased
at a rapid rate.

Alhambra is amenity oriented (for example, there is a $50.00
per unit assessment to an open space fund for the Recreation Department when building permits are issued). There is a strong
feeling of identification on the part of local citizens with Alhambra

rather than with Los Angeles.[34] City administrators and officials associate this feeling of city pride with a high percentage of home ownership. This attitude is perceived as an attribute, thus there is a strong single-family orientation to the community leadership. To further develop this civic pride orientation, the Planning and Building Department is encouraging the development of condominiums rather than multifamily rental units.

While the 1970 median family income for the city was $11,004, one official estimated that 3,000-4,000 family units in Alhambra were receiving welfare assistance. About 35 percent of the population is elderly, and it is likely that a large percentage of the welfare families fall into this category. Most of the remainder of the welfare recipients are commonly believed to be from the 15-20 percent of the population making up the Mexican-American community. And yet it is difficult to physically identify any low-income or slum area. There is no area concentration in the city of low-income families; they are almost randomly dispersed throughout the community.

The central business district, or CBD, is often discussed when local officials are talking of future developments. And yet there really is no physical CBD--the business district consists of miles of strip zoning along the two major east-west arteries. The CBD is made up of small specialty shops and restaurants. It appears quite prosperous with very few vacant stores. It is a retail center of sorts--78 percent of the retail income comes from the San Gabriel Valley, not just from Alhambra. And yet most businesses are small, highly personalized, locally owned shops.

While Alhambra is a dormitory community, it is a balanced one with a sizable industrial base. The Alhambra Industrial Center, a 370-acre area in the western section of the city, has been the location of over 200 industries for a number of years.[35] The Industrial Center has not escaped the trend of deterioration and decline common to many such areas. Fragmented land ownership patterns, high land cost, parking shortages, etc., moved the center to a point of "critical obsolescence."[36] To stimulate redevelopment in the industrial area, Alhambra established the Alhambra Redevelopment Agency in 1968 (functional beginning in 1969) to provide the "opportunity for marshalling and implementing all the diverse private and public efforts essential to the revitalization of the Industrial Center."[37] While concerned with the upgrading of the public areas within the center, the main job of the agency is land assembly for industrial users. The agency therefore has the power of eminent domain within the project area. Financing is accomplished through a tax increment plan under the Community Redevelopment Law of the State of California.[38]

The agency only acquires land when it has a buyer. It purchases small individual land parcels from the owners based upon an appraised valuation (or uses the power of eminent domain and court proceedings) and assembles the land that it then sells to the industrial developer/user. Much like the federal urban renewal program, it usually sells the land at a lower price than the acquisition costs.

The Politics of Housing and Renewal

Politically, Alhambra is a highly conservative community. In 1964, the local newspaper, the Alhambra Post-Advocate, supported the candidacy of Barry Goldwater for the presidency.[39] With a voter turnout of almost 90 percent, Goldwater carried Alhambra with 15,638 votes to Johnson's 14,263.[40] In 1968 the Post-Advocate endorsed Richard Nixon for president--"Nixon has key to future."[41] Nixon carried Alhambra with 16,668 votes to 10,858 for Humphrey and 1,424 votes for George Wallace.[42]

The city seldom has referendum elections. Bond issues generally fail. The city paid cash for its new city hall complex in 1960, for example, and will pay cash for a new library in the near future. Alhambra even once turned down the offer of a free Carnegie Library. Very status-quo oriented, the community resists change. They utilize few federal programs because they do not want the "federal strings." While located in Los Angeles County, the city exhibits the Orange County conservative orientation.

There is an association of area governments (COG), but the city, though a member, has little to do with the association. Since the power of the association is in the area of federal grant approval, and since Alhambra never applies for federal grants, there is little participation by the city in the association. The city does, however, keep up with the association's transportation plans as it is in this area where the decisions of the association can affect the community.

Local election issues are usually concerned with the maintenance of private property and with keeping down the property tax rate. Residents are almost infected with an all-pervasive norm concerned with "keeping up private property." The norm is often voiced by the newspaper--everyone talks about it. The city has a stringent nuisance ordinance that is strictly enforced as is the local noise ordinance.[43] Though the city is older, and certainly not wealthy by California standards, the "keep up private property" norm has kept Alhambra a virtually slumless city. The norm is not only a characteristic of the long-time Anglo residents, but it is also characteristic of the newer Mexican-American community as well.

Public housing and urban renewal have never really been issue areas in the community. The author could find no evidence of public housing as a public issue. It apparently was never considered. Urban renewal was suggested, however, by Gruen Associates as a

possible vehicle for the industrial redevelopment project.[44] Renewal
never became a public issue, although it was considered at length in
the planning for the Redevelopment Agency.

Urban renewal was never publicly put forth as an alternative
for the Redevelopment Agency. As one official put, "it was extremely
doubtful that the community would approve such a program if it went
to referendum as it was certain to do." Some members of the city
council also opposed it on ideological grounds (the "federal strings"
argument). Another reason given by a number of officials and administrators was that Alhambra's priority for renewal funds would
be too low--that it would delay the project much too long.

Conclusions

A study of the City of Alhambra suggests several reasons for
the lack of urban renewal and public housing programs. The city
really has no need for renewal and no wish for public housing.

Physically, the city has not deteriorated the way many other
U.S. cities have. This is probably the result of a number of factors.
First, the old zoning laws, while certainly not perfect, did allow for
an orderly and quality development of the community. While zoning
laws are not usually a key to community development, in this case
the zoning laws were probably an important factor in the local development.

A second factor peculiar to Alhambra was its small size--only
7.6 square miles, which is completely surrounded by other incorporated communities. The small size of the community allows for
close supervision and control of the physical development of the city.
City officials and administrators were able to keep an eye on community development in the normal course of doing business, or through
merely living in the city. The limited physical area of Alhambra
undoubtedly produced a strict control on potential blight and deterioration within the community.

Probably the most important reason that Alhambra has not
experienced decay has been the norm concerning the maintenance of
private (and public) property. The strict nuisance ordinances are
strongly supported by the community. The average citizen believes
that lawns should be maintained, that cars should not be parked on
the street at night, and that air conditioning units should not be too
loud. Ordinances such as Alhambra's nuisance ordinance cannot be
effectively enforced without broad community support. In Alhambra
this support not only exists, but the all-pervasive "keeping up private property" norm defines the community's lifestyle.

In many respects Alhambra is quite provincial. While it exists
in a large metropolitan area, it sees only its own problems. The city

has no interest in public housing. Low-income people are not solic-
ited--they are seen as a liability. Problems in Los Angeles are not
seen as problems for Alhambra (except for transportation planning).
The city is "not in any hurry for social change," as one administrator put it. The citizens of Alhambra are apparently proud of their
community and their way of life and do not want to do anything that
might change it.

Alhambra voting patterns confirm the use of the Goldwater vote
as a measure of local political attitudes operating in opposition to the
use of federal grants. Apparently the Goldwater vote is indicative of
a kind of "local independence" operating against intergovernmental
ties.

Alhambra may also indicate certain weaknesses in variable
selection for the quantitative analysis. It appears that the land area
of the city may be an important quantitative measure not heretofore
considered.

Vallejo

Vallejo, California, was one of the smaller suburban cities receiving more urban renewal funds and constructing or leasing more
low-income public housing than the quantitative models had predicted.
Like Alhambra, Vallejo is unique in many respects. Here, however,
the physical characteristics of the city that ultimately led to the need
for an urban renewal program (and low-rent housing) were primarily
economically based.

Physical Characteristics

During the 1960s, Vallejo had three operating urban renewal
projects. The first, Marina Vista, was a waterfront/downtown
project of approximately 125 acres. The second project, Flosden
Acres, was a rehabilitation project of about 70 acres in an outlying
residential area. The third was a concentrated code enforcement
project of 359 housing units in South Vallejo and in the McKinley
School areas. No public housing units were constructed in Vallejo
during the 1960s, although approximately 600 units were leased
under the Section 23 program.

Marina Vista, Vallejo's first and largest urban renewal project, unquestionably explains the city's positive renewal residual of
$2,914,423. This one project alone had an estimated gross project
cost of $15.2 million. With a net project cost of $10.5 million, the
city received (or would receive) approximately $7 million from the
federal government.[45]

Marina Vista is a downtown urban renewal project of 125 acres consisting of 24 former city blocks and approximately a mile of waterfront on the Mare Island Strait. By 1950 the broad area between the central business district and the waterfront was characterized by dilapidated commercial buildings and overcrowded, antiquated living quarters. The center of the area, lower Georgia Street and lower Virginia Street, made up the "sporting" area for the workers at the Mare Island Naval Shipyards during World War I and World War II. As normal times returned, Vallejo "cleaned up" the vice in the area and all that remained were many largely vacant and dilapidated structures. The shoreline was almost completely abandoned and was choked with mud and debris.

The first major phase in the project was the acquisition of the 337 separate parcels of land in the area--largely through negotiated price settlement rather than eminent domain. Second, the Redevelopment Agency assisted over 500 families, individuals, and businesses in relocation forced by the renewal project. The third phase of the program was the removal of all buildings from the site. Over 600 structures required demolition. This phase was completed between 1961 and 1963.

Once the area had been completely cleared, and before the land was offered for sale, the topography of the area was completely changed. A major hill was leveled and a million cubic yards of earth were redistributed. Some 25 acres of land were reclaimed from mudflats and tons of mud were cleared from the shoreline. [46]

By 1972 the project was 95 percent complete with most of the land having been sold, leased, or committed by 1968. Included in the development were a new post office, civic center, library, and city hall. Also included in the area were four apartment complexes of some 618 units, and a number of new office buildings, service stations, banks, and a supermarket. The new 5,000-foot concrete seawall and promenade deck heightened the waterfront development. Marina Vista includes two new parks and many original sculptures, fountains, and works of art. Restaurants, a local yacht club, and a ferry terminal constitute a portion of the waterfront development. [47]

The project was a massive undertaking for such a small community and required a large commitment on the part of the city. Marina Vista now has a reputation as an example of a successful urban renewal project--many cities have sent local officials and administrators to Vallejo to view the project.

Low-income housing in Vallejo has been another matter. During World War II roughly 15,000 public housing units were constructed in Vallejo, housing a population of some 40,000 people. The units were constructed to house the workers at the Mare Island Shipyards and were commonly called Lanham War Housing. After the war the

Lanham housing was slowly torn down until all projects had been demolished with the exception of one. The city kept this one project, Floyd Terrace, consisting of 1,000 units--all either one or three bedrooms. The Vallejo Housing Authority ran this project for roughly seven years until the mid-1960s when the project was closed and eventually demolished.

Several years elapsed before Vallejo once again provided low-rent public housing. Through the Section 23 leased-housing program, the city now leases approximately 600 units from private owners which it operates as low-rent public housing. As of early 1973, there were some 1,200 families on the waiting list for public housing.

Vallejo's housing presents the city with more of a problem than did Alhambra's. Some 13 percent of the housing is classified unsound with 42 percent of the structures being 20 years old or older.[48] Nonetheless, the general housing condition is not critical in the same sense that it is in many older Eastern cities. Like most cities, there is a definite shortage of low-rent housing (that is, the 1,200 families on the waiting list for public housing). The problem is somewhat compounded by the fact that 45 percent of the families in Vallejo have incomes under $7,000 per year (the national average is 40 percent).[49]

The Politics of Housing and Renewal

Local political attitudes in Vallejo were significantly different than those found in Alhambra. While Goldwater carried Alhambra by some 1,375 votes, in Solano County, Johnson defeated Goldwater by a margin of more than two to one (Johnson, 21,438 votes and Goldwater, 9,418 votes).[50]

Similarly, urban renewal found an easy acceptance in Vallejo-- so little opposition developed that the Redevelopment Agency was established by vote of the city council rather than through local referendum. The renewal project itself (and thus the establishment of the Redevelopment Agency) had wide popular support. The original proposal for a downtown renewal project came from the Downtown Association, an association of local merchants. The association wanted James D. Richardson, the executive director of the Housing Authority, to direct the project. The city council established the Redevelopment Agency and appointed Richardson as executive director. The board of directors of the Housing Authority was also appointed as the board of the Redevelopment Agency. However, this setup soon became unworkable and separate boards were appointed for Redevelopment and Housing although one administration (and Richardson) served them both.

Support for the Marina Vista project was widespread. Virtually all of the candidates in the 1961 city council election were in favor of "going ahead with renewal."[51] In the 1965 election, one incumbent councilman ran on his record of support for redevelopment--"rooted out 22 blocks of tired dilapidation and crime-breeding blight in exchange for an emerging, true, gleaming new vista."[52]

The Redevelopment Agency, in addition to managing the renewal program, made every effort to keep the Marina Vista project constantly before the people. The former executive director said, "I would talk to anybody," meaning that he would discuss the project with any group, coffee club, etc., to "sell" the redevelopment program. The agency developed an elaborate one-hour slide show using three projectors simultaneously and approximately 540 slides. The elaborate show, followed by a question-and-answer period, was designed to keep the community informed about the progress and programs of the agency. They made a "fetish" of ground-breakings or openings with large luncheons or dinners. The city council was constantly kept up to date on the projects' progress. "There wasn't six weeks went by, whether they liked it or not, that the city council and their wives were[n't] invited to a little story presentation. . . ." Elaborate brochures were printed explaining in graphic detail all elements of the project and projecting the eventual benefits to the community.[53] The agency thus made public relations an important part of the overall program.

While broad public acceptance and support may have been characteristic of urban renewal, it was not characteristic of public housing--especially not low-income (as opposed to housing for the elderly) public housing. During the period between 1960 and 1970, public housing became an election issue only once during the period. One candidate for the city council, Robert Doran Boot, campaigned on a housing platform: "Low rent housing--we need it NOW."[54] "Low-rent housing for the senior citizens and all those who need it."[55] Another candidate in the 1963 election, Les Fisk, called for "a study to determine what the real need is for low-rent housing."[56] Fisk was elected, Boot defeated.

One major elected official was queried concerning the reasons for the demolition of Floyd Terrace. The response was, "The economy was good--it was time for them [the tenants] to stand on their own feet."

In the late 1960s some pressure did develop for additional low-income housing. In a Forum for Community Development in 1969, the issue of low-rent housing was highlighted. The operations officer for the Vallejo Housing Authority outlined the procedure necessary before any public housing could be built in Vallejo: "State law requires approval of a ballot referendum at the polls before any city can construct public housing. This particular type of referendum measure requires a two-thirds 'yes' vote."[57] The chairman of the Vallejo Community Action Committee did not believe that such a

119

referendum would pass since "the minority people who need homes are in the minority and 85 percent of the community won't do a darn thing about it."[58] The chairman of the Solano County Economic Opportunity Council added that "there has been no vocal commitment from anyone in the city for public housing. We are aware that most of the programs would require a referendum but we have city officials who do not commit themselves. The measure will not pass without city support."[59]

Conclusions

The high positive residual in urban renewal receipts was the direct result of the Marina Vista project. Marina Vista was no small undertaking for a community the size of Vallejo. It was large in area and was financially ambitious. Marina Vista was not a trial project in any sense of the word. The success of the project in large part can be attributed to the executive director of the Redevelopment Agency, James D. Richardson. His competence and political skill undoubtedly made a major contribution to not only the successful completion of the project, but to the broad community support as well. While acknowledging that he "couldn't get by with this today," Richardson supervised a massive land clearance project in the early 1960s. Faced with 125 acres of rubble and leveled buildings, what else could the city council candidates of 1961 do but voice their approval of "going ahead with renewal"? They had little choice at that point.

Being a salesman, as well as an administrator, was one of Richardson's strong points--and, indirectly, reflected the good judgment of the Downtown Association in promoting him for the position of executive director. Through the public relations efforts of the agency, the Marina Vista project was viewed with some measure of community pride.

The positive housing residual indicates some of the difficulty in total reliance on census-type data and statistical analysis. While it outwardly appeared that Vallejo had increased its stock of public housing by more than 300 units over what had been predicted, Vallejo had actually decreased its public housing inventory. The HUD report accurately reported the initial occupancy of 557 Section 23 units, but it did not report the demolition of the 1,000-unit Floyd Terrace project. Thus, when considering the total stock of public housing, Vallejo did not have a positive residual of 300 units, it actually had a negative residual of 700 units.

The housing program is thus not a success--it serves merely as a replacement program. The community norms concerning public housing are exemplified by the attitudes of the elected leaders.

Low-income public housing is simply not wanted. As one administrator put it, low-income housing is "politically infeasible" while
Section 23 housing is "tolerated." And yet the community is not as
heartless as it seems. In many ways, Vallejo exemplifies the successful application of the provision of low- and moderate-income
housing through the below market interest rate programs. The application of these programs in Vallejo will be discussed at length in
Chapter 7.

Beaumont

Beaumont, Texas, provides an example of a medium-sized,
Southern, central city having negative renewal and public housing
residuals. Like Alhambra, Beaumont has never had an urban renewal program, but it has a public housing authority and has had low-
rent public housing since 1937. In a geographic sense, Beaumont is
very similar to Vallejo. It, too, is located on a ship channel and is
heavily dependent upon one industry. Downtown Beaumont looks very
much like "lower Georgia Street" (before urban renewal).

Physical Characteristics

During the 1960s it became evident that Beaumont's economy
was running into trouble. City population declined by 1.4 percent
and the economy of the Beaumont-Port-Arthur-Orange SMSA went
into a period of relative stagnation. The retail function of the central business district has been steadily declining over the past decade
with many of the retail businesses leaving the core area for suburban
shopping centers. As a result, empty storefronts in the central
business districts are the rule, rather than the exception.

New police and library buildings are presently under construction in the downtown areas. The municipal building and the Jefferson
County Courthouse are both located in the central business district
but both are outdated and in need of replacement.[60]

> The exodus of retail establishments from the CBD,
> coupled with the closing of many other businesses
> (three old hotels in the CBD are closed for transit
> trade), a lack of cultural facilities, and generally
> the failure to reinvest in the CBD, have resulted
> in a serious problem of decay and deterioration.
> The CBD does not have a hotel, meeting facilities,
> or a good public restaurant.[61]

A housing study by the Beaumont Chamber of Commerce indicates that there are between 9,000 and 11,000 substandard structures in the City of Beaumont. An area referred to as "Old Beaumont" was recently inspected by the city and 20 percent of the structures were found to be substandard. One of the prime factors for the substandard determination is lack of proper bathroom facilities, or lack of a bathroom entirely. Some 80 percent of the structures in Old Beaumont do not have hot water heaters. [62]

Beaumont has 650 units of public housing of which 150 are reserved for the elderly. There are virtually no vacancies in any of the housing projects. The Beaumont Housing Authority reported a waiting list of approximately 400 applicants. The only development of public housing units in the 1960s was the construction of 150 elderly units in the early 1960s; however, at the time of this research the Housing Authority had a proposal before the city council to lease 500 units (to be built especially for this program) to help alleviate the housing shortage.

Beaumont has two projects financed under Section 236 (of the Housing Act of 1968). Washington Manor has 150 units and Virginia Manor 110. A rent supplement program is also in operation and rent supplement tenants are in both 236 projects. [63]

Surprisingly for a city with a population of more than 100,000, Beaumont has no official master plan. In 1960 a comprehensive plan for the city was prepared by Harland Bartholomew and Associates but it was never adopted by the city. [64] It was not until 1971 that the city even adopted a minimum housing code. [65] The city planning department still operates without a master plan or long-range planning. A complete inventory of housing is not available, although the city is making application for federal 701 funds to complete this inventory. The planning department does not really plan, it controls (through zoning, etc.). "We have a city hall [administration] that follows--we have no advocacy function--it's not wanted," is the way one administrator put it.

The Politics of Housing and Renewal

Jefferson County (Beaumont) has traditionally been a Democratic (although conservative) stronghold. In the 1964 presidential campaign, for example, voters in the county gave Johnson 61 percent of the vote (44,584) to Goldwater's 39 percent (28,771). [66] Since President Johnson was a native Texan this might have been expected, even in a county that an outsider might associate with a Goldwater type of conservatism.

A more conservative trend was evident in the 1968 election when Hubert Humphrey received only 38.6 percent (30,032) of the total vote. The combined vote for Richard Nixon with 33.4 percent (26,007) and George Wallace with 28.0 percent (21,824) was more nearly what was expected.[67] George Wallace made significant inroads in this conservative Democratic area.

Housing. In spite of the fact that housing, especially low-rent housing, is in critical supply in Beaumont, there was no organized political pressure for more public housing during the 1960s. Attitudes toward the housing problem are best described by the Chamber of Commerce report. While there is apparently a realization of the need for more public housing for the elderly, additional public housing for low-income families is another matter. The Chamber report concludes that "many say it makes little sense to place large welfare families in new buildings, because rehabilitated dwellings can be provided at far less cost. Therefore, we may wish to direct our efforts towards something along the Code Enforcement Program lines of rehabilitation."[68] The report indicates a general reluctance concerning the construction of additional low-rent public housing. As a Chamber official put it, "From talking with the local people involved in low-cost housing, the general consensus is doubtful that federal housing programs are the best solution to the housing problem for the poor."[69]

Urban Renewal. Beaumont provides an interesting study of urban renewal politics because the issue, or the attempt to establish an urban renewal authority in Beaumont, was submitted to a vote of the people twice during the 1960s. On June 14, 1960, the urban renewal issue was defeated 8,898 to 1,581 and again on November 18, 1967, it was defeated by a vote of 12,503 to 2,946.

The first attempt to establish a renewal authority in Beaumont promoted urban renewal as a tool to effect "slum clearance." The urban renewal campaign appeared to be characterized by three phases: The first was media editorial support; the second was characterized by the emergence of support by local elites and civic groups; while the third was the emergence of a strong opposition. The local newspaper, the Beaumont Enterprise, could hardly be considered liberal, especially in the area of civil rights[70]--and yet the Enterprise was a strong supporter of the urban renewal effort. In an editorial discussing some of the common arguments against renewal, the editor asked, "Since when is it pampering to make it possible for an American child to live better than a rat?"[71] A later editorial appealed to the citizens of Beaumont to support urban renewal with the argument that urban renewal funds came from Beaumont taxpayers, so this money should be spent in Beaumont.[72] Two days later, the paper ran a page-one article showing the U.S. Chamber of Commerce's support for renewal.

Urban Renewal is characterized by the Chamber of
Commerce of the United States as "probably the
most creative and constructive tool with which to
attack problems of community deterioration" in a
statement cited in letters now being distributed to
members of the local chamber.[73]

Unfortunately for the renewal backers, the neighboring community of Port Arthur had recently established an urban renewal agency
but renewal was running into serious opposition from large groups of
citizens. The Enterprise reported some of this opposition: "Although no one in the audience was allowed to speak, sentiment among
the Negroes was definitely anti-Urban Renewal."[74] With vocal citizen opposition the agency in Port Arthur was having difficulty in obtaining project approval from the city council.[75]

The second phase of the renewal campaign began early in June
1960 with the emergence of elite and organizational support for the
coming referendum: "The Beaumont Chamber of Commerce's en-
dorsement last year of Urban Renewal was reaffirmed by Elmo
Beard, president, in the current issue of Spotlight, the organization's
official publication."[76] The local chapter of the American Institute
of Architects unanimously approved a resolution favoring urban renewal in Beaumont,[77] and the Beaumont Building and Construction
Trades Council endorsed renewal and urged its approval.[78]

As the referendum date approached, ads urging approval of
the referendum appeared in the Enterprise. On June 7, in a full-
page ad, the Beaumont Council Committee, "Twenty well-known
Beaumonters selected from all walks of life . . . ,"[79] urged renewal
adoption. Advertisements urging adoption appeared several more
times prior to the referendum.[80]

By June 7 the opposition began to organize publicly. Initial
public opposition appeared in the form of "letters to the editor" in
the Enterprise and generally urged the use of local tools for redevelopment and housing improvement.[81] Opposition came from local
realtors:

Since the Urban Renewal Program firmly establishes
Federal interference in Local affairs, insures an
unsound Federal and Local spending program, and
contains a questionable concept of the right of
eminent domain for use by private purposes, the
Beaumont Board of Realtors recommends the re-
jection of the program in the election of June 11,
1960.[82]

On June 10 the Enterprise reported renewal opposition from the Beaumont Academy of Medicine and a group called the Property Owners and Landlords Association. [83] And finally, on the day of the referendum, the Enterprise carried large advertisements opposing urban renewal from the Beaumont Citizens for Responsible Government, the Beaumont Academy of Medicine, and the Beaumont Retail Lumber Dealers Association. [84]

Renewal was soundly defeated by the voters of Beaumont with 1,581 votes for urban renewal and 8,898 against. The issue was rejected by a margin of 5.5 to 1 and failed to carry even a single voting box. [85]

Undaunted, the urban renewal supporters tried again in 1967 --this time with a change of tactics. Instead of supporting renewal on the slum clearance issue, the second attempt was linked to the expansion of Lamar Tech. Again the Beaumont Enterprise supported the renewal proposal, [86] but this time the opposition efforts coalesced at an earlier date, primarily through the vehicle of the Republican party. The Beaumont Republican Municipal Policy Committee declared its "total opposition to federal Urban Renewal and urged every responsible citizen to vote against it in the Nov. 18 special election. "[87] Support for renewal again came largely from the business community with the board of directors of the Beaumont Junior Chamber of Commerce, the Action Now Committee (much like the Beaumont Council Committee of the 1960 attempt), the board of directors of the Beaumont Chamber of Commerce, the Baptist Ministers Union of Beaumont, and (this time) the Beaumont Board of Realtors. [88]

The mayor and three of the four city councilmen were active in their support of urban renewal. [89] In an attempt to rally support for renewal, approximately 10 days before the referendum, Mayor Jack Moore named the nine members he would appoint to the urban renewal board should the issue be approved. He said that all of the prospective board members had the unanimous approval of the city council. [90] The mayor's selections were hailed by both the Action Now Committee and the Beaumont Enterprise. [91]

In addition to providing editorial support for the issue, the Enterprise gave page-one coverage to stories concerning the success of Port Arthur's urban renewal project and printed a lengthy article on how renewal was able to help solve the growth problems of the University of Texas. [92] The point of this article was obvious--what worked well in Austin (home of the University of Texas) could work equally well in Beaumont for Lamar Tech's expansion.

In addition to opposition from the Republican Policy Committee, the local American Legion Post "declared its opposition to federal Urban Renewal as 'inimical to and contrary to' the basic constitutional rights of all citizens." Opposition also came from a group called the Beaumont Citizens for Responsible Government.[93] Scare tactics were prevalent. One large advertisement addressed to "All Beaumont Business Men" warned that "according to recent studies, most businesses forced to close by federal urban renewal, never re-open their doors because it is too costly to comply with zoning laws."[94] Feeling the pressure, the Action Now Committee responded with a letter to the Chamber of Commerce claiming that slumlords were behind the move to kill urban renewal.[95]

Slumlords or no slumlords, urban renewal failed by a margin of more than 4 to 1: 12,503 votes against, 2,946 in support of renewal. Dr. Dale C. Hager, chairman of the Beaumont Republican Policy Committee that opposed the referendum hailed the election results as "a great victory for the small businessman and home-owner . . . a mandate from the people to replace the present city administration."[96] Renewal in Beaumont was not dead, however; in the next city council election, urban renewal was to be a major issue. The effects of this renewal attempt on the outcome of the 1968 city council election will be covered in Chapter 5.

Conclusions

Beaumont, when examined on the basis of the predictive measures, indicated negative housing and renewal residuals. Like Alhambra, the negative residuals appeared to be based largely on local attitudes operating in opposition to federal grant programs. Again, this attitude appears to be measured by a large vote for Barry Goldwater in 1964. And yet in the renewal model (Figure 3.1), the independent effect of the Goldwater vote was only -.23. In cities such as Beaumont, however, local attitudes appear to dominate over the physical characteristics of the city as determinants of grant use.

Alhambra and Beaumont suggest that there is some "threshold" point where local political attitudes become the dominant determinant of grant use. It is probable that in the overwhelming majority of cities, physical characteristics are the primary determinants of grant use. On the other hand, in the small number of cities exhibiting highly conservative political philosophies, it appears that local attitudes are the major determinants.

Austin

Austin, the capital city of Texas, was eminently successful in its urban renewal and public housing endeavors during the 1960s.

Renewal and housing efforts in Austin contrast sharply with Beaumont. Like Washington, D.C., Austin was created as a capital city. Since its founding in 1839, Austin has been primarily a government center --the city is headquarters for most state agencies and state institutions (such as the University of Texas). As a by-product, almost 200 private associations also have their headquarters in the city. In 1960 the government employed 21,700 of the 79,000 persons in the Austin labor force. As a government center, Austin has certain difficulties with its tax base as 52 percent of the property in the city is tax exempt. [97]

Physical Characteristics

During the decade of the 1960s Austin had five operating urban renewal projects. The University East project cleared an area of approximately 40 city blocks of some 310 structures. The land will eventually be sold to the University of Texas for campus expansion. As might be surmised from the name of the project, University East, the area is located directly east of the University of Texas. Many of the residences in the area were in good physical condition, so in order to save as many of the dwelling units as possible, the Urban Renewal Agency tried to sell the structures to be moved and rehabilitated wherever possible. With a total of 302 residential dwelling units, 87 structures were moved and rebuilt in this manner. The project will add approximately 98 acres to the University of Texas campus and will also provide land for the widening of Interstate Highway 35 through the area. The Department of Housing and Urban Development has appropriated $8.8 million as its two-thirds contribution toward the project.

The Brackenridge project of some 45 city blocks is located adjacent to, and to the east of, the State Capitol complex. Brackenridge is bordered on the north by the University of Texas and the University East project. Approximately 20 city blocks in this project will go to the University of Texas for expansion of the campus. Another major portion of the project land will be used for the expansion of the city-owned Brackenridge Hospital and for the allied medical and health facilities adjoining it. As with University East, land along the eastern border of the project will be provided for the widening of Interstate Highway 35 while some lots on the southern end of the project will be made available for private and public redevelopment. This project had a federal appropriation of $9.0 million.

The Kealing project was Austin's first residential urban renewal project. Located in the eastern part of the city in a predominantly black area, Kealing combined clearance and rehabilitation techniques (emphasis was on the clearance). Forty-two substandard houses were rehabilitated and 52 new homes were constructed on cleared land. The area also contains a new 100-unit low-cost rent-supplement housing project.

The Blackshear project area is located directly south of, and adjacent to, the Kealing area. While designated a project area, work in the Blackshear area remained at a virtual standstill during the 1960s. There are 356 structures in the 61.6-acre area of which 200 are considered to be dilapidated. Political pressure from the residents of the Blackshear area forced the Urban Renewal Agency to abandon the conventional urban renewal approach it had originally planned for the area and to adopt a Neighborhood Development Program.

The fifth project, Glen Oaks, was initiated in 1963 to lessen the problems associated with the flooding of a creek through the area and to eliminate poor housing conditions. Land in the flood plain of the creek will be converted to an open green space to serve as a drainage area as well as for recreational activities. A total of $12.0 million was appropriated by HUD for the three residential renewal areas. [98]

The Housing Authority of the City of Austin operates eight housing projects consisting of 1,050 units. Two of the projects are designed specifically for the elderly and both were built in the late 1960s. The authority maintains a waiting list of approximately 1,200 families (approximately 300 elderly).

The City of Austin gave a high priority to the upgrading of housing within the city during the 1960s. Housing problems have been attacked through the use of a number of tools: public housing, concentrated code enforcement, model cities, as well as through urban renewal. Success has been such that the number of units lacking some or all plumbing facilities decreased by approximately 70 percent during the 10-year period. [99]

Earlier in this chapter a strong independent statistical relationship was noted between public housing and urban renewal. This relationship had been expected for two reasons: (1) to provide low-rent housing for families relocated because of urban renewal projects, and (2) to provide replacement housing for the low-rent housing destroyed in the urban renewal areas. It was thus expected that most urban renewal projects, especially those in predominantly residential areas, would make provisions for public housing on the land being redeveloped. None of the five Austin urban renewal projects had provisions for additional public housing. The reason for this apparent lack of concern for low-income families is found in the Texas urban renewal laws: "No real property acquired under the provisions of this Act shall be sold, leased, granted, conveyed or otherwise made available for any public housing." [100] Thus while

Austin may have wanted to allocate space in one or more of the urban renewal areas to public housing, state law prohibited such allocation.

The Politics of Housing and Renewal

Austin voters exhibited substantial differences in voting behavior from Beaumont voters. Austin voting was along much more traditional Democratic lines. In the 1964 presidential elections, Travis County voters gave overwhelming support to President Johnson with 69 percent of the vote (44,058) to Goldwater's 31 percent (19,838).[101] In 1968 Hubert Humphrey received 48.1 percent (39,667), Nixon 41.6 percent (34,309), and Wallace 10.2 (8,424) of the vote.[102] While Nixon did considerably better in Austin than he did in Beaumont, George Wallace did not fare nearly as well. The third-party candidate was thus not as influential in the more cosmopolitan Austin as in Beaumont.

On December 5, 1959, the voters of Austin approved urban renewal in the City of Austin by a narrow 55-vote margin, one of the closest elections in Austin's history. The final count was 3,424 votes for the renewal issue and 3,369 against. The low voter turnout of less than 20 percent of the city's electorate apparently indicated voter indifference to the renewal issue.[103]

Opposition to the renewal issue generally came from real estate interests, a group called the Austin Taxpayers Association, and certain religious groups.[104] Editorial support for urban renewal was provided by both Austin newspapers[105] with most political leaders of the community also supporting the issue.[106]

During the 1961 city council elections urban renewal was not a significant issue as the referendum election of 1959 was at the time tied up in litigation. Virtually all candidates supported "slum clearance and urban renewal" if the courts validated the election.[107] The clearance program was subsequently upheld.

During the campaign for the 1963 city council elections the Austin League of Women Voters sought the opinion of the candidates on the issue of urban renewal. "Austin has launched its Urban Renewal program with the initiation of Kealing and Glen Oaks (Boggy Creek) projects. What is your position on these projects?"[108] Only one candidate indicated any opposition--Paul W. Stimson, Place 3, who also ran on a platform opposing fluoridation.[109] Stimson was defeated.

Urban renewal was not an issue in the 1965 city council campaign; there was little public discussion of the issue. In the 1967 campaign two of the candidates for city council had public comments on renewal. M. Z. Collins, Place 3, "urged a re-shaping of the Urban Renewal program which he said was 'in bad shape,'"[110] and

Jasper Glover, Place 4, supported the concept of renewal but believed that Austin's program "is being run wrong and the people are suffering."[111] Again, both candidates were defeated.

The council election of 1969 brought the issues of urban renewal, model cities, and public housing into the public view more than any campaign during the 1960s. D. R. Price, ranch developer and investor, running against long-time liberal councilwoman Emma Long, "suggests that urban renewal here has not been successful, especially in its endeavors to relocate people in better conditions than they previously had."[112] Price favored a strong code-enforcement program. In Place 6, East Austin real estate broker Robert B. Smith "proposed a review of 'inequities' in the Urban Renewal program."[113] Candidate for Place 3, Jimmy Lee Ball, suggested that "before the city spends large sums of money on rejuvenating low-income areas of Austin . . . the council should initiate a 'neighborhood clean-up' campaign to get people 'to help themselves.'"[114]

Incumbent councilman Travis LaRue jumped places to face Mayor Harry Akin in Place 4. He made model cities a prime target and called the project an "extension of Urban Renewal and could end up costing the city as much as urban renewal."[115] In Place 7 Les Gage, termed the "liberal" candidate by his opponent Warren Smith, wanted to revamp Austin's low-cost housing efforts. Smith, on the other hand, was "not inclined to support give-away projects like model cities."[116]

Mr. Price defeated Mrs. Long in Place 1 and Mr. LaRue defeated the mayor in Place 4. The other renewal critics were not elected. "Liberal" Les Gage won by a substantial majority.[117]

In spite of the fact that the urban renewal issue was frequently discussed in the 1969 campaign, it was not the real issue. The real issue in this election was open housing in Austin. In the late 1960s the city council passed an open housing ordinance, but the ordinance was subsequently voided by a referendum vote of the people. This was the underlying issue of the 1969 campaign. The 1969 election was an attempt by the opponents of the ordinance to remove the open housing supporters from the council and replace them with more conservative members. In this they succeeded.

Urban renewal, however, became a very heated issue in certain limited segments of Austin--so much so that one project was delayed for a number of years and nearly canceled.[118] This project (Blackshear) will be discussed at length here and again in Chapter 7. In general, however, urban renewal apparently never ranked as an important issue for the majority of the population in the city of Austin.[119]

Blackshear. Blackshear was the third residential urban renewal project attempted in Austin. The first two, Kealing and Glen Oaks,

were "slum-clearance" type projects, and Blackshear was scheduled
for the same type of clearance. A number of the Blackshear residents formed an organization to fight the project (called the Blackshear Residents Organization, BRO). With the assistance of legal
aid and University of Texas faculty and students, the BRO was able
to keep the project tied up in the federal courts for a number of
years. A major complaint of the residents concerned the attitude of
the renewal authority and disputes over relocation procedures. Finally HUD, tired of the constant delay, insisted that the Renewal
Agency either come to agreement with the BRO or cancel the project.
The Renewal Agency changed the project to an "NDP type" project
(neighborhood development program) and reached a lengthy agreement with the BRO concerning relocation.[120] The issue, however,
was complicated by the emergence of a second resident organization,
the Blackshear Residents for Individual Property Rights, whose members were anxious to sell their property to the Renewal Agency.
This organization, obviously, was made up largely of Blackshear
property owners.

To best understand the failure (or success, depending upon
one's normative philosophy) of Blackshear, it is necessary to examine the attitudes of the project residents. Such a study was undertaken by Allen Williams of the University of Texas. Williams found
that 45.2 percent of the residents would dislike being forced to move
and that, of those who would either not mind moving or would like to
move, the primary dissatisfaction with the neighborhood was based
on the physical environment.[121]

Some 57 percent of the Blackshear residents had some knowledge of urban renewal while another 12.9 percent had a reasonably
good knowledge. Of those having some knowledge of renewal, approximately 50 percent had unfavorable attitudes toward the program.
Furthermore, unfavorable attitudes toward renewal were highly associated with a dislike toward moving. A number of the respondents
expressed anxiety over their expected relocation, not knowing when
or how it was to be accomplished.[122]

Kealing and Glen Oaks forced approximately 652 household relocations in East Austin. Criticism of the relocation efforts in these
projects came from a variety of sources.[123] Concern from a portion of the community at-large (especially legal-aid attorneys and
university faculty and students) brought expert assistance to the
Blackshear residents. The residents were then able to organize
effectively to change the direction and concept of the Blackshear
project. One administrator, however, attributed the Blackshear
changes more to "agitation by students and faculty" at the university
rather than to the desires of the residents.

The Positive Residual

While the Blackshear project provides an example of the application of political pressure to delay and change a project, in general
Austin has had a highly successful (in terms of funds received) program. This is largely attributed to the high dollar cost associated
with the two university-connected projects--University East and
Brackenridge. Some claim that the long personal relationship between
the executive director of the Urban Renewal Agency and President
Johnson was a major factor in obtaining quick HUD approval for these
two large and expensive projects. Another theory suggested that the
"University and Chancellor Frank Irwin were 90 percent and 150 percent" responsible for the two projects. There was a very close relationship between the City of Austin and the University of Texas (the
administration, not necessarily faculty or students). In fact, it was
the city that first approached the university concerning the possibility of using the urban renewal program for university expansion.
The university had been given special power of eminent domain by the
state legislature within a given area of the city for expansion, but
instead of the university undertaking the expansion itself through
this eminent domain (at a much higher cost), the university and the
city cooperated in the present urban renewal effort. In fact, one administrator claims "that the city government is dominated by the University and the State Legislature." Unquestionably, the University of
Texas (particularly Chancellor Frank Irwin) was extremely influential
in Texas politics and in the two renewal programs. The extent of the
involvement, however, cannot be documented as all sources interviewed were not able to delineate the exact relationships that might
bear on this investigation, although most sources believed that the
influence of the chancellor was a major factor in renewal success.

Housing

Two housing projects for the elderly comprised the only housing
projects built in Austin during the 1960s. The Lakeside Apartments
consisting of 164 units were first occupied in 1967, and the Rosewood
Addition consisting of 32 units was initially occupied in 1966. In addition, the Housing Authority received a program reservation for
1,000 units of public housing (750 family and 250 elderly) in February
1966. The Housing Authority's first project, known as TEX 1-9, was
for 300 units to be constructed on land the authority had purchased in
East Austin. The Blackshear Residents Organization, "as represen-
tatives of all Mexican-American and Negro residents of Austin," sued
to halt planning and construction of the project on the basis that the
project would perpetuate racial segregation in the City of Austin.[124]

The court noted that racial segregation was the official policy of the Housing Authority between 1938 and 1967--even the elderly projects of the 1960s were intended to be segregated with Lakeside for Anglos and Rosewood Addition for blacks. Moreover, the court found that HUD was aware of and condoned the Housing Authority's occupancy system despite knowledge that similar action by a local authority violated rights guaranteed by the Fifth Amendment to the Constitution.[125] The court held

> that both the Housing Authority and HUD are charged with the affirmative obligation to further the national housing policy expressed in the 1964 and 1968 Civil Rights Acts and that . . . the selection and approval of the Project TEX 1-9 site produced a decision that failed to consider that policy . . . and must therefore be set aside.[126]

This decision forced the Housing Authority to reexamine its site selection procedures and caused a delay in implementing construction of the 1,000 units. The Board of Directors of the Housing Authority took little action during the 1960s while awaiting the Blackshear decision. Thus the 1,000-unit program reservation became a program of the 1970s and is therefore beyond the scope of this investigation.

Syracuse

Like Austin, Syracuse had substantial positive residuals for both public housing and urban renewal.[127] Unlike Austin, however, Syracuse is typical of large central cities in that it is declining in population (-8.7 percent between 1960 and 1970)[128] and is faced with deteriorating physical facilities and a relative increase in low-income population.[129] Unlike many other cities, however, the property tax base is not shrinking[130]--primarily due to the success of the urban renewal programs in the city.

The City of Syracuse listed a number of goals in its 1968 _Workable Program_. The first two areas of emphasis pertained to renewal and housing:

1. The most sensitive and vital goal is the provision of new or rehabilitated housing for low and medium income groups, including in-migrants, relocatees, and racial minorities. . . .
2. Rebuilding the commercial and business core of the City into an attractive, functional, and

vibrant area is a prerequisite for rebuilding the
City, and by necessity will continue to rate as a
high priority goal. [131]

Physical Characteristics

During the decade of the 1960s, urban renewal in Syracuse was
directed almost entirely toward downtown redevelopment. While only
one project was in the middle of the central business district, virtually all of the other financially significant projects were on the
fringes of the CBD and were essentially business (or government)
redevelopments. Syracuse had five renewal projects in various stages
of development during the decade.

The Near East Side project was the first full-scale urban renewal project in Syracuse (there was a small trial project in the mid-
1950s). An area of some 100 acres immediately to the east of the
central business district, Near East Side was a clearance project
forcing relocation of large numbers of families and businesses. The
area was formerly considered blighted, having a large number of
substandard structures. Redevelopment in the Near East Side area
includes numerous office complexes, a state Public Safety Building,
a garage, three apartment complexes including 318 units for middle-
and low-income tenants, a State Mental Hygiene Department hospital,
as well as a museum, a motel, and theaters.

The second local project came into being as a result of a campaign promise for a downtown renewal project. Downtown One was
designed to redevelop and renew the commercial, retail, and office
core of the central business district. Included in Downtown One will
be the MONY project (a multistory office complex and associated
garage), a major department store, and numerous stores, offices,
and apartments (Clinton Plaza).

The Clinton Square urban renewal project was the third downtown project in Syracuse. It was also designed to renew a business
and civic area within the central business district. Redevelopment
in Clinton Square included a major department store, two banks, a
newspaper printing and publishing plant, and several office complexes. [132]

The first of two residential projects, Thorden Park East, is a
190-acre residential Concentrated Code Enforcement Project coupling
the rehabilitation of structures with public improvements.

Finally, the Syracuse Hill NDP is a 410-acre project in the
Syracuse University area. The project will facilitate expansion
plans of the university and medical complex and will renew or con-
serve blighted residential and commercial facilities within the
area. [133] Started in the late 1960s, this project was not in operation

long enough to have an impact on the city's urban renewal success during the decade under study.

Urban renewal in Syracuse has not operated to help the poor secure adequate and fair-cost housing. Urban renewal (especially the Near East Side project) razed far more low-income housing units through slum clearance projects than it has constructed. The consequent tighter housing supply has caused an increasing concentration of poor families in adjacent areas.[134]

Despite new housing developments and apartments and the fact that Syracuse has been losing population, both homeowner and renter vacancy rates decreased between 1964 and 1967. The rental vacancy rate of 4.6 percent in 1960 decreased to 3.6 percent in 1964, and then to 2.7 percent in 1967. (A rate of 5 percent is generally considered acceptable.) Although Syracuse had been experiencing a tight housing market, approximately 5,500 people in the city were displaced and relocated between 1959 and 1969.[135]

The Syracuse Housing Authority operated six housing projects plus a leased housing program during the 1960s. Four of the projects operate under federal housing laws while two are state-funded housing developments. Syracuse had a total of 2,436 public housing units (not including leased housing) by 1970--of these, 1,124 units were for the elderly. Of the 2,436 units, almost half (1,058) were initially occupied during the 1960s. In addition to the James-Geddes Homes opened in 1961, a 500-unit project, Central Village, was initially occupied in 1963, and the 364-unit Toomey-Abbott Towers for the elderly was opened in 1969. In addition, a scattered-site leased housing was approved in April 1968 by the Syracuse Common Council. The authority began leasing the first of a scheduled 94-unit program for large families in September 1968.[136]

The Politics of Housing and Renewal

Syracuse provided an example of an anachronism in its voting behavior during the 1960s. The city constantly supported Republican candidates at the local and state levels while supporting the Democratic candidates for president. In 1964 Syracuse gave overwhelming support to President Johnson with 63,113 votes (72 percent) to Goldwater's 24,912 (28 percent).[137] The city also voted Democratic in 1968 with Humphrey polling 38,210 votes (52 percent) to 31,564 for Nixon (43 percent) and 3,250 votes for George Wallace (5 percent).[138] Locally, however, the Republican party dominated the Common Council and the mayor's office throughout the 1960s (until 1969).

Housing and renewal as public issues were quite different in Syracuse than they were in the Western and Southern cities visited.

For one thing, housing was a much more salient issue in Syracuse while renewal was the subject of little public controversy. Secondly, neither issue made a substantial impact on the local political scene until 1969.[139] In 1961 there was some controversy involving these grant programs. Unsuccessful candidate for president of the Common Council, William Rafter (Dynamic party), cited a pressing need for more "government sponsored housing." Both major parties, however, indicated support for increased urban renewal efforts. Two of the Democratic candidates for councilman-at-large campaigned for expansion of the renewal program and William Walsh, the Republican candidate for mayor, pledged a downtown urban renewal program if elected (he was). While not attacking renewal expansion directly, Joseph Grosso, Dynamic party candidate for mayor, condemned the past Republican administration for its failure to adequately take care of those displaced by urban renewal.[140]

It was not until 1969 that urban renewal emerged again as a significant issue. With an increasing minority population coupled with the "white flight" to the suburbs, the trend in the later 1960s was away from Republican domination of local politics. In 1969 the voters of Syracuse elected Democrat Lee Alexander mayor--the first Democratic mayor in Syracuse in 16 years. The Republicans also lost control of the Common Council with the Democrats gaining a 6-3 majority.[141] The future direction of the city's urban renewal program was a major issue in the campaign. As Lee Alexander put it: The major difference between Gualtieri (Republican candidate for mayor) and himself is that Gualtieri proposed to "continue to concentrate on downtown development, while he [Alexander] will put some of the resources into the neighborhoods."[142] One administrator noted that the Democratic timing was perfect--in 1969 HUD was shifting its urban renewal emphasis from redevelopment to neighborhood preservation. The Democratic party in Syracuse was able to predict this shift and capitalized on it.

The renewal approach taken by Syracuse was closely patterned after the successes in Philadelphia and New Haven. To insure citizen involvement and program approval, a 35-member citizens group, the Citizens Council for Urban Renewal, sought to represent the thinking of a wide variety of civic-interest groups within the city.[143] The Citizens Council is the mandated citizen participation group in relation to the overall development of the urban renewal program. While praised in its early years by officials of the Federal Housing and Home Finance Agency,[144] the city admits to a major weakness of the council: "It strives to increase representation of the poor and black populations by membership in its committees. It has tried to win inner city representation, to little avail."[145]

Renewal supporters attempted to give political and administrative muscle to the program in its early stages. John Searles, the former head of the Washington, D.C., Urban Renewal Agency, was brought to Syracuse to head up the Metropolitan Development Association (MDA)--a sort of super chamber of commerce. The MDA was primarily an organization of downtown businessmen trying to promote the growth of downtown Syracuse. As director of the MDA, Searles was able to "get things moving." His knowledge of the urban renewal program and his friendships in Washington made him especially helpful in securing quick project approvals.

Syracuse also brought in George Schuster as the second director of the Urban Renewal Agency. Schuster spent a number of years working under Edward Logue, the highly reputed renewal director in New Haven, and brought a wealth of experience and ability to the Syracuse program. Searles and Schuster, through their reputations and abilities, were able to keep the renewal program "professional" rather than political.

Nor can the influence of local businesses be discounted, especially local banks and real estate interests. The apparent influence of one firm, Eagan Real Estate, a local broker and developer, was mentioned by several sources.

In Syracuse there was apparently a consensus favoring (downtown) development--especially among community elites. Literally no opposition developed to any of the downtown projects. The Near East Side project was typical of many large projects of that era-- it was essentially a "Negro removal" program. The black community in Syracuse at that time was small and politically weak and was not able to generate effective opposition.

Another factor that undoubtedly accounts for a high level of urban renewal expenditures is the amount of the local contribution necessary. In some states (for example New York, Pennsylvania, Connecticut) a portion, often half, of the local contribution is matched by state grants. Thus cities in states such as New York are able to double the size of their urban renewal projects for a given dollar.

The influence of Syracuse University on urban renewal in that city contrasts sharply with the influence of the University of Texas on Austin's program. Ties between the university and the city were "unimportant." Rather than taking pride in the university, it was often referred to as the "Little Red Schoolhouse on the Hill." During the 1960s, the city administration was thoroughly Republican and, rightly or wrongly, the university was perceived as Democratic. The relationship between the two institutions was thus often strained.

Another cause of substantial renewal receipts in the city was inaccurate cost estimates. Project costs were occasionally grossly understated. The original estimated purchase price for the 456 parcels in the Near East Side project was approximately $18.9 million. Final land cost in the project area was in excess of $32.0

million--a figure almost twice that of the original estimate.[146] Almost 60 percent of the property owners went to court for settlement rather than accept the price negotiated with the Renewal Agency. This was obviously a long and costly process.

Unlike Vallejo or Austin, Syracuse attempted to utilize its public housing program to provide homes for those displaced by urban renewal. As far back as 1956 the city began planning for additional public housing to be constructed and ready for occupancy in time to assist those displaced by renewal. In proposing a 319-unit addition to the James-Geddes Homes project, the Housing Authority, supported by Arthur J. Reed, the Urban Renewal director, recommended Common Council approval of the project "on the basis of long range need tied to the city's slum clearance and renewal program."[147] The Common Council agreed and approved the project.[148]

The State of New York also offered the City of Syracuse a $6.6 million state public housing contract for construction of 400 new units in the Near East Side. The Housing Authority, however, told the mayor that it "definitely does not want" the state contract. Authority Chairman Jacob C. Lattif said, "We definitely do not want to use the state contract. We have sufficient public housing as such."[149]

As the Near East Side project moved into execution, however, the city recognized the need for additional public housing. This led to the construction of the additional 500-unit Burt Street Housing Development (Central Village).[150]

The Citizens' Council on Urban Renewal reported a continuing shortage of low-income housing in early 1964 leading the commissioner of Urban Improvement to promise, "The city contemplates no new projects which will displace large numbers of families until an adequate supply of housing is available to meet the resulting needs."[151]

The mid-1960s were characterized by an attempt at retrenchment. Syracuse Mayor William Walsh pushed for increased public housing--but in the suburbs of Syracuse rather than in the central city. Walsh suggested "that the Syracuse Housing Authority be expanded into the towns so that housing can be built there or that new legislation be sought to permit a county-wide authority." He suggested that the city "should take a look at those best able to provide this housing."[152] A growing number of community organizations began pressing for an increase in the public housing stock--primarily through the scattered site concept. The Syracuse Area Council of Churches, the Community Chest, the Human Rights Commission, the League of Women Voters, CORE, NAACP, the Urban League, and other such organizations urged the city to seek additional public housing in the form of scattered site units.[153] The pressure groups were successful--the Syracuse Housing Authority embarked upon a program

in the late 1960s to lease scattered-site housing units from private
owners for use as public housing for low-income families.[154]

Conclusions

Renewal in Syracuse had a definite business orientation. The
program was designed primarily to revitalize the downtown commercial area and, to this end, experienced and effective administrators
were imported to assure the program's success. Political support
was provided by the Metropolitan Development Association and
through the citizens committee appointed by the mayor. Unlike Austin,
the local university was not influential in renewal--the "Little Red
Schoolhouse" avoided the issue. Another aspect of renewal success
(when measured by dollars received) was the drastic increase in dollar costs of the projects (particularly Near East Side) over the original estimates. This of course meant increased funds from the federal government.

Unlike the other cities studied thus far, Syracuse had a definite
interest in public housing. Two factors are believed to have accounted for this interest: First, the city recognized its future relocation problems and tried to schedule public housing construction so
that it would help alleviate the pressures caused by relocations;
second, community support for low-income housing was well organized. The civic action pressure groups in Syracuse were much
more active and effective than they were in many other cities. This
pressure undoubtedly contributed significantly to public housing expansion during the 1960s.

Buffalo

The City of Buffalo provides an interesting comparison to
Beaumont and Syracuse--the two other cities characterized by urban
deterioration. Buffalo, the largest of the cities analyzed through
field study, had both negative housing and negative urban renewal
residuals. And yet Buffalo was somewhat successful in renewal and
housing; it is merely that the need (predicted grant use) was much
greater than the city's grant success.

Physical Characteristics

During the 1960s Buffalo had a total of six urban renewal projects in various stages of completion. Of the six, only three are
federally assisted, the other three are supported entirely by the city.
In addition, Buffalo has two federally assisted code enforcement
projects.

The population of the City of Buffalo declined by 74,451 during the 1960s. At the same time, there has been a significant increase in the proportion of low-income persons residing in the community. The adverse impact of these two factors has been a declining tax base coupled with an increased demand for city services.

Like Alhambra, Buffalo's land area is restricted--the city has had no significant change in boundaries since 1853. Buffalo ranked 20th in population in 1960, but has the smallest land area of any of the 29 largest cities.

During the decade, Buffalo lost almost 11,000 housing units--mostly as a result of urban renewal, highway construction, or code enforcement.

In spite of the decrease in population, Buffalo faces a critical housing situation. City officials estimate that 18 percent of the city's housing supply is substandard or deficient. From the standpoint of housing vacancy, a June 1968 Post Office survey estimated an overall vacancy rate of only 0.7 percent in the City of Buffalo. Between 1960 and 1970 Buffalo lost 10,797 housing units (-6.1 percent). Toward the end of the decade there was a slight improvement with an increase of 1,486 (0.9 percent) units between 1966 and 1970.[155]

Urban renewal has had some impact on the overall housing situation. The Ellicott project was the first redevelopment project in the State of New York. Ellicott covers 161.4 acres and was predominantly a clearance project although some rehabilitation was included. Ellicott was a deteriorating residential and commercial area located on the eastern fringe of the central business district. The development program consists of 1,444 low and moderate housing units, new and expanded recreational facilities, and a new commercial plaza.

The Waterfront project borders the central business district on the west, and as its name suggests, is located on the shores of Lake Erie. Like Ellicott, Waterfront was predominantly a clearance project with some rehabilitation. Waterfront called for 3,000 new housing units for the elderly and low/moderate-income families. Also included are two seawalls and land reclamation projects, a new elementary school, commercial plaza, office tower, motels, parking garage, and hospital expansion. The total project covers 292.8 acres and began in 1962.

The Oak Street project was the third of the three federally assisted renewal projects in Buffalo. Consisting of 161.2 acres, Oak Street was also predominantly a clearance project with selected rehabilitation. It is located adjacent to, and to the north of, the downtown area. Oak Street development includes 1,544 low or moderate housing units, residential rehabilitation, hospital and medical facility expansion, parking, and commercial development.

Downtown (phases I and II) were total clearance projects in the
heart of the central business district encompassing 15 acres. Both
projects were financed entirely by the city with no federal assistance.
Financing cost to the city was approximately $6 million. Phase I de-
velopment included the "Main Place" enclosed shopping mall and
underground parking garage, the Erie County Bank Tower, the M and
T Bank Building, and the Church Street extension, and Cathedral
(mini)park. Phase I is the only renewal project that was entirely
complete at the time of the field observation. Phase II calls for a
retail/office complex, office tower, and pedestrian plaza.

The Industrial Park pilot project was a nonassisted project of
41.4 acres of clearance and rehabilitation to provide sites for light
industrial development. Industrial Park achieved a very limited
success.

Maryland Street/West was a nonassisted total clearance project
located adjacent to and north of the Waterfront redevelopment. A
small project, 12 acres, Maryland Street provided space for the
construction of a 240-unit tower apartment building and 52 townhouse
units.

In addition, Buffalo had plans for a Neighborhood Development
Program encompassing 1,281 acres. As this program was not under-
way during the 1960s, it is beyond the scope of this study.

The Allentown/Lakeview concentrated code enforcement project
covered 350 acres of predominantly residential property. The project
was located immediately north of the central business district and
west of the Oak Street area. Allentown/Lakeview brought 2,655
structures into code compliance with federal loan and grant assistance.

The second code enforcement project was Hamlin Park, an area
of 271.3 acres. This project brought 2,622 structures into compliance.[156]

Public housing in Buffalo has historically been accepted by the
public but yet has had an unusual cycle of development. Low-income
housing in Buffalo began with the Kenfield project in 1937, and public
housing construction under both federal and state laws continued
through 1959. After Talbert Mall, a state-aided project with an
initial occupancy date of November 1959, no public housing projects
were constructed until the 35-unit Schwab Terrace for the elderly
was opened in July 1966. Only two other small projects were opened
during the decade--Kelly Gardens, consisting of 44 units opened in
March 1967, and Kowal Apartments, consisting of 24 units opened
in December 1968. Both Kowal and Kelly Gardens were elderly projects. Thus public housing construction during the decade amounted
to only 103 units, all for the elderly.

Between January 1970 and August 1972 the Buffalo Municipal
Housing Authority opened an additional five housing projects consisting of 436 units, again all for the elderly.[157]

The Buffalo Authority is also unique in one other respect from other authorities studied--it has leased out one of its housing projects to a private company that now operates the project for moderate-income tenants. Dante Place, a low-income family project of 616 units constructed as a state-aided project was opened in October 1952. Like so many of the high-rise apartment-type projects of that era, Dante Place was constructed in an isolated area and it soon became a project noted for its high crime rate and increasing vandalism. The authority could not cope with the social problems associated with the project and was also unable to provide satisfactory project maintenance; so the project was vacated and leased to a private developer who renovated the apartments and converted it to moderate-income housing.

By 1970 two other state-aided high-rise projects were well into a cycle of high deterioration with Talbert Mall (763 units) being 21.2 percent vacant and Ellicott Mall (590 units) 8.5 percent vacant. By 1972 the state-aided high-rise projects were almost 50 percent vacant. To counter this trend, the Housing Authority was attempting to convert one of the projects from family occupancy to an elderly project. In addition, the Housing Committee of the Regional Planning Board recommended that the Ellicott Mall and Talbert Mall projects be converted to cooperatives and sold to the tenants.[158]

Not including Dante Place, the Buffalo Municipal Housing Authority had 6,670 units in 22 projects under management by August 1972. Virtually all of the family-type projects in Buffalo were constructed prior to 1960 and all of the elderly units were constructed since 1965.[159]

The Politics of Housing and Renewal

The city of Buffalo has been a traditional Democratic stronghold in national, state, and local elections. In the 1964 presidential election, Johnson defeated Goldwater by a margin of 5-1--Johnson received 172,592 votes (80 percent) to Goldwater's 43,628 (20 percent).[160] In 1968 Humphrey also received a substantial majority, carrying Buffalo with 119,279 votes (66 percent) to 480,079 for Nixon (27 percent) and 13,025 votes for George Wallace (7 percent).[161]

Although Buffalo had been a Democratic stronghold for years, in 1961 the Republican candidate was elected mayor. Chester Kowal, the Republican and Liberal party candidate, was able to take advantage of a split in the Democratic party and win the election. The incumbent mayor, Frank A. Sedita, failed to win the Democratic nomination for mayor and ran as an independent. The Democratic vote was thus split between the Democratic candidate and the incumbent mayor, allowing Kowal to emerge as the winner. The Democrats, however, were still able to maintain an 11-4 margin in the Common Council.[162] During the campaign virtually all candidates supported the urban renewal program. Ethnic divisions within the population proved to be the major issue.[163]

The results of the 1961 election provided the city of Buffalo with four years of frustration and delay in the city's urban renewal efforts. Bickering between the mayor's office and the Common Council over renewal contracts was characteristic of the Kowal administration. The federal government finally became so dissatisfied with the program in Buffalo that it threatened to withhold certification (and funds).

The Buffalo Courier Express reported that the Ellicott project was in a state of "utter and unbelievable confusion." The urban renewal commissioner and the mayor wanted to sell the 160-acre project to a developer unacceptable to the Democratically controlled Common Council while the council wanted a developer who was unacceptable to the Republican mayor. The reporter commented: "Perhaps it would be different if one party controlled both the mayor's office and the legislative branch."[164]

The difficulty over the selection of renewal developers led to a legal squabble over who had the power to award contracts--the administration or the council. In June 1963 the Common Council awarded the development contract for the Ellicott project to the First Hartford Realty Corporation. The mayor called the action illegal and vetoed the contract.[165]

Ellicott was not the only disputed project. The same sort of difficulty existed over the development of the Industrial Park pilot project. In November 1963, after two years of bickering and delays, the mayor finally approved development of the industrial park.[166]

In the 1965 election for mayor, Frank A. Sedita (this time the candidate of the Democratic and Liberal parties) defeated Roland R. Renzow, the Republican candidate, by a margin of 11,759 votes-- 92,950 for Sedita to Penzow's 81,191 votes. The Common Council remained Democratic by the same 11-4 margin.[167] Renewal was an important part of the Democratic platform for the election: "We are convinced that the future of our city depends in large measure upon getting our urban renewal program back on the track."[168]

The Buffalo Evening News complained bitterly about the city's lack of urban renewal progress, noting a consultants' report concerning "the detrimental effects of 'political discord' and 'a negative attitude towards urban renewal,' by citizens in bogging down Buffalo's program."[169] The News also recommended the formation of an urban renewal agency to remove political pressure from the renewal program.[170] The paper later complained that "for more than 10 years, Buffalo has watched in vain for signs, however small, of urban renewal's ideal result."[171]

Several years later, the renewal program still showed little progress. James P. Kavanaugh said the Buffalo program was an "impossible blend of politics and redevelopment and has caused the city to become 'a disgrace in urban renewal throughout the country.'" When asked if the City Charter could be revised to make the Urban Renewal Department autonomous, Kavanaugh replied, "It'll never happen here. People who have to take it out of politics are in politics."[172]

In the 1969 election for mayor, Frank Sedita easily won his third term as mayor by defeating Republican candidate Mrs. Alfreda Slominski by more than 20,000 votes.[173] Mrs. Slominski's

> often-recorded antipathy toward federal grant programs, further, prevented her from posing solutions to the many problems besetting Buffalo in a convincing manner. While her campaign literature pointed with outrage to lagging urban renewal, blighted housing and poorly equipped playgrounds, her votes against harnessing federal aid to relieve these ills muddled the issue.[174]

Conclusion

During the 10-year period under study, Buffalo lagged far behind expected urban renewal receipts and public housing construction. Concerning public housing, the negative residual may have been illusory. While Buffalo added only 103 public housing units during the 1960s, it was possible that a flurry of construction in the late 1960s might result in large numbers of initial occupancies in the early 1970s. Such was not the case, however. Only 436 units were initially occupied between January 1970 and August 1972.[175] Public housing construction in Buffalo, then, followed the same pattern as did the private housing sector. Neither public nor private housing supplies kept pace with the demand.

The limited number of public housing units constructed during the 1960s is in part also explained by the Housing Authority's reluctance "to attempt such an undertaking until the image of public housing has improved, as well as the social problems presently being encountered in some of its projects."[176]

The negative residual noted in Buffalo's renewal program during the decade was unquestionably caused by political factors. For the four-year period beginning with the election of a Republican mayor along with a Democratic Common Council, the urban renewal program in Buffalo came to a virtual standstill. With urban renewal under the control of the mayor's office in what is commonly known as a "machine city," the awarding of development contracts became a major political issue. Republican-supported developers could not win approval from Democratic Common Council and Democratic-supported developers could not win the approval of the Republican mayor. Renewal in Buffalo thus ground to a halt. The frustration and delay caused by the political nature of the renewal process in Buffalo is probably a major determinant of the negative renewal residual. The quantitative measures of reformism do not adequately capture this type of political conflict. The findings in Buffalo suggest that renewal and housing can become major sources of conflict in unreformed cities having a mayor of a different political party from the council majority. If data were available on a city-by-city basis concerning this type of split, the Buffalo case suggests that such a variable might be important in explaining additional amounts of the unexplained variance in grant use.

Another deterrent to renewal in Buffalo is related to the critical housing shortage in the city. There simply was no relocation housing available for the displaced of proposed renewal projects.[177] Thus little additional renewal could be undertaken until the present projects were far enough along to provide adequate low-rent housing.

CONCLUSIONS AND CONTENTIONS

The review of the literature in Chapter 2 suggested a number of hypotheses pertaining to the relationship between the outputs of the political system, in this case housing and renewal success, and measures of the city's profile. Specifically:

1. Public housing construction and urban renewal expenditures are positively related to city size and industrialization.
2. Public housing construction and urban renewal expenditures are negatively related to measures of city socioeconomic status.
3. Central cities exhibit significantly higher levels of public housing construction and urban renewal expenditures than do suburban cities.

The first hypothesis obviously cannot be rejected. The underlying dimension of city size and manufacturing is undeniably the major determinant of the use of public housing and urban renewal grants. This dimension contributed substantially and significantly to the explained variance of the grant programs both independently and through the intervening political system variables. The findings here thus substantiate relationships suggested by other scholars.

It was also expected that public housing and urban renewal would be related (negatively) to measures of socioeconomic status. Such was not the case. The factor containing significant variable

145

loadings commonly associated with socioeconomic status (Status, Wealth, and Education) was not significantly related to either public housing or urban renewal at the zero order level. When controlling for other variables in the renewal and housing models, the factor still showed no significant independent relationship with grant use. Status, Wealth, and Education was, however, related to urban renewal grant use through three of the intervening variables--two state-level variables and one measure of local political attitudes. This factor was not as influential in the housing model because it was related to public housing construction only through the housing difficulty scale. Thus socioeconomic status makes only a minor contribution to the explained variance in urban renewal and public housing. What influence it does exert is through the intervening political variables. Status, Wealth, and Education (low) is negatively related to both renewal and housing difficulty as expressed by state laws, while both renewal and housing difficulty are negatively related to the dependent variables. Thus, cities with low status (presumably those needing housing and renewal the most) are located in states where the state recognizes the need for these grants and puts few impediments in the way of city participation. These cities, in turn, then have higher levels of housing and renewal success. This type of relationship exemplifies intergovernmental cooperation stimulated by the physical characteristics of the city but made "operable" by the political system

It was also noted that central cities exhibit higher levels of public housing construction and urban renewal receipts than do suburban cities. One profile factor, termed Central City, contained substantial variable loadings of variables normally associated with urban-core cities. To further test the validity of the factor as a measure of the central city/suburban dichotomy, the factor scores were correlated with the metropolitan status dichotomous variable (Table 3.18). The significant r of -.50 substantiated the isolation of central city characteristics. Central City (the factor score) was correlated with renewal and housing success but was found not to be significantly related to either dependent variable at the zero order level. Once all of the variables in both the renewal and housing models were held constant, however, Central City was found to have a small but significant independent relationship with both housing and renewal. Central City was also related to urban renewal through the federal variable and the two variables representing local political culture. In the housing model, Central City was related to public housing through one federal and one state variable. Central City was thus positively related to model cities designation (the federal variable) that, in turn, was positively related to both housing and renewal success. It is thus noted that cities with central city characteristics are most likely to have been designated a "model city" by the federal government. The high priority given to the grant applications of the model cities by the federal approving authorities in turn stimulates housing and renewal success by the central cities.

The findings thus far generally support previous research findings. While examining grants in a slightly different vein, the studies concerning the importance of city size as a determinant of grant use by Segal and Fritschler and by Hebert and Bingham are generally substantiated. The relationships between the other profile factors and grant use also provide general support for the housing and renewal work of Aiken and Alford. While Aiken and Alford were dealing with individual variables rather than the underlying dimensions presented here, nonetheless, the overall conclusions are very similar to those of this study.

The remaining hypotheses suggested relationships between the system outputs and the intervening variables. Specifically:

4. Public housing construction is positively related to urban renewal expenditures.

5. Cities located in the same state with a HUD regional office exhibit higher levels of public housing construction and urban renewal expenditures than do cities in states without HUD regional offices.

6. Public housing construction and urban renewal expenditures are positively related to the ease with which citizens are able to participate in the programs as authorized by state enabling legislation.

7. Public housing construction and urban renewal expenditures are negatively related to reformism in city government.

8. Public housing construction and urban renewal expenditures are directly related to community political and social attitudes.

Urban renewal was closely related to public housing construction/leasing. Other than Size/Manufacturing, urban renewal independently explained the largest amount of the variance in public housing. In addition, renewal served as an intervening variable for a portion of the influence of Urban Density and Size/Manufacturing, two of the three factors that also showed an independent relationship with public housing. Several of the case studies also exemplified this relationship. In Syracuse it was noted that public housing construction was often programmed to coincide with the need for relocation housing generated by urban renewal. Buffalo, on the other hand, exemplified the use of renewal land to provide sites for public housing (albeit elderly housing).

The location of HUD regional offices was not related to grant success. Although the Oakland Task Force report suggested that cities located near HUD offices might expect some increased priority/ success in the grantsman game, this study found no such relationship.

State laws, and the rapidity with which local renewal agencies were established, play an important role in renewal and housing success. Legal impediments to the use of federal urban renewal programs (through state laws and state enabling legislation) significantly affect the level of grant use. This was also found to be the case with public housing construction/leasing.

There was a noticeable difference between renewal and housing success and the early establishment of local authorities. Those cities establishing renewal agencies rapidly (after 1949 authorization) had higher levels of renewal success during the 1960s than their slower counterparts. Apparently the long lead time between project initiation and the receipt of federal funds along with the probability that such cities would have more projects in the execution stage than the latecomers explains this relationship. With housing construction/leasing, on the other hand, those cities that were late in establishing local housing authorities constructed/leased more units during the 1960s than their earlier counterparts. This is also logical as HUD authorizations for new public housing construction during the 1960s was probably higher for cities with no public housing (or low levels of housing) than for cities with established and sizable programs.

The findings concerning reform measures in city government were disappointing. Local reformism was not independently related to urban renewal success while only the election type was related to public housing. Nonpartisan elections were the only reform measure found to be related to public housing. It is quite possible that public housing is a partisan political issue with, as a general rule, Republicans opposing housing construction and Democrats supporting it. Apparently, without party support the issue is diffused, and higher construction/leasing levels are possible. This supports the previous finding of Lineberry and Fowler that reformism (at least this one reform measure) tends to minimize the impact of cleavage indicators on public policy. The analysis in this chapter did not, however, support Lineberry and Fowler's contention that reformism is additive.

Local community attitudes were shown to have important relationships to urban renewal grant use but were of little significance in determining levels of public housing construction. The attitudes of suburbanites, for example, was found to be anathema to urban renewal. Of interest also was the apparent difference in the types of conservatism indicated by the Goldwater and Wallace votes. While recognizing the dangers in oversimplifying the meanings attributed to votes for political candidates, nonetheless, the vote for Goldwater was taken as a rough measure of a basic ideological conservatism concerning the activities of government, and the Wallace vote was used as a rough measure of racism in the community. While more will be said in Chapter 8 concerning racism, the Wallace vote was not related to either housing or renewal success. Communities with a high vote for Goldwater, on the other hand, were not prone to utilize federal urban renewal programs. There apparently exists a community attitude concerning the scope of government activity, captured by the vote for Goldwater, that explains a reluctance to utilize federal urban renewal programs. Alhambra and Beaumont both strongly supported Goldwater's candidacy, and both communities rejected the use of federal urban renewal. Beaumont, on the other hand, gave moderate support to George Wallace while Alhambra voters strongly rejected his appeal.

The case studies of urban renewal and public housing success closely followed other case study literature. Cities such as Vallejo, Austin, and Syracuse were exemplified by capable and energetic administrators, high degrees of political support for the programs, and a general downtown or business orientation and/or domination. The other cities either exhibited local norms or attitudes that were in conflict with federal renewal and housing programs (Beaumont and Alhambra) or were characterized by serious political in-fighting and administrative bungling caused by the programs becoming "too political," as was the case with Buffalo.

One conclusion here becomes extremely important. The case study approach tends to inflate the importance of the "political hero" or the "super administrator" in the grant process. Richard Lee and Edward Logue probably made very little difference in New Haven's urban renewal program, just as James Richardson in Vallejo or George Schuster in Syracuse probably made less of an impact than the case study approach might lead one to believe. No matter who was running the show in any of these cities, it is most probable that the cities would have had successful urban renewal and public housing programs and, in terms of development, would probably not be much different than they are today. Unquestionably, the physical characteristics of the city are the important determinants of grant use. These characteristics are "filtered through" the political environment, made up of federal, state, and local decisions and attitudinal constraints, to determine patterns of grant use. Good administration or bad administration probably makes little difference.

The general flavor of Buffalo's renewal and housing programs was set by the city's physical profile, not by its politics. Political squabbling, poor administration, and corruption may help account for the negative residual in the program, and had Richard Lee and Edward Logue been in Buffalo instead of New Haven, Buffalo might have had a more successful program. The point is, in an $87 million program, the $87 million is of primary importance, not a $9 million negative residual. The residual is of undeniable importance when attempting to explain as much of the program variation as possible, but it must be kept in its proper perspective. Overreliance on qualitative case studies tends to convey the erroneous impression that the factors that might serve to explain the residuals (for example, politics, good administration, citizen support, etc.) are more important than the true determinants.

NOTES

1. U.S. Department of Housing and Urban Development, Urban Renewal Directory: As of December 31, 1970 (Washington, D.C.: Government Printing Office, 1971).

2. U.S. Department of Housing and Urban Development, Consolidated Development Directory, Report S-11A (Washington, D.C.: U.S. Department of Housing and Urban Development, 1970).

3. R. J. Rummel, Applied Factor Analysis (Evanston, Ill.: Northwestern University Press, 1970), p. 148.

4. Ibid., p. 385.

5. Seven cities had missing data.

6. Thirty-three cities had missing data.

7. Robert L. Lineberry and Edmund P. Fowler, "Reformism and Public Policies in American Cities," American Political Science Review 61 (September 1967): 701-16. Data source was The Municipal Year Book 1960 (Chicago: International City Managers' Association, 1960), pp. 84-90.

8. Predicted Urban Renewal Funds = (-1285000 x Reformism) + (3954800 x Central City) + (6810600 x Urban Density) + (2273300 x Status, Wealth, and Education) + (20285000 x Size/Manufacturing) + (-2130400 x Commuting/Growth) + (1616700 x Liberalism Factor) + 13455121. Predicted Public Housing Construction/Leasing = (-56.249 x Reformism) + (232.19 x Central City) + (450.14 x Urban Density) + (39.262 x Status, Wealth, and Education) + (2069 x Size/Manufacturing) + (-137.95 x Commuting/Growth) + (-36.303 x Liberalism Factor) + 816.6.

9. U.S. Department of Housing and Urban Development, "Execution Project Number by State," Transmittal Notice MC-24, February 1970 (Mimeographed).

10. U.S. Office of Economic Opportunity, Catalog of Federal Domestic Assistance (Washington, D.C.: Government Printing Office, 1970), p. 969.

11. "Dates of Enactment of State Housing Authorities Laws," and "Dates of Enactment of State Urban Renewal Laws." Attachments to letter from Deborah Greenstein, Program Analyst, Housing Management Research Division, Department of Housing and Urban Development, November 3, 1972.

12. Municipal Year Book 1960, pp. 89-117.

13. Metropolitan status is not normally considered a measure of attitude. It was used as an attitudinal variable in this instance in an attempt to capture different attitudes based upon residential location. See Scott Greer, The Urbane View: Life and Politics in Metropolitan America (New York: Oxford University Press, 1972) for a discussion of these differing attitudes.

14. Richard L. Cole, "The Urban Policy Process: A Note on Structural and Regional Influences," Social Science Quarterly 52 (December 1971): 651.

15. See Denton E. Morrison and Ramon E. Henkel, eds., The Significance Test Controversy: A Reader (Chicago: Aldine, 1970).

16. Robert P. Groberg, Centralized Relocation: A New Municipal Service (Washington, D.C.: National Association of Housing and Redevelopment Officials, 1969), p. 4.

17. U.S. Congress, House, Committee on Banking and Currency, Basic Laws and Authorities on Housing and Urban Development (Washington, D.C.: Government Printing Office, 1969), p. 370.

18. Alhambra Chamber of Commerce, 1972-73 Community Factbook (Whittier, Calif.: Frank Clement, 1972); Alhambra Chamber of Commerce, Alhambra California Facts (Alhambra: Chamber of Commerce, 1972); Margaret J. Dutcher and Robert Studer, History of Alhambra (Alhambra: Chamber of Commerce, n.d.).

19. U.S. Department of Commerce, Bureau of the Census, General Social and Economic Characteristics: California (Washington, D.C.: Government Printing Office, 1972).

20. Alhambra, Factbook, p. 9.

21. Bureau of the Census, California.

22. Vallejo Chamber of Commerce, Vallejo, California (Encino, Calif.: Windsor Publications, 1971); Vallejo Chamber of Commerce, Vallejo, California (Vallejo: Solano County Board of Supervisors, n.d.).

23. U.S. Department of Commerce, Bureau of the Census, General Social and Economic Characteristics: Texas (Washington, D.C.: Government Printing Office, 1972).

24. Central City Development Corporation, Beaumont Central City Analysis: Advance Information Kit (Beaumont, 1972) (Mimeographed).

25. Bureau of the Census, Texas.

26. Austin Chamber of Commerce, Austin's Remarkable Growth Pattern (Austin, 1972) (Mimeographed); Austin Chamber of Commerce, General Demographic Trends (Austin, 1972) (Mimeographed); "Community Profile: Austin, Texas" (Austin, 1972) (Mimeographed).

27. U.S. Department of Commerce, Bureau of the Census, General Social and Economic Characteristics: New York (Washington, D.C.: Government Printing Office, 1972).

28. Department of City Planning and Department of Urban Improvement, A Community Renewal Program: Syracuse, New York (Syracuse: City of Syracuse, N.Y., n.d.).

29. Syracuse Governmental Research Bureau and Metropolitan Development Association, Profile of Central New York (Syracuse: Syracuse Governmental Research Bureau and Metropolitan Development Association, 1973), p. 117.

30. Bureau of the Census, New York.

31. Nathaniel S. Keith and Marcou, O'Leary and Associates, Inc., Buffalo Community Renewal Program Extension for the City of Buffalo, New York (Buffalo: City of Buffalo, N.Y., n.d.), p. 11.

32. "Buffalo," Encyclopedia Americana, 1970, IV, 712-16.

33. Victor Gruen Associates, Alhambra 1985: A General Plan for Alhambra, California (Los Angeles: Victor Gruen Associates, 1965), p. 7.

34. Ibid., p. 8.

35. Alhambra Industrial Directory (Alhambra: Alhambra Chamber of Commerce, 1972).

36. Gruen Associates, Alhambra Industrial Redevelopment: A Design and Implementation Framework (Los Angeles: Gruen Associates, August 1970), p. 2.

37. Ibid.

38. Alhambra Redevelopment Agency, Redevelopment Plan for the Industrial Redevelopment Project (Alhambra, May 26, 1969), p. 4 (Mimeographed).

39. Post-Advocate (Alhambra, Calif.), November 2, 1964, p. 1.

40. Post-Advocate, November 4, 1964, p. 1.

41. Post-Advocate, October 29, 1968, p. 2-B.

42. "How Valley Cities Voted," Post-Advocate, November 8, 1968, p. 6-A.

43. Ordinance No. 070-3480, "An Ordinance of the Alhambra City Council Amending the Alhambra City Code by Adding a New Chapter 6-26 Pertaining to Maintenance of Property, and Property Nuisances and by Repealing Chapter 6.28 Thereof," City of Alhambra, California, July 7, 1970; Ordinance No. 071-3512, "An Ordinance of the Alhambra City Council Amending the Alhambra Municipal Code by Adding Thereto a New Title 18 Prohibiting Emission or Creation of Noise Beyond Certain Levels and by Repealing Sections 9.04.010 and 9.04.020 Thereof," City of Alhambra, California, April 6, 1971.

44. Gruen Associates, Alhambra 1985, pp. 87-93.

45. Redevelopment Agency of the City of Vallejo, Marina Vista (Vallejo, Calif.: Gibson Publication, n.d.), p. 13.

46. Ibid., p. 1.

47. Ibid., pp. 2-11.

48. Vallejo Planning Department, Neighborhood Analyses: Vallejo, California (Vallejo, 1966) (Mimeographed); Vallejo Planning Department, 1967 Special Census Release (Vallejo, 1968) (Mimeographed).

49. Charlotte Pruitt, "Vallejo is Facing a Housing Dilemma," Vallejo Times-Herald, April 20, 1969, pp. 1, 4.

50. Vallejo Times-Herald, November 4, 1964, p. 1.

51. Vallejo Times-Herald, April 5, 1961, p. 1.

52. Sunday Times-Herald, April 4, 1965, p. 6.

53. Redevelopment Agency, Marina Vista; Redevelopment Agency of the City of Vallejo, Urban Design for Marina Vista: A Redevelopment Project for the Urban Renewal of Downtown Vallejo, California (Vallejo, Calif.: Gibson Publications, n.d.).

54. Vallejo Times-Herald, April 1, 1963, p. 12.

55. Vallejo Times-Herald, April 2, 1963, p. 10.

56. Vallejo Times-Herald, April 1, 1963, p. 13.

57. Pruitt, "Housing Dilemma," p. 4.

58. Ibid.

59. Ibid.

60. Central City Development Corporation, Beaumont Analysis, pp. 2-5-2-8.

61. Ibid., p. 2-9.

62. J. Earl Brickhouse, A Low Cost Housing Study of Beaumont, Texas (Beaumont: Chamber of Commerce, April 25, 1972), p. 1 (Mimeographed).

63. Ibid., pp. 3-5.

64. Central City Development Corporation, Beaumont Analysis, pp. 2-29.

65. Brickhouse, Low Cost Housing Study, p. 1.

66. Richard M. Scammon, ed., America Votes 7 (Washington, D.C.: Governmental Affairs Institute, 1968), p. 383.

67. Richard M. Scammon, ed., America Votes 8 (Washington, D.C.: Governmental Affairs Institute, 1970), p. 386.

68. Brickhouse, Low Cost Housing Study, p. 15.

69. Ibid.

70. An editorial, for example, took issue with Democratic National Chairman Paul Butler's "radical ideas on civil rights." Beaumont Enterprise, May 3, 1960, p. 1.

71. Beaumont Enterprise, April 3, 1960, p. 6A.

72. Beaumont Enterprise, June 1, 1960, p. 6.

73. "U.S. Chamber's Urban Renewal Approval Cited," Beaumont Enterprise, June 3, 1960, p. 1.

74. Willis Swearinger, "Urban Renewal Meet Recesses at Port Arthur," Beaumont Enterprise, June 2, 1960, p. 1.

75. Beaumont Enterprise, June 4, 1960, p. 1.

76. "Board Reaffirms C-C's Urban Renewal Stand," Beaumont Enterprise, June 6, 1960, p. 1.

77. "Urban Renewal Approved by Architect Unit," Beaumont Enterprise, June 7, 1960, p. 1.

78. Beaumont Enterprise, June 10, 1960, p. 1.

79. Beaumont Enterprise, June 7, 1960, p. 7.

80. Beaumont Enterprise, June 9, 1960, p. 2; June 10, 1960, p. 34.

81. Beaumont Enterprise, June 7, 1960, p. 4.

82. Beaumont Enterprise, June 8, 1960, p. 13; June 9, 1960, p. 37.

83. Beaumont Enterprise, June 10, 1960, pp. 3, 6.

84. Beaumont Enterprise, June 11, 1960, pp. 3, 8, 16.

85. Beaumont Enterprise, June 12, 1960, p. 1.

86. Beaumont Enterprise, November 3, 1967, p. 8.

87. Beaumont Enterprise, November 1, 1967, p. 2.

88. Beaumont Enterprise, November 1, 1967, p. 1; November 5, 1967, p. 4A; November 10, 1967, pp. 1, 9; November 14, 1967, p. 7.

89. Beaumont Enterprise, November 17, 1967, p. 1.

90. Beaumont Enterprise, November 5, 1967, p. 1.

91. Beaumont Enterprise, November 8, 1967, p. 6.

92. Beaumont Enterprise, November 5, 1967, pp. 1-2; November 9, 1967, pp. 1, 5.

93. Beaumont Enterprise, November 8, 1967, p. 1; November 12, 1967, p. 10A.

94. Beaumont Enterprise, November 10, 1967, p. 17.

95. Beaumont Enterprise, November 14, 1967, p. 30.

96. Sunday Enterprise, November 19, 1967, p. 4A.

97. David M. Olson, "Austin: The Capital City," in Urban Politics in the Southwest, ed. Leonard E. Goodall (Tempe: Institute of Public Administration, Arizona State University, 1967), pp. 23-24.

98. "Urban Renewal Special," Austin American-Statesman, August 27, 1972, pp. 4-5, 7.

99. City of Austin, 1972-1973 Workable Program (Austin: City of Austin, 1972), pp. 37-41.

100. Art. 12691-3, Section 3, Acts 1957, 55th Legislature, p. 704, Ch. 298, Vernon's Annotated Revised Civil Statutes of the State of Texas, Volume 2B (Kansas City, Mo.: Vernon Law Book Company, 1963), p. 375.

101. Scammon, America Votes 7, p. 384.

102. Scammon, America Votes 8, p. 369.

103. Bill Woods, "Urban Renewal Wins With 55-Vote Margin," Austin American-Statesman, December 6, 1959, pp. 1, A-4.

104. Ibid.; Austin American, December 4, 1959; Austin Statesman, December 4, 1959.

105. Austin American, December 2, 1959, p. A-4; Austin Statesman, December 1, 1959, p. A-4; December 3, 1959, p. A-4.

106. Austin Statesman, December 3, 1959, p. A-15; Austin American, December 4, 1959, p. 1.

107. Austin American-Statesman, March 26, 1961, pp. B1, B5.

108. Austin American-Statesman, March 31, 1963, pp. D1, D3.

109. Ibid.

110. Austin American-Statesman, March 12, 1967, p. D-1.

111. Ibid.

112. Austin American, March 23, 1969, p. 16.

113. Ibid.

114. Ibid.

115. Ibid.

116. Ibid.

117. Austin American, April 7, 1969, p. 1.

118. J. Allen Williams, Jr., "The Effects of Urban Renewal Upon a Black Community: Evaluation and Recommendations," Social Science Quarterly 50 (December 1969): 703-12; J. Allen Williams, Jr., Blackshear Diagnostic Survey: A Description and Problem Analysis (Austin: The Urban Renewal Agency of the City of Austin, June 1968) (Mimeographed).

119. Charles M. Bonjean, "Dimensions of Power Structures: Some Problems in Conceptualization and Measurement," in Future Directions in Community Power Research: A Colloquium, ed. Frederick M. Wirt (Berkeley: Institute of Governmental Studies, Universityof California, 1971), pp. 19-42. For a general discussion of Austin politics in the 1960s, see David M. Olson, Nonpartisan Elections: A Case Analysis (Austin: Institute of Public Affairs, University of Texas, 1965).

120. Amended Memorandum of Understanding (Austin: Urban Renewal Agency of the City of Austin, July 1, 1972) (Mimeographed).

121. Williams, Blackshear Diagnostic Survey, p. 172.

122. Ibid., pp. 192-201.

123. Ibid.; Williams, "Effects of Urban Renewal."

124. Memorandum Opinion: Blackshear Residents Organization, et al. vs. Housing Authority of the City of Austin, et al., Civil Action No. A-70-CA-51 (Austin: United States District Court, Western District of Texas, Austin Division, Filed December 3, 1971), p. 1 (Mimeographed).

125. Ibid., p. 5.

126. Ibid., p. 14.

127. For a description of community power in Syracuse, see Roscoe C. Martin et al., Decisions in Syracuse (Bloomington:

Indiana University Press, 1961); Linton C. Freeman, Patterns of Local Community Leadership (Indianapolis: Bobbs-Merrill, 1968); H. George Frederickson and Linda Schluter O'Leary, Power, Public Opinion, and Policy in a Metropolitan Community: A Case Study of Syracuse, New York (New York: Praeger, 1973).

128. Syracuse Governmental Research Bureau, Profile of Central New York, p. 17.

129. Housing Committee of the League of Women Voters of Metropolitan Syracuse, Housing in Onondaga County: Present Facts and Future Goals (Syracuse: League of Women Voters, February 1969), pp. 1-2.

130. Gene Goshorn, "Syracuse tackles problem head-on," Syracuse Herald-American, January 2, 1966.

131. A Workable Program for Community Improvement: 1968 Progress Report for the Elimination and Prevention of Slums and Blight in Syracuse, New York (Syracuse: City of Syracuse, 1968), p. 18.

132. Syracuse Governmental Research Bureau, Profile of Central New York, pp. 14-16.

133. Workable Program, Syracuse, p. 21.

134. League of Women Voters, Housing in Onondaga County, p. 1.

135. Ibid., p. 4.

136. Ibid., pp. 19, 5.

137. Syracuse Post-Standard, November 4, 1964, pp. 1-2.

138. Syracuse Post-Standard, November 6, 1968, p. 1.

139. Syracuse Post-Standard, November 1, 1969, p. 8.

140. Syracuse Post-Standard, November 2, 1961, p. 24.

141. Syracuse Post-Standard, November 5, 1969, p. 1.

142. Syracuse Post-Standard, November 1, 1969, p. 8.

143. See Freeman, Patterns of Leadership, for background information.

144. "Renewal Council Praised," Syracuse Post-Standard, November 2, 1962.

145. Workable Program, Syracuse, Citizen Involvement, p. 3.

146. Joseph A. Porcello, "UR condemnation," Syracuse Herald-Journal, July 16, 1968.

147. Joseph V. Ganley, "719 Units Can Now Be Built," Syracuse Post-Standard, May 17, 1956, pp. 1, 25.

148. "Council Accepts $4.5 Million Federal Housing Aid," Syracuse Post-Standard, May 29, 1956.

149. Joseph V. Ganley, "City Holds Off State Housing," Syracuse Herald-Journal, April 23, 1959, p. 3. Under federal housing, the city government is not responsible for housing authority financial losses. Under New York state housing, however, if the state sponsored projects are losing money, the city is required to make up the loss.

150. "Action Asked in Urban Renewal Problems," Syracuse Post-Standard, July 30, 1961, pp. 1, 31.

151. Eleanor Rosebrugh, "Housing Needs Are Reviewed," Syracuse Post-Standard, April 15, 1964.

152. Joseph V. Ganley, "See city public housing as ending," Syracuse Herald-Journal, May 31, 1965.

153. Eleanor Rosebrugh, "Scattered Site Housing Urged," Syracuse Post-Standard, August 12, 1966.

154. Eleanor Rosebrugh, "Expect Housing Action," Syracuse Post-Standard, December 9, 1966.

155. Keith et al., Buffalo Community Renewal Program, pp. 11-19.

156. Frank Stahl, Reflections: A Summary of Urban Renewal Activities in Buffalo, New York 1971/1972 (Buffalo: Department of Urban Renewal, 1972), p. 18.

157. Buffalo Municipal Housing Authority, Data on Occupied Projects Under Management, 1972 (Buffalo: August 1972) (Mimeographed).

158. Housing Committee of the Erie and Niagara Counties Regional Planning Board, Technical Report on Housing in the Erie-Niagara Region: First Year Study (Grand Island, N.Y.: Erie and Niagara Counties Regional Planning Board, June 1970), pp. 1-17.

159. Buffalo Municipal Housing Authority, Data on Occupied Projects.

160. Buffalo Courier Express, November 4, 1964, p. 1.

161. Buffalo Courier Express, November 6, 1968, p. 1.

162. Buffalo Courier Express, November 8, 1961, p. 1.

163. Buffalo Courier Express, November 1, 1961, pp. 7, 36; November 5, 1961, pp. 5, 14.

164. Dick Hirsch, "Buffalo Renewal in Utter Confusion," Buffalo Courier Express, June 2, 1963, pp. 1B, 5B.

165. "Mayor Vetoes Second Ellicott Project Action," Buffalo Courier Express, June 6, 1963, p. 11.

166. "Kowal Approves Industrial Park Work," Buffalo Courier Express, November 2, 1963, p. 1.

167. Buffalo Courier Express, November 3, 1965, p. 1.

168. Buffalo Courier Express, October 19, 1965, p. 32.

169. Frank Buell, "20-Year Program of Urban Renewal Projected for City," Buffalo Evening News, April 19, 1965, p. 1.

170. At this time the city's urban renewal program was operated by the Department of Urban Renewal--a line department within the city administration. The Buffalo Evening News recommended that renewal be handled by a semiautonomous agency as was the case in most cities.

171. Frank Buell, "New Ideas Needed to Breathe Life into Renewal Phantoms," Buffalo Evening News, August 18, 1965, p. 39.

172. Dominic Merle, "Renewal Delays Tied to Council," Buffalo Evening News, December 2, 1968, p. 28.

173. Buffalo Courier Express, November 5, 1969, p. 1.

174. Douglas Turner, "Sedita Win Caps Masterful Effort," Buffalo Courier Express, November 5, 1969, p. 1.

175. Buffalo Municipal Housing Authority, Data on Occupied Projects.

176. Workable Program 1970/1972 (Buffalo: City of Buffalo, 1969), p. 11B.

177. Keith et al., Buffalo Community Renewal Program, p. 33.

CHAPTER

4

EFFECTS OF
HOUSING AND RENEWAL
ON LOCAL BUSINESS

Thus far this study has attempted to provide some insight into the patterns of use of federal grants to local government—specifically urban renewal and public housing grants. This chapter and the remaining chapters will be concerned with the second of the two major research questions: What impact have these grants actually had on cities? This chapter will deal with one of the four broad areas of hypothesized grant effects: the effects on local business.

There is one significant methodological difference between Chapter 3 and the chapters dealing with grant effects. Chapter 3 attempted to isolate the city physical and social characteristics, along with the political characteristics, which would explain the variation in the dependent variables, namely, urban renewal and public housing. The chapters concerning grant effects, however, are not attempting to explain a large percentage of the variation in the dependent variables, only that variance explained by renewal and housing grants.

One hypothesized effect of urban renewal and public housing to be discussed in this chapter, for example, is the effect of these grants on residential construction. The dependent variable, then, is residential construction. However, the purpose of this study is not to "explain" the variation in residential construction, or to predict construction, but merely to isolate the effects of renewal and housing on this construction.

In this chapter, and in the remaining chapters concerned with grant effects, environmental influences not contained in this analysis are probably the major determinants of most of the effects being considered. Many factors affect local construction levels, for example, but this study is only concerned with two of those factors: urban renewal and public housing. For this reason, multiple regression and correlation is not a particularly appropriate methodological technique. Simple and partial correlation coefficients provide more appropriate analytical tools.

Two measures were selected as representative of general business conditions within the cities. One such measure was the unemployment rate. In theory at least, both renewal and public housing programs are stimulative to general business activity. If renewal and housing programs were large enough to substantially affect business conditions within a community, they should be associated with a low unemployment rate. The unemployment rate for each city was obtained from the 1970 census.[1]

The other area of economic activity expected to benefit from urban renewal and public housing was the area of residential housing construction. The number of new housing units authorized in permit-issuing places from 1960 through 1970 was selected as an indicator of residential construction.[2]

BIVARIATE RELATIONSHIPS

Table 4.1 shows the zero order relationship between the grant programs and the indicator of the city's economic vitality, the unemployment rate. Neither urban renewal receipts nor public housing construction/leasing were significantly related to unemployment.

TABLE 4.1

Zero Order Product Moment Correlation Coefficients
between Grant Use and Unemployment

	Percent Unemployed, 1970
Urban renewal	0.037
Public housing	0.015

Both renewal and housing, however, were significantly related to residential housing construction as is shown in Table 4.2. Both relationships were quite substantial with the coefficient between renewal and housing permits of $r = .59$ and between public housing and housing permits of $r = .73$. Temporal ordering became a significant problem here--especially in the relationship between public housing construction and housing permits. Obviously, the housing permit comes before housing construction and occupancy in the temporal sequence. Just how much before is another question. There is no "average" construction time that can be assumed to exist between permit issuance and unit occupancy in public housing. The variables determining the time lag could not be built into a model. They include method of bid (for example, turnkey vs. conventional bidding), climatic conditions, number of units in the project, specifications, material shortages, type units (that is, high-rise or single family units), etc. Rather than risking adoption of an invalid time-series sequence that could produce erroneous conclusions, the data were not temporally ordered. Both independent variables and the dependent variable cover the entire 1960-70 time frame. The reader, then, must recognize these limitations to the data.

TABLE 4.2

Zero Order Product Moment Correlation Coefficients
between Grant Use and Housing Construction

	Housing Permits, 1960-70
Urban renewal	0.591*
Public housing	0.733*

*Significant at the .05 level.

At the zero order level, urban renewal and public housing programs apparently do not make enough of an impact on the local economy to affect overall economic vitality as measured by the unemployment rate. On the other hand, both programs are significantly and substantially related to housing construction. The unanswered question is, however, whether these relationships are independent or are indicative of other possible relationships within the model. Is the relationship between urban renewal and housing construction independent or does the coefficient of $r = .59$ actually show the relationship between City Size/Manufacturing and housing construction?

MULTIVARIATE RELATIONSHIPS

To test the independence of the zero order correlations, partials were computed between renewal and housing (as independent variables) and the economic indicators, while controlling for the five city profile factors and all of the individual political variables. Since the use of the reformism score and the Local Culture factor in Chapter 3 tended to hide important relationships, all of the individual political variables were included in the computation. Table 4.3 shows the independent relationships between grant use and local economic vitality. Both correlation coefficients are negative as expected; however, public housing was found to be independently related to the unemployment rate when controlling for the other variables in the model. The relationship (r = .13) was not high enough, however, so that public housing construction/leasing can be considered a real determinant of employment. The multivariate relationships here generally verify the zero order correlations.

TABLE 4.3

Partial Correlation Coefficients Showing Independent Relationships between Grant Use and Unemployment

	Percent Unemployed, 1970
Urban renewal	−0.047
Public housing	−0.133*

*Significant at the .05 level.

Partials were also computed between grant use and housing construction (Table 4.4). Both urban renewal and public housing were found to be significantly and independently related to housing construction--but this time in a negative direction with r = -.25 and r = -.24 respectively. Thus high levels of renewal receipts and public housing construction/leasing are independently related to a reduced number of housing permits.

It had been expected that urban renewal and public housing might be independently related to housing construction--but in a positive direction. This was not the case. The relationships between housing permits and each of the variables in both the renewal and housing models, while controlling for all others, was then examined for a possible key to the negative coefficients. Tables 4.5 and 4.6 present the partial coefficients. No other unusual relationships are apparent. Size/Manufacturing is once again a dominant influence; but this is certainly no surprise.

TABLE 4.4

Partial Correlation Coefficients Showing Independent Relationships
between Grant Use and Housing Construction

	Housing Permits, 1960–70
Urban renewal	−0.247*
Public housing	−0.238*

*Significant at the .05 level.

TABLE 4.5

Partial Correlation Coefficients Showing Independent
Relationships between Renewal Model Variables
and Housing Construction

	Housing Permits, 1960–70
Status, Wealth, and Education (low)	−0.223*
Central City	0.155*
Urban Density	0.142*
Size/Manufacturing	0.792*
Commuting/Growth	0.040
Model city	0.099
HUD office in state	0.060
Renewal difficulty	−0.020
Years since 1949 for URA	0.055
Years since 1960 for enabling legislation	0.013
Form of government	−0.153*
Representation	0.037
Type of election	0.121*
Wallace vote	−0.127*
Goldwater vote	0.044
Elazar's political cultures	−0.020
Metro status	−0.124*
Urban renewal	−0.247*

*Significant at the .05 level.

TABLE 4.6

Partial Correlation Coefficients Showing Independent
Relationships between Housing Model Variables
and Housing Construction

	Housing Permits, 1960-70
Status, Wealth, and Education (low)	-0.233*
Central City	0.200*
Urban Density	0.183*
Size/Manufacturing	0.733*
Commuting/Growth	0.020
Model city	0.130*
HUD office in state	0.118*
Urban renewal	-0.201*
Housing difficulty	-0.036
Years since 1937 for LHA	0.110
Years since 1960 for enabling legislation	0.101
Form of government	-0.175*
Representation	0.032
Type of election	0.156*
Wallace vote	-0.145*
Goldwater vote	0.053
Elazar's political cultures	-0.019
Metro status	-0.124*
Public housing	-0.238*

*Significant at the .05 level.

There is a plausible explanation for the negative relationships, nevertheless. Recall that in Chapter 3, Central City, Urban Density, and Size/Manufacturing were positively related to, and significant contributors to, the explained variance in both urban renewal and public housing. The conditions isolated by these factors are descriptive of the older, stagnant, and decaying core cities. The political and government officials respond to the physical conditions and deterioration of the city by heavily participating in federal programs such as urban renewal and public housing in an attempt to "get things moving again." The same characteristics (Central City, Urban Density, and Size/Manufacturing) are also indicative of higher levels of housing construction.

Let us now compare two hypothetical cities, both of which have roughly the same factor scores on the aforementioned three factors--but with one city in reasonably sound economic health and the other characterized by a badly deteriorating economic condition. One indicator of this deteriorating economic condition (with socioeconomic factors held constant) is a low level of housing construction (building permits). In this situation, the political officials in the economically weak city might be inclined to favor large doses of federal construction money to aid the economic situation.

In this context, then, the problem may merely be one of failure to account for the time lag. Under the same controls used in this chapter, it is possible that high levels of renewal and housing from 1960 through 1970 might be independently associated with an increase in building permits during the period 1970 through 1980, while at the same time exhibiting the negative association found here during the 1960 through 1970 period.

QUALITATIVE ANALYSIS

The business and economic effects of the public housing and urban renewal programs were also examined through the case study approach. In part the case studies suggest a strong economic orientation to the programs--especially urban renewal.

Vallejo

At best, the economic effects of urban renewal and public housing on a given community are difficult to measure. This is especially true of suburban communities such as Vallejo, which usually hire out-of-town developers for large local projects. It is much more likely that larger central cities would be able to hire local architects and construction firms than would cities of Vallejo's size. For example, San Francisco (31 miles away) would undoubtedly have little difficulty in hiring local firms for renewal and housing work, while there may be no local firms in Vallejo capable of handling much of the complex renewal work. Thus the economic effects of Vallejo's renewal and housing programs undoubtedly reach well outside the local community.

During the 11-year period from January 1960 through the end of 1970, the City of Vallejo issued 11,930 construction permits.[3] Without even considering commercial construction in the Marina Vista area, the residential construction of 618 dwelling units in the area accounted for roughly 5 percent of the total construction in the city during the 11-year period. With almost as much commercial zoning as residential in the area, commercial construction probably accounted for another 4 percent of the total construction.

During the 1960s approximately 600 housing units were taken off the private rental market when they were leased to the Vallejo Housing Authority for Section 23 low-income housing. Concerning housing in Vallejo, the Vallejo Chamber of Commerce advises that "housing, both for sale and for rent, is not plentiful. . . ."[4] Conservatively assuming that the removal of 600 units from the rental market generated a 50 percent replacement construction of 300 units, public housing operations in the city could conceivably have accounted for 2.5 percent of the construction in the city during the period.

In addition, it is likely that the generation of demand for the construction of single-family dwellings had a greater impact for local contractors than did a large portion of the renewal work. Construction of the $3.0 million John F. Kennedy Library in the Marina Vista area is a case in point. Architects in association for the library were Beland, Gianell, and Associates of Vallejo and Marquis and Stoller of San Francisco. General contractor was the firm of Christensen and Foster of Santa Rosa.[5] Thus a large portion of the $3.0 million cost of the library went to firms located out of town.

Urban renewal is often thought to attract industry and commerce to a city. The Marina Vista project in Vallejo did not prove to be significant in this regard. Most of the businesses in the project are Vallejo firms relocating from other parts of the city. The relocations appear to be generating large numbers of vacancies in commercial buildings--vacancies that are not being filled by new businesses.

Overall, it is reasonable and conservative to conclude that urban renewal and public housing probably accounted for a minimum of 10 percent of the construction in Vallejo between 1960 and 1970. While the total construction generated by the urban renewal project far exceeded the construction generated by public housing, it is likely that a higher percentage of the construction dollars accounted for by public housing remained in the city than was the case with urban renewal monies.

While the ability of renewal and housing to generate construction in Vallejo might be easily accepted, there is some question as to the overall effect on business: Thus far, the overall effect of both renewal and housing on commercial and industrial activity within the city appears to be marginal. A note of caution, however, is necessary here--it is really too early to try to measure the effects of the renewal project on attracting new industry and commerce. The value of Marina Vista in improving the overall business climate and in providing an attractive city for commercial and industrial firms probably cannot be determined until the end of the 1970s.

Austin

While Austin, like Vallejo, had positive renewal and housing residuals, the economic climate of the two cities was distinctly different. Vallejo had a much more fragile economy, relying to a large extent on defense spending for economic health. While Austin's economy is also government dominated, the economy is affected (by Bergstrom Air Force Base) but not dominated by defense expenditures.

The most important economic difference between Vallejo and Austin, however, was in the growth rate. While Vallejo was expecting an improved economic condition as a result of urban renewal and housing, Austin was not. Austin's population growth rate between 1960 and 1970 was a phenomenal 35 percent--the highest in Texas. The National Planning Association predicts a continuing growth of 34 percent for the 1970-80 decade--the nation's third highest for cities over 250,000 population.

Austin's total employment increased by 5.5 percent between 1960 and 1970, approaching a figure of 140,000. The city unemployment rate has been among the lowest in the state, ranging between 2 and 3 percent, while the national rate has been between 5 and 6 percent.[6]

During the 11-year period from 1961 through 1971, the City of Austin issued some 46,809 building permits (for dwelling units). Of this total, 7,524 permits were issued during 1971--the highest figure for the 11-year period.[7] Recall that Vallejo, during the 11-year period 1960 through 1970, issued 11,930 construction permits.

With residential construction of only 152 units in Kealing and less than 100 units (prior to 1971) in Glen Oaks,[8] the construction impact of urban renewal and public housing in Austin has been minimal. In this regard, Austin has not utilized these programs to generate local area construction. In fact, one official reports a severe shortage of contractors in the city--contracts go begging as the city builders have all the work they can handle. There were rumors in Austin concerning excess profits on some of the transactions in the University East project--especially concerning purchase, removal, and rebuilding of apartment units. These charges, however, were unsubstantiated by this investigation.

Overall, urban renewal and public housing in Austin have apparently had little effect upon the business and economic climate of the city. Analysts have examined Austin's growth and economic factors and have come up with the simple conclusion that "'people just like to live in Austin.' Residents who had originally planned a temporary stay, such as former governors, university students and servicemen, regularly choose Austin as the place to make their home."[9]

In the mid 1960s there was some talk of a "downtown" convention center that would require the use of urban renewal to clear a 16-block area. This proposal effectively died. Major opposition from the local business community coupled with the probable high costs of land acquisition killed the proposal. Redevelopment in the downtown area of Austin appears to be a continuing process. With the city's strong economic climate, private redevelopment has encompassed a total area of some 10-12 square blocks. There is a common belief in the city that the "inner city [downtown] will correct itself"; and given the economic climate of Austin, this is probably true.

Austin thus represents the unusual--the use of urban renewal and public housing for noneconomic purposes. With Austin's high growth rate and continuing economic expansion, renewal in the city was not proposed with the primary goal being economic growth. The major effects of Austin's programs will be discussed in Chapters 5 and 6.

Syracuse

The changes in the business and economic climate of downtown Syracuse appear to be based largely on the urban renewal program. One former administrator believes that the "only real development in Syracuse is due to renewal."

Total employment in downtown Syracuse increased from approximately 20,500 in 1950 to 25,000 in 1962 and then decreased again to 23,000 in 1970. Between 1958 and 1963, the number of retail stores in the downtown area declined by 17 percent and retail sales dropped by $2 million.[10] After this drop in sales in the early 1960s the retail business in downtown Syracuse improved considerably. The decline in downtown employment between 1962 and 1970 was accounted for primarily by a change in merchandising methods-- not in problems in the retailing business. Office employment in the central city increased during the period, largely as a result of the urban renewal project.

While renewal undoubtedly helped the downtown business climate in the long run, in the short run there were some detrimental effects. Between January 1961 and January 1964, urban renewal relocated a total of 147 businesses--119 of which relocated within the City of Syracuse. Another 117 businesses were forced to discontinue their operations rather than relocate because of age, high rents, or inability to relocate their marginal businesses. Of these businesses, 35 were one- or two-man operations. Of the 35, 11 ceased operations because of "age of the proprietors or inability to adjust business operations to suit new neighborhoods and no suitable location available for reasons other than price."[11]

The Citizens' Council on Urban Renewal claims that these businesses were "typically marginal" and were generally operated by "aging owners who decided to retire rather than relocate." The council noted that offsetting this is "cumulative evidence many of the businesses that have relocated in other sections of Syracuse have modernized their establishments and expanded their plants with the result that they are experiencing increased sales and profits."[12]

Housing construction in Syracuse during the decade was weak, with federal reports indicating that only 6,620 housing units were authorized by permit from 1960 through 1970.[13] With 1,058 units of public housing constructed over the 11-year period, public housing accounted for over 15 percent of the residential construction in Syracuse.

Urban renewal was responsible for approximately 5 percent of the nonresidential construction in the entire Syracuse SMSA during the decade. With existing or planned development of $57.4 million in urban renewal, nonresidential construction has been significantly stimulated by renewal-generated building.[14] When considering the effect only on the City of Syracuse rather than the entire SMSA, renewal was undoubtedly responsible for well over 10 percent of the business and commercial construction in the city.

Buffalo

Renewal and housing in Buffalo have had an obvious short-term effect on the city's business community. Financing for the city's urban renewal projects alone amounts to $82.1 million, while code enforcement projects account for another estimated $5.3 million.[15] Unquestionably, $87.4 million in urban renewal will generate substantial amounts of construction--both residential and commercial. And yet federal sources report only 2,816 housing units authorized by permit from 1960 through 1970 in the City of Buffalo.[16] The execution of Buffalo's urban renewal projects of the 1960s is generating housing construction in the 1970s. During the period from 1970 through 1975 Buffalo was expected to construct 6,100 new housing units--the majority being for low- and moderate-income families and constructed on land made available through urban renewal. Four projects--Ellicott, Maryland Street West, Waterfront, and Oak Street--alone will provide sites for 5,150 of the units.[17] It was some 24 years ago in 1949 that Congress passed urban renewal legislation. It is hard to believe that New York's first project, Ellicott, had not been closed out by February 1973, the date of the field observation. The small, by today's standards, 160-acre project has exemplified the slowness of the renewal process in Buffalo.

The Buffalo projects where substantial progress has been made show no evidence of attracting much outside commerce and industry to the city. The vast majority of the tenants and owners in the new developments have merely relocated from other sections of the city (although many have expanded their operations).

The Industrial Park pilot project has been weak by any standard The city found it difficult to move the land once it was purchased and does not now plan any more projects of this type.

CONCLUSIONS AND CONTENTIONS

Chapter 2 posed a number of hypotheses to examine the effects of public housing construction and urban renewal grants on the business and economic environment of the community. Specifically:

1. A city's economic vitality is positively related to public housing construction and urban renewal expenditures.
2. Total housing construction is positively related to urban renewal expenditures.
3. Total housing construction is not related to public housing construction.
4. Property values are positively related to urban renewal expenditures.

Public housing construction appears to be independently, although weakly, related to employment within a city--those cities having high levels of public housing construction during the 10 years between 1960 and 1970 were likely to have lower unemployment rates than cities with low levels of public housing construction/leasing. This relationship was not noted in the case of renewal, however. The 1970 unemployment rate is apparently independent of the level of urban renewal receipts.

The second and third hypotheses are both rejected. Housing and renewal successes during the decade were both independently and negatively related to housing construction. Urban renewal and public housing programs unquestionably "cause" some housing construction; however, cities with high overall construction levels are not the cities achieving unusual success in either housing or urban renewal.

While public housing construction is able to exert a small independent influence on the employment rate, in general these programs (renewal and housing) are not associated with the short-term economic health of the community. Cities unquestionably use urban renewal and public housing (especially urban renewal) as tools to improve the local business climate and to develop the local economy. Deteriorating cities (such as Beaumont), especially those without urban renewal programs, see urban renewal as some kind of a magic formula that will transform a worn-out dying community into a thriving metropolis. This just does not happen. There are segments of the local economy that receive short-run economic benefits from renewal and housing--notably local banking interests, real estate firms, developers, investors, and specialized (and large) construction and architectural firms. Renewal and housing are, in the short run, unable to make a sick city well. It is possible in the long run, say over 30 years, that these grants can at least assist in the economic turnaround of a city. It is apparent, however, that the time lag necessary for this transition is much longer than this author had originally supposed.

One note of caution, however. There do appear to be cities, and Syracuse is a prime example, that are in a cycle of development where the city is transitioning from a healthy economic status into a stage of deterioration and decay. If grant programs are applied soon enough, and in large enough quantity, it appears that the decay can be reversed in a very short period of time. Timing in this instance is probably extremely important. The author's natural pessimism thus attributes the judicious application of renewal and housing grants in Syracuse to sheer luck rather than to any careful planning on the part of local officials.

The case studies also suggest that the "residential requirement" of urban renewal law is probably not being applied quite the way that Congress intended. Many of the so-called residential projects border the central business district and are really commercial redevelopments. While these projects may meet all of the technical requirements of the law, their purpose is obvious--to augment the central business district. The required number of housing units may be provided but in most instances single family units and/or two or three family dwellings are replaced by apartment towers or townhouses and the like, leaving plenty of land available for the real purpose of the redevelopment project.

Data were not available to evaluate the relationships between property values and urban renewal on any systematic basis, thus only tentative suggestions are made on the basis of the findings generated from the field studies. In all cases (even in Downtown One in Syracuse), the property values of the redeveloped land and the associated structures were higher after redevelopment than before redevelopment. Renewal was also generally found to have a beneficial effect on the property values within two or three blocks of the renewal project. Thus renewal favorably affects property values in and around the project. But what about the rest of the city? In Vallejo and Buffalo a few administrators and officials complained that the majority of the businesses moving into the redeveloped areas were merely relocating from other parts of the city. As these firms moved, vacancies were created in the areas they were moving from and property values began to decline. While the evidence of such situations gathered during this study is so sketchy that no conclusions should be drawn, a note of caution suggests that examination of the effects of urban renewal on property values should cover more than the redevelopment itself and a two- or three-block surrounding area-- especially in the case of commercial renewal projects.

NOTES

1. U.S. Department of Commerce, Bureau of the Census, General Social and Economic Characteristics: U.S. Summary (Washington, D.C.: Government Printing Office, 1972), pp. 1-566 to 1-570.

2. U.S. Department of Commerce, Bureau of the Census, New Housing Units Authorized by Local Building Permits, Annual Summary 1960-1961, Construction Reports C40-38 (Washington, D.C.: Government Printing Office, 1962); U.S. Department of Commerce, Bureau of the Census, Housing Authorized in Individual Permit Issuing Places Construction Reports C40-50 (Washington, D.C.: Government Printing Office, 1963); U.S. Department of Commerce, Bureau of the Census, Housing Authorized in Individual Permit-Issuing Places 1964, Construction Reports C40-74 (Washington, D.C.: Government Printing Office, 1964); U.S. Department of Commerce, Bureau of the Census, Housing Authorized by Building Permits and Public Contracts 1966, Construction Reports C40/C42-66-13 (Washington, D.C.: Government Printing Office, 1967); U.S. Department of Commerce, Bureau of the Census, Housing Authorized by Building Permits and Public Contracts 1968, Construction Reports C40-68-13 (Washington, D.C.: Government Printing Office, 1970); U.S. Department of Commerce, Bureau of the Census, Housing Authorized by Building Permits and Public Contracts 1970, Construction Reports C40-70-13 (Washington, D.C.: Government Printing Office, 1971).

3. Vallejo Chamber of Commerce, Fact Card No. 8 (Vallejo: Chamber of Commerce, n.d.).

4. Vallejo Chamber of Commerce, Vallejo, California (Vallejo: Solano County Board of Supervisors, n.d.).

5. John F. Kennedy Library (Vallejo: Public Library System, n.d.).

6. Front Runner for the New Decade (Austin: Chamber of Commerce, January 24, 1972), p. 1. (Mimeographed).

7. Housing and Apartment Development: Austin, Texas (Austin: Chamber of Commerce, February 21, 1972) (Mimeographed).

8. "Urban Renewal Special," Austin American-Statesman, August 27, 1972, pp. 4-5, 7.

9. Living At Its Best (Austin: Chamber of Commerce, n.d.), p. 1.

10. Gene Goshorn, "Syracuse tackles problem head-on," Syracuse Herald-American, January 2, 1966.

11. "Renewal Group Reports 147 Businesses Moved," Syracuse Post-Standard, January 12, 1964.

12. Ibid.

13. See footnote 2, above.

14. Goshorn, "Syracuse tackles problem."

15. Frank Stahl, Reflections: A Summary of Urban Renewal Activities in Buffalo, New York 1971/1972 (Buffalo: Department of Urban Renewal, 1972), p. 18.

16. See footnote 2, above.

17. Nathaniel S. Keith and Marcou, O'Leary and Associates, Inc., Buffalo, Community Renewal Program Extension for the City of Buffalo, New York (Buffalo: City of Buffalo, n.d.), pp. 34-35.

5

EFFECTS OF
HOUSING AND RENEWAL
ON LOCAL POLITICS
AND GOVERNMENT

Urban renewal and public housing were hypothesized to affect significantly local government and politics, in particular, government employment, local finances, and political stability.

GOVERNMENT EMPLOYMENT

Grants to local government, specifically housing and renewal grants, were expected to be stimulative of government employment. The first area of interest was the relationship between housing, renewal, and the size of the city planning department. It was expected that the planning requirements associated with public housing and urban renewal would stimulate the city to expand the size of its planning staff. The size of the city planning staff was available for 148 of the 310 cities as of January 1971.[1] It was also expected that housing and renewal grants would stimulate overall government employment in both common and variable functions.[2] Renewal and housing were expected to be directly related to the number of employees in variable functions because housing and renewal authority employees are included in the variable category. It was also expected that the demand for municipal services fostered by renewal and public housing projects would stimulate employment in the common functions. The number of full-time employees in both common and variable functions is as of October 1969.[3] The segment of common functions where pressure for increased services was expected to be greatest was in the area of parks and recreation. As a consequence, the final measure of local government employment to be examined in relation to housing and renewal was the number of full-time park and recreation employees as of October 1969.[4]

Table 5.1 shows the zero order relationships between grant measures and measures of city government employment. As expected, all relationships were significant and substantial. At the zero order level, there is no question but that grants are related to government employment. The real question, however, is whether grants are independently related to employment levels.

TABLE 5.1

Zero Order Product Moment Correlation Coefficients
between Grant Use and Measures of
City Government Employment

	Urban Renewal	Public Housing
Size of city planning staff	0.702*	0.784*
Number of park and recreation employees	0.731*	0.816*
Number of employees in common functions	0.547*	0.378*
Number of employees in variable functions	0.750*	0.763*

*Significant at the .05 level.

To test the independence of the relationships, partial correlation coefficients were computed between the employment measures and renewal and housing while holding the city profile factors and political variables constant. When controlling for all other variables, the positive zero order relationships reversed themselves and became negative. That is, all of the statistically significant relationships under controlled conditions (except the relationship between urban renewal and the number of employees in common functions) were negative (Table 5.2). Public housing was significantly and negatively related to all four measures of public employment while renewal was negatively related only to the size of the city planning staff and was positively related to the number of employees in common functions. No significant relationship existed, however, between renewal and either the number of employees in variable functions or the number of park and recreation employees.

TABLE 5.2

Partial Correlation Coefficients Showing Independent
Relationships between Grant Use and Measures
of City Government Employment

	Urban Renewal	Public Housing
Size of city planning staff	−0.268*	−0.529*
Number of park and recreation employees	−0.077	−0.199*
Number of employees in common functions	0.186*	−0.404*
Number of employees in variable functions	0.046	−0.354*

*Significant at the .05 level.

Recall that in Chapter 4 there was a significant and positive
relationship between grants and residential construction at the zero
order level, but that once controls were introduced through the use
of partial correlation coefficients the relationships between the variables were found to be negative. The same general pattern of reversal is noted here between grants and government employment.
Tables 5.3 and 5.4 show the relationships between all model variables and the size of the city planning staff. The planning staff
variable was selected for detailed examination because the most
dramatic reversal occurred with this variable. No unexpected relationships are noted. In Chapter 4, explanation of the reversal suggested that cities with major problems of deterioration, stagnation,
and decay responded to the problems through heavy grant use and
that the time period necessary for a city to reverse its deterioration
process was so long that housing construction, as an economic indicator, did not have time to respond. Such is probably also the case
with public employment. Again, Central City, Urban Density, and
Size/Manufacturing are descriptive of urban stagnation and decay and
are independently related to grant use. It is thus suspected that
these same cities (those characterized by stagnation and decay)
would be deficient in the area of public employment and, under controls, housing and renewal would be negatively related to employment characteristics.
The fact that urban renewal was positively related to the number of employees in common functions and was not significantly

related to the number of employees in variable functions while housing was negatively related to both also poses some interesting possibilities. It is quite possible that these relationships are indicative of a difference in demand systems. With urban renewal's apparent business orientation, it is possible that renewal does not place a demand for services upon municipal government. On the other hand, low-income public housing should impose a high demand for personal services (and thus municipal employment) upon local government. Quite possibly, however, a lengthy lead time exists before local government responds to pressures for these services--especially to pressures from low-income families. It is likely that public housing constructed during the 1960s places a demand on the city for services (police, fire, recreation, welfare, etc.)--demands that are largely unmet for a lengthy time period--a longer period than the 10 years considered in this study.

TABLE 5.3

Partial Correlation Coefficients Showing Independent
Relationships between Renewal Model Variables
and Size of the City Planning Staff

Status, Wealth, and Education (low)	−0.017
Central City	0.262*
Urban Density	0.551*
Size/Manufacturing	0.900*
Commuting/Growth	0.215*
Model city	−0.007
HUD office in state	0.142
Renewal difficulty	−0.070
Years since 1949 for URA	0.111
Years since 1960 for enabling legislation	−0.185
Form of government	−0.174
Representation	−0.095
Type of election	0.062
Wallace vote	−0.209*
Goldwater vote	0.021
Elazar's political cultures	−0.035
Metro status	−0.377*
Urban renewal	−0.268*

*Significant at the .05 level.

TABLE 5.4

Partial Correlation Coefficients Showing Independent
Relationships between Housing Model Variables
and Size of the City Planning Staff

Status, Wealth, and Education (low)	-0.051
Central City	0.380*
Urban Density	0.658*
Size/Manufacturing	0.901*
Commuting/Growth	0.169
Model city	0.115
HUD office in state	0.241*
Urban renewal	-0.198
Housing difficulty	0.002
Years since 1937 for LHA	0.210*
Years since 1960 for enabling legislation	0.095
Form of government	-0.233*
Representation	-0.188
Type of election	0.193
Wallace vote	-0.249*
Goldwater vote	0.014
Elazar's political cultures	-0.036
Metro status	-0.399*
Public housing	-0.529*

*Significant at the .05 level.

INTERGOVERNMENTAL TRANSFERS

A review of the economic literature concerning federal grants
suggested that cities tending to utilize programs such as housing and
renewal are also likely to participate heavily in other federal-local
grant programs. Such was indeed the case. Zero order correlation
coefficients between renewal and housing and intergovernmental revenue received in 1969-70[5] were r = .81 and r = .89 respectively
(Table 5.5).

Since other studies have shown the overwhelming importance
of city size in grant use, partials were computed, again controlling
for city profile factors and political variables. As expected, the
positive relationship was reduced but remained statistically significant (Table 5.6). Both correlation coefficients were approximately

the same in spite of substantial differences in the types of intergovernmental transfers involved. Housing authorities receive annual contributions from the federal government based upon debt retirement costs and the number of low-income, disabled, and elderly tenants it houses. Renewal grants, on the other hand, are not annual grants but are based upon project execution. Housing construction then would be directly related to 1969-70 intergovernmental transfers because the total intergovernmental transfer funds include the housing subsidies. Renewal funds received between 1960 and 1970, however, need not be related to intergovernmental transfers in 1969-70 (fiscal year 1970). There is thus a strong reason to suspect a stimulative relationship between renewal, housing, and intergovernmental transfers.

TABLE 5.5

Zero Order Product Moment Correlation Coefficients
between Grant Use and Intergovernmental Transfers

	Intergovernmental Revenue Received
Urban renewal	0.807*
Public housing	0.887*

*Significant at the .05 level.

TABLE 5.6

Partial Correlation Coefficients Showing Independent
Relationships between Grant Use and
Intergovernmental Transfers

	Intergovernmental Revenue Received
Urban renewal	0.306*
Public housing	0.301*

*Significant at the .05 level.

CITY INCOME, EXPENDITURES, AND DEBT

Both public housing and urban renewal are hypothesized as having a major impact on local government finances. Critics of the housing program often claim that public housing is costly in that it removes property from the tax rolls while at the same time increasing the demand (thus expenditures) for city services. A major benefit attributed to urban renewal (theoretically) has been that renewal improves the city's tax base and helps increase city income. On the other hand, renewal is also likely to increase a city's debt and total expenditures because of the one-third city matching requirement of the renewal grants. Cities might be expected to float a bond issue to pay the matching share or to pay for in-kind contributions.

The changes in per capita income, expenditure, and debt between 1960 and 1970 were computed from census figures[6] and are shown in Table 5.7. All measures showed a substantial increase during the 10-year period. These changes in per capita income, expenditure, and debt were computed as the dependent variables, and housing and renewal were again the independent variables. The results of the zero order correlations are contained in Table 5.8. A significant and positive relationship was found to exist between both housing and renewal and almost all of the financial change variables.

Public housing was not significantly related to changes in city property taxes. Apparently the amount of property removed from tax rolls by public housing construction is so small as to have no effect on the tax base. In general, however, the zero order relationships tend to confirm the arguments against public housing--that is, public housing is costly in terms of general tax increases because it increases the demand (and thus expenditures) for the city services and raises bonded debt.

TABLE 5.7

Change in Per Capita City Incomes, Expenditures,
and Debt between 1960 and 1970 for Cities
over 50,000 Population

	Mean Change	Standard Deviation	Minimum Code	Maximum Code
General revenue	96.03	77.03	-15.78	579.90
City taxes	47.36	38.10	-24.20	300.55
Property tax	32.61	36.99	-24.12	183.46
General expenditures	101.25	91.36	-102.41	672.00
Total debt	118.96	126.15	-131.11	807.05

TABLE 5.8

Zero Order Product Moment Correlation Coefficients
between Grant Use and Changes in Per Capita
City Incomes, Expenditures, and Debt

	Urban Renewal	Public Housing
General revenue	0.467*	0.328*
City taxes	0.339*	0.219*
Property tax	0.179*	0.096
General expenditures	0.437*	0.301*
Total debt	0.270*	0.152*

*Significant at the .05 level.

Renewal is also associated with increased debt and expenditures; but it is credited with increased tax revenues, not by increasing the tax burden on the individual citizen, but by increasing city property values. However, it is again important to look with suspicion on these simple correlations. The close relationship between the selected grant programs and the city profile factors may be hiding the true relationships between the grant programs and financial changes in the city.

This was very much the case as is shown by the partials in Table 5.9. The partials were again computed by controlling for the city profile factors and the political variables. Under controls, virtually all of the significant relationships between public housing construction/leasing and changes in city finances disappeared. Low-income public housing does not, then, provide a drain on the local tax base by significantly and independently affecting either property taxes, total city taxes, or general revenue. Additional public housing does not increase general expenditure levels, nor is it significantly related to total debt. In other words, increased levels of public housing within a city do not bring about significant changes in the city government's financial structure (in itself).

Such is not the case with urban renewal. Renewal was significantly and independently related to all five of the changes in city financial structures. Urban renewal was found to be significantly related to increases in city total debt. Cities apparently increase debt levels to produce matching funds or to pay for in-kind contributions for local urban renewal programs.

TABLE 5.9

Partial Correlation Coefficients Showing Independent
Relationships between Grant Use and Changes in
Per Capita City Incomes, Expenditures, and Debt

	Urban Renewal	Public Housing
General revenue	0.220*	−0.109
City taxes	0.160*	−0.064
Property tax	0.119*	0.022
General expenditures	0.226*	−0.063
Total debt	0.226*	−0.046

*Significant at the .05 level.

Renewal receipts were also found to be independently related
to all three revenue measures: change in per capita property tax
($r = .12$), change in per capita city taxes ($r = .16$), and change in
per capita general revenue ($r = .22$). Urban renewal is apparently
an effective tool to increase income from property taxes without
placing substantial additional burden on the local taxpayer. The increase in property tax receipts is probably brought about by increased property values in and around urban renewal projects.
There also appears to be some type of multiplier effect at work.
Notice the change in the relationships between renewal and the revenue measures with renewal having the closest independent relationship with the dependent variable at the highest revenue level (general
revenue). This suggests the possibility that renewal is also related
to other city revenue measures such as increased city sales tax receipts, or increases in intergovernmental revenue.

With the relationships shown above concerning changes in debt
and revenue, it is only logical to assume that renewal would be associated with changes in expenditures. This was the case with a
coefficient of $r = .23$ between the variables.

POLITICAL STABILITY

The numberous case studies of renewal and housing efforts in
cities throughout the country indicated that a number of city administrations based their political campaigns on housing and renewal
issues. It was thus expected that large amounts of renewal funds

received would aid incumbent administrations in reelection efforts. It was also expected that large amounts of low-income housing construction would be detrimental to an administration's reelection, although this hypothesis is not as clear-cut. It is also probable that public housing architectural and construction contracts stimulate contractor campaign contributions to incumbents. In any event, some relationship was expected.

To test the hypothesis a simple stability scale was developed based upon the number of mayors each city had between January 1960 and January 1970. This information was obtained simply by recording the mayors' names every year between 1960 and 1970 and then totaling the number of different mayors for each city.[7] The crudity of this measure must be emphasized. Some cities have two-year terms for mayor while others have four-year terms. In many manager cities the mayor's office is rotated between councilmen. Nonetheless, while the scale is admittedly crude and covers a very short time period, it will hopefully differentiate between cities with high and low political stability in the mayor's office.

Zero order product moment correlation coefficients were computed between the political stability scale and urban renewal and public housing. Both urban renewal and public housing showed a low but significant negative relationship with the stability rating with $r = .14$ and $r = .13$ respectively (Table 5.10). Renewal and housing successes thus appear to contribute to increased political stability in city politics.

TABLE 5.10

Zero Order Product Moment Correlation Coefficients
between Grant Use and Mayors' Longevity

	Number of Mayors, 1960-70
Urban renewal	−0.141*
Public housing	−0.129*

*Significant at the .05 level.

Once again, however, the independence of the relationships becomes important. Do renewal and housing contribute to political stability or does the relationship merely reflect a relationship between stability and one of the demographic or political variables? Partials were again computed controlling for the city profile and the political variables. The relationship between grant success and stability disappeared (Table 5.11). Grant success apparently does not have an independent effect upon mayors' tenure.

TABLE 5.11

Partial Correlation Coefficients Showing Independent
Relationships between Grant Use and
Mayors' Longevity

	Number of Mayors, 1960–70
Urban renewal	−0.031
Public housing	−0.034

Partials were also computed between the stability measure and each of the independent variables in both the renewal and housing models, while controlling for all other variables. Only two correlation coefficients in the renewal model were statistically significant at the .05 level. Stability was independently related to Urban Density ($r = .12$) and form of government ($r = .25$). Three coefficients in the housing model were significant: housing difficulty ($r = .13$), form of government ($r = .24$), and metro status ($r = -.11$). The major determinant of turnover in the mayor's office appears to be the presence of the city manager form of government rather than unsuccessful renewal or housing programs.

QUALITATIVE ANALYSIS

Information obtained during the field studies generally supported the quantitative conclusions. In most cases the relationship between increased city revenue and urban renewal success was the most clear-cut and obvious. While housing and renewal were not quantitatively related to political stability, both issues were found to be important determinants of political stability/instability in several of the cities.

Vallejo

A Vallejo Redevelopment Agency publication, in discussing the Marina Vista project, stated that "the main objective of a redevelopment or urban renewal plan is to sell or lease the project land to private developers so it can be returned to the tax rolls as quickly as possible. "[8] The approximate assessed valuation of all of the property in the renewal area in 1960 prior to redevelopment was $1.5 million. The agency expected assessed valuation in the area to equal $5.0 million by 1970 and between $5.5 million and $6.0 million by 1980.[9] In spite of the fact that large amounts of the land in the Marina Vista area would be devoted to public use, one administrator expected an increase in the overall tax base of 5 to 1--that is, for every $100,000 in assessed valuation before redevelopment, $500,000 in assessed valuation was expected after redevelopment. There has already been a tax gain from the Marina Vista project although it is not as large as expected.

One administrator said that the overall financial effects of the renewal project are still unknown. The old area was run-down, but it was entirely built-up. While the new area has large amounts of land devoted to public use, the assessment values in the area generally increased and property values within a two-block circumference around the project (approximate) increased.

The same administrator believes that there have been detrimental effects from Marina Vista that must also be considered. The project, in some ways, drained the remainder of the downtown. "Most of the businesses in the new area are from the old downtown." This has led to larger numbers of vacancies in the older areas and has been a direct cause of a downward assessment in surrounding areas.

Park and recreation maintenance costs to the city were undoubtedly increased by the addition of two city parks--the $9\frac{1}{2}$-acre Memorial City Park, and the smaller U.S.S. Independence Park. These, along with the seawall promenade and the Town Square (plaza), undoubtedly increased the need for maintenance. Renewal thus placed increased demands for services on the Parks and Recreation Department, although their responsiveness to these demands has been questioned.

Beaumont

Beaumont provides an excellent case study into the political effect of an urban renewal election. Recall that Dale C. Hager, chairman of the Beaumont Republican Policy Committee that opposed urban renewal, called the 1967 election "a mandate from the people to replace the present city administration."[10]

Both 1968 candidates for mayor were critical of the urban renewal effort. One of the candidate's advertisements for mayor headlined: "You Saw Jim McFaddin On The Firing Line Fighting Urban

Renewal--YOU KNOW Where He Stands."[11] Even the more moderate candidate, James D. McNicholas, accused the city council of holding a "secret meeting" to plan for the urban renewal election prior to a public hearing on the election.[12] Although McNicholas was the Democratic candidate for mayor, he took pains to disassociate himself from the slate of four Democratic candidates for city council. Fear of an urban renewal backlash caused him to campaign independently of the other party candidates. McNicholas was victorious but only by a slight margin.[13]

A slate of four "Independent" candidates opposed the Democratic ticket for the city council. All four Independents were elected. Included were two Republicans, Dale C. Hager and Ken Ritter--both members of the Beaumont Republican Policy Committee that had been so strongly opposed to urban renewal.[14]

A former local official claimed that the Democratic slate was defeated by "the John Birchers who coalesced for the 1967 renewal election." Urban renewal was the main issue in the 1968 election and the incumbent councilmen were defeated because they had supported the renewal effort. In Beaumont, he claims, renewal is associated with communism. He believes that the citizens never really understood the issues, they only heard the catch phrases--"Communism; they can take your house; and federal control by the Easterners."

This criticism appears to have some validity. In a 1968 survey of community attitudes by the Beaumont Jaycees, one question asked, "Do you understand most aspects of Urban Renewal?" The responses split almost evenly with 48.5 percent indicating "no."[15] Citizens apparently recognize that Beaumont is in trouble, nevertheless. In response to "Do you feel that Beaumont has kept up with most cities in general improvements?" approximately 60 percent of the respondents said "no."[16]

The major supporters of urban renewal had been the "chamber of commerce types" or the downtown businessmen. With the second defeat of urban renewal at the polls, what could they do to start the local economy moving forward again?

To attempt to reverse the decline in the central business district, the Central City Development Corporation (CCDC) was formed in June 1971 by civic and business leaders interested in revitalizing the deteriorating Beaumont central business district. The goal of the CCDC is to create a downtown that Beaumont can be proud of and a central business district that will contribute to the overall growth of the community. Toward this end the CCDC is concentrating in two major areas:

> Our effort will be to help establish a comprehensive
> plan of action for the Downtown Area that will pro-
> vide direction for future projects involving land use,

transportation, utilities, community facilities, private development, etc. The other major effort of CCDC will be to implement projects to meet the urgent and pressing problems currently facing Central City.[17]

The CCDC, then, performs a number of functions that are normally associated with a city planning department. One knowledgeable businessman calls the city planning effort "grossly inadequate." He said that the "city hasn't planned--there is no real master plan, only an inventory, and that is no good." The CCDC thus is an attempt by the business leaders of Beaumont to compensate for the inadequacies of the city planning department and to search for alternatives to federal urban renewal that might assist in downtown revitalization. Toward this end, the CCDC engaged the services of the Urban Land Institute of Washington, D.C., to

    a. evaluate the redevelopment prospects for the Central Business District;
    b. evaluate the present plans now being designed by governmental agencies that will affect Central City;
    c. and to suggest priorities and programs designed for immediate and long-range implementation in the development of the Central Business District into an active center of the city.[18]

At the time of this investigation the Urban Land Institute had just completed its visit to Beaumont and was in the process of preparing its report.

Urban renewal, as a public issue in Beaumont, has had far-reaching effects on political and government institutions. The issue itself forced a dramatic change in the political make-up of the city council. In fact the issue probably accounted for, at least in part, a charter amendment that changed Beaumont city elections from nominally partisan to true nonpartisan elections. Failure of the renewal election also forced the business community to develop a "shadow administration" in the form of the CCDC, which has been forced to perform many of the planning functions normally associated with city government.

Austin

In Chapter 3 it was noted that some 52 percent of the land in Austin was devoted to public use and that this created certain revenue problems for the city. The five urban renewal projects in Austin, far from attempting to increase the tax base, transferred large amounts of land from private to public use--in fact, much of this land was prime commercial and multifamily residential property.

While the Renewal Agency claimed that urban renewal tripled the assessed tax valuation in the Kealing area,[19] improving the tax base was never an issue in Austin's renewal programs. Quite simply, a city that has historically devoted much of its land to the public weal has had to find a revenue source other than the property tax. In Austin's case the city relies on utility income.

The loss of property tax revenue as a result of urban renewal and the subsequent University of Texas and Brackenridge Hospital expansion was not a major issue because Austin's income is derived primarily from annual transfers from the city-owned municipal utility (electricity) and water plants. Austin, with this type of financial diversity, is apparently able to approve urban renewal projects that other cities might find financially unacceptable. The form of Austin's renewal program was thus, in part, shaped by the city's ability to devote additional land to public use without having to be overly concerned with the expected tax loss.

Syracuse

Urban renewal has unquestionably assisted the City of Syracuse in avoiding many of the financial problems facing other older U.S. central cities. Unlike many other cities, the property tax base in Syracuse is not shrinking. Between 1953 and 1965, urban renewal was responsible for $57.4 million in existing or planned development. During this time period the city has received in excess of $39 million in federal renewal grant funds.

Ultimately, renewal is expected to produce a six-fold increase in tax assessments. Former Renewal Commissioner George B. Schuster estimated that "the $5 million in assessments urban renewal has taken off the city tax rolls will be replaced with a solid $30 million in new assessments."[20]

Some citizens do not agree with this contention, however. One knowledgeable citizen, for example, does not believe that urban renewal (Downtown One in particular) has increased downtown property values all that much--primarily because the project removed some rather expensive property from the tax rolls to begin with. Another factor, he believes, was the governing Republican administration that, in many cases, gave the new users of the redeveloped property abnormally low tax assessments.

In the late 1960s Syracuse became a city in political transition --moving from a Republican-dominated city toward a more independent orientation. While the voters undoubtedly wanted a change in 1969, urban renewal was a substantial issue in the community and was at least a contributing factor in the change of administrations. The Democratic candidate for mayor called for a change in the pattern of urban renewal--he wanted "to do something for the neighborhoods." The local Democrats were able to predict a trend in HUD away from redevelopment and toward neighborhood preservation and were able to politically capitalize on this shift in federal policy.

Buffalo

There are three basic goals to Buffalo's urban renewal program: revitalization of the central business district, the development of standard low-income housing, and increasing the property tax base. One of the major problems of the city administration has been a declining tax base coupled with growing responsibilities to provide social services and economic opportunities to Buffalo's residents.[21]

Revitalization of the central business district through renewal obviously goes hand in hand with an increasing tax base. The only difficulty with a program of this type, coupling business or industrial development renewal projects with a program to expand the tax base, might be program delays. Phase I of the Downtown renewal project exemplified proper operation of the renewal program. Land was purchased by the city (and thus temporarily removed from the tax rolls), cleared, sold, and redeveloped in a relatively short period of time--thus the tax income lost during the redevelopment cycle was minimized and was more than made up by the increased tax returns after redevelopment. Ellicott and the Industrial project did not conform to this standard, however. In both projects (but especially Ellicott) land was purchased and cleared by the city (and removed from the tax rolls) and remained as city-owned vacant land for many years. Renewal, when operated in this manner, further serves to destroy the tax base.

It is often suggested that two of the renewal objectives operate in conflict with each other--that attempts to increase the tax base are anathema to the development of low-income housing as much of the low-income housing will require various forms of real estate tax abatement. This contention is not necessarily true as exemplified by Buffalo's Maryland Street West project. This project area (12 acres), of which one-third was city owned, returned $7,108 in taxes per year prior to redevelopment. After completion, the project was expected to return $71,000 per year in taxes, even after tax abatements.[22] Increases of this magnitude are possible through judicious site selection. By redeveloping land that is currently producing low tax yields, or that is tax-exempt by reason of public ownership, large tax increases are possible. In addition, payment in lieu of taxes of 10 percent of shelter rents is paid on housing developed by the New York State Urban Development Corporation and the Buffalo Housing Authority. [23] In many cases this 10 percent payment amounts to more than the prior tax yield.

CONCLUSIONS AND CONTENTIONS

A review of the housing and renewal literature suggested a number of hypotheses concerning the effects of housing and renewal on politics and government:

1. Public employment is positively related to urban renewal expenditures and public housing construction.
2. Urban renewal expenditures and public housing construction are stimulative of other grant use.
3. City tax revenues are directly related to urban renewal expenditures.
4. Political stability is negatively related to public housing construction.
5. Political stability is positively related to public housing construction.

The study had originally hypothesized that public employment would be positively related to measures of government employment--the theory being that housing and renewal would generate a demand for services and the city would respond through increased personnel levels. However, the findings in Chapter 4 suggested that the hypothesis might be invalid and the situation might be reversed; that is, urban renewal and public housing are negatively related to levels of government employment. Once controls were introduced, this was indeed the case. Thus, instead of renewal and housing generating a demand for services (and personnel) met by the city, renewal and public housing are indicative of cities with serious problems--one being lower services and personnel levels.

Renewal and housing grants were found to be significantly related to the level of intergovernmental transfers. It is not possible to conclude absolutely from this relationship that housing and renewal grants are stimulative of the use of other federal grants as renewal and housing grants are themselves a portion of the intergovernmental transfers. There is reason to suspect, however, that because of the nature of the renewal and housing grants, there is a stimulative relationship between renewal, housing, and other intergovernmental transfers.

The most important finding generated by this chapter has been the relationship between grants and changes in city financial measures. There was no independent relationship between public housing and changes in city financial measures. This might very well have been expected in spite of the criticisms of public housing opponents. Urban renewal, on the other hand, was independently related to positive increases in city financial measures. Renewal is positively related to increases in per capita property tax receipts, city tax receipts, and general revenue. This does not necessarily mean, however, that renewal is associated with changes in the tax rate. This evidence simply suggests the effectiveness of urban renewal in increasing city revenue. The relationship does suggest one other possibility that in all fairness must be mentioned. If high renewal levels are indicative of city deterioration, it is possible that cities are increasing their tax rates, and thus revenue measures, in response to deteriorating conditions and increased demand for services. The qualitative evidence from the case studies, although limited by the small number of cities visited, does seem to support the first contention--that is, renewal serves as an effective tool to increase city revenues.

There may be a financial drawback associated with renewal, however. As expected, urban renewal was related to positive increases in per capita city debt. Cities apparently increase bonded debt to pay for their cash or in-kind contributions.

Urban renewal and public housing have been shown to be important political issues in local government. In spite of exceptions such as Beaumont, however, both issues do not affect stability in the mayor's office to any significant degree on a nationwide basis. Renewal and housing may be important issues to the voters; however, the voters do not turn out the mayor because of renewal or housing success or failure. Other factors, such as type of government, are the important determinants of local political stability.

NOTES

1. James Hannah, Expenditures, Staff, and Salaries of Planning Agencies, 1971 (Chicago: American Society of Planning Officials, April 1971), pp. 21-24.

2. Common functions include highways, police, fire, sewage and sanitation, parks and recreation, libraries, financial administration, water, and general control. Variable functions include all of those functions not normally performed by municipal governments: education, airports, port facilities, corrections, urban renewal, public housing, welfare, health and hospitals, utilities, etc.

3. The Municipal Year Book 1971 (Washington, D.C.: International City Management Association, 1971), pp. 190-202.

4. Ibid.

5. U.S. Department of Commerce, Bureau of the Census, City Government Finances in 1969-70 (Washington, D.C.: Government Printing Office, 1971).

6. Ibid., and U.S. Department of Commerce, Bureau of the Census, County and City Data Book 1962 (Washington, D.C.: Government Printing Office, 1962), pp. 476-575.

7. Mayors' names were obtained from The Municipal Year Book for 1960, 1962, 1964, 1966, 1968, and 1970.

8. Redevelopment Agency of the City of Vallejo, Marina Vista (Vallejo, Calif.: Gibson Publications, n.d.), p. 3.

9. Ibid., p. 12.

10. Sunday Enterprise, November 19, 1967, pp. 1, 4A.

11. Beaumont Enterprise, May 12, 1968, p. 15A.

12. Beaumont Enterprise, May 10, 1968, p. 8.

13. Beaumont Enterprise, May 15, 1968, pp. 1, 5.

14. Ibid.

15. The Beaumont Jaycees, Beaumont Community Attitude Survey (Beaumont: The Beaumont Jaycees, March 15, 1968), p. 18. (Mimeographed.)

16. Ibid., p. 17.

17. CCDC (Beaumont: Central City Development Corporation, n.d.), p. 1.

18. CCDC Newsletter 1 (Beaumont: Central City Development Corporation, November 1972).

19. "Urban Renewal Special," Austin American-Statesman, August 27, 1972, pp. 4-5.

20. Gene Goshorn, "Syracuse tackles problem head-on," Syracuse Herald-American, January 2, 1966.

21. Nathaniel S. Keith and Marcou, O'Leary and Associates, Inc., Buffalo Community Renewal Program Extension for the City of Buffalo, New York (Buffalo: City of Buffalo, N.Y., n.d.), p. 11.

22. Ibid., pp. 24-25.

23. Ibid.

CHAPTER

6

EFFECTS
OF HOUSING AND
RENEWAL ON CITY
LAND USE PATTERNS

Low-income public housing and urban renewal projects undoubtedly affect city land use patterns since the elimination of slums
and blight are major goals of both programs. The ever-increasing
number of renewal and housing case studies point to enormous
changes in land use patterns based upon these federal grant programs. The question, however, is: Is there a difference in land
use patterns between cities that utilize housing and renewal programs and those that do not? Do renewal and housing programs
cause a change in city land use?

LAND OWNERSHIP PATTERNS

The predominant difficulty in attempting to assess the impact
of renewal and housing grants on the physical makeup of U.S. cities
is the lack of data available on a nationwide basis. In spite of severe
limitations in this area, some data were available that might be useful in hypothesis testing. It is expected, for example, that urban renewal and public housing (especially urban renewal) operate in such
a way as to transfer land from private to public use. Public housing
unquestionably transfers land from private to public use in that low-
income housing projects are usually built on land purchased from the
private sector.

The urban renewal process also involves the transfer of land
from private ownership to the urban renewal agency. The agency re-
tains the land for a limited time period (for clearance and development) and then sells it to the new developer/user. In a great many
cases at least part of the renewal land is sold to public agencies for
civic centers, schools, park land, playgrounds, public housing sites,

etc. In effect, then, urban renewal may serve as a device to transfer land from the private to the public sector.

Allen Manvel recently reported the results of a land use survey in a number of large U.S. cities.[1] One of the items reported in the survey was the percent of total city land that was privately owned. Unfortunately, each city reported this percentage as of the date they last compiled this data so there was no uniform effective date the data were gathered. Generally, however, cities reported the percentage as of a date between 1961 and 1967. Another limitation to the data was the small number of cities having usable data. Only 74 cities had useful (for this study) responses on this item. While ideally this study would be concerned with the change in land ownership between 1960 and 1970, data limitations force certain constraints. Nonetheless, it was felt that the land use patterns that were available would provide some indication of changes in use brought about by housing and renewal programs.

Zero order correlation coefficients were computed showing the relationships between urban renewal, public housing, and land ownership. Both renewal and housing were significantly and negatively related to private land ownership with $r = -.47$ and $r = -.37$ respectively (Table 6.1). The amount of land cities devoted to public use is thus related to both urban renewal and public housing programs. The relationship between renewal and land ownership was expected, but the relationship between public housing and land ownership was somewhat of a surprise. With public housing accounting for only 1 percent of all the housing units in the country, it was not likely that public housing construction would account for the substantial zero order relationship found.

TABLE 6.1

Zero Order Product Moment Correlation Coefficients
between Grant Use and Land Ownership

	Percent of Land Privately Owned (N = 74)
Urban renewal	−0.474*
Public housing	−0.369*

*Significant at the .05 level.

Partial correlation coefficients were computed to test the independent relationships between housing and renewal and land use patterns. Again, the city profile factors and political variables were held constant. As expected (see Table 6.2), the relationship between public housing and land use disappeared (r = .02), but urban renewal was still significantly related to land ownership (r = -.33). While the possibility that this relationship is caused by the temporary holding of land by renewal agencies cannot be discounted, it is much more likely that the relationship reflects a trend toward devoting increasing amounts of land to public enterprises among cities using urban renewal programs.

TABLE 6.2

Partial Correlation Coefficients Showing Independent
Relationship between Grant Use and Land Ownership

	Percent of Land Privately Owned (N = 74)
Urban renewal	−0.332*
Public housing	0.017

*Significant at the .05 level.

PARK AND RECREATION LAND

As another test of the relationship between grant use and public land holdings, changes in park and recreation land were examined. The Bureau of Outdoor Recreation of the U.S. Department of the Interior was able to provide data on park and recreation land for a number of U.S. cities for both 1960 and 1970.[2] Two indices of change in the number of acres of recreation land in each city were selected: the change in the number of acres of school recreation land between 1960 and 1970, and the change in the number of acres of city park and recreation land between 1960 and 1970. Once again the number of cases subjected to analysis was substantially reduced with data for only 96 cities available concerning school recreation areas and 146 cities concerning city park land. Survey research was utilized to gather the data in both 1960 and 1970. Since this analysis is concerned with change, each city would have had to provide the required information both in 1960 and again in 1970 to be included in the analysis. Most cities did not do this.

Most cities responding in both 1960 and 1970 increased both their number of acres of school recreation land and their number of acres of city park land between 1960 and 1970. The mean increase in school recreation land was 123 acres--from a mean of 113 acres in 1960 to a mean of 236 acres in 1970. The change ranged from a loss of 728 acres to an increase of 3,640 with a standard deviation of 473.

The mean increase in city park land was 770 acres with a 1960 mean of 1,440 acres and 2,318 acres in 1970.[3] The change ranged from a loss of 8,281 acres to a gain of 23,616 with a standard deviation of 3,192 acres.

Product moment correlation coefficients were computed between housing, renewal, and the measures of change in recreation land. At the zero order level, only one relationship was found to be significant. As shown in Table 6.3, only urban renewal was significantly related to changes in city park land ($r = -.22$) while neither urban renewal nor public housing were related to changes in school recreation land.

TABLE 6.3

Zero Order Product Moment Correlation Coefficients
between Grant Use and Changes in Amount
of Recreation Land

	Acres of School Recreation Areas (N = 96)	Acres of City Park and Recreation Land (N = 146)
Urban renewal	−0.105	−0.220*
Public housing	−0.020	−0.113

*Significant at the .05 level.

When partials were computed, again controlling for the city profile and political variables, urban renewal was found to be significantly related to changes in both school ($r = -.34$) and city ($r = -.21$) recreation areas (Table 6.4). Both measures of change were again found to be independent of public housing construction/leasing.

TABLE 6.4

Partial Correlation Coefficients Showing Independent
Relationship between Grant Use and Changes
in Amount of Recreation Land

	Acres of School Recreation Areas (N = 96)	Acres of City Park and Recreation Land (N = 146)
Urban renewal	−0.340*	−0.213*
Public housing	−0.145	−0.029

*Significant at the .05 level.

Partials were then computed between the change measures and each of the independent variables in the renewal model. Other than urban renewal, Size/Manufacturing was the only other variable independently related to the change in school recreation acres (r = .33). The change in park land fared little better, with Elazar's political cultures being the only other variable showing an independent relationship with the change in city park and recreation land (r = .16).

It is not difficult to posit an explanation for the negative relationship between renewal and the measures of change in city recreation land. When controlling for profile measures and political variables, urban renewal success is significantly related to low levels of park and recreation land acquisition. It is very likely that the negative relationship is merely a matter of city priorities. Cities finding themselves in serious economic/social difficulties probably give priority to the types of public projects that will stimulate economic growth rather than concentrating on amenities such as the acquisition of park land.

It might also be possible that urban renewal is associated with central cities and that suburban cities, expanding in both population and physical size, were emphasizing park-land acquisition. This possibility did not prove out. There was no significant relationship between growth in park land and change in city size (square miles) between 1960 and 1970 or the metropolitan status dichotomous variable.

QUALITATIVE ANALYSIS

Once again the case studies analysis provided general support for the quantitative findings. Cities appeared to use renewal as a tool to expand public land, although this was not found to be true in communities with a shortage of vacant land. Little relationship was noted between park land and renewal or public housing.

Vallejo

The overall physical effects of the Marina Vista urban renewal project have been described at length in Chapter 3. Marina Vista dramatically changed the face of Vallejo, turning an area of dilapidated structures into an impressive example of redevelopment. Earlier in this chapter an independent relationship was found to exist between urban renewal and the percent of publicly owned land in the city. Vallejo appears to confirm this finding. The Marina Vista project converted large amounts of land from private to public use. Included in this changeover were two parks, post office, library, town square, parking lots, seawall promenade, boat launching ramp, and a possible civic center complex. Of the 124.6 acres in the project, approximately 81 acres are devoted to public uses.[4]

Renewal in Vallejo was not associated with a dramatic increase in park land. Only 12.1 acres of the renewal area was utilized for parks, courts, and plaza.[5] Conforming to the trends noted in the quantitative analysis, Vallejo did not show a dramatic increase in park land during the 10-year period.

Austin

Urban renewal in Austin also fit the pattern noted in the quantitative analysis with regard to the relationship between renewal and the percent of land within a city devoted to public use. The two University of Texas-connected projects, University East and Brackenridge, will transfer almost 200 acres of valuable property from private to public uses. In addition, the Kealing project increased the size of the site of the Kealing Junior High School from 4.8 acres to 20.5 acres with an associated park, playground, and pool. The Glen Oaks project will eventually convert the flood-plain area of Boggy Creek into an open green space.[6] Urban renewal in Austin, then, appears to conform to the national trend.

There was no noticeable relationship between urban renewal and park land in Austin during the 1960s. Three projects, Brackenridge, Kealing, and Glen Oaks, slightly increased the amount of park land in the city; however, the overall effect of the increase was minuscule. Austin has 10 major parks and 40 playgrounds with a total of over 6,566 acres of park land.[7] Like Vallejo, however, there did not appear to be any significant relationship between park land and urban renewal in Austin.

Syracuse

Renewal in the City of Syracuse provides an interesting contrast in land use patterns when compared to Vallejo and Austin. Syracuse does not exemplify the quantitative relationship noted between urban renewal success and land devoted to the public. Very little of the urban renewal land was converted from private to public use through the renewal process. A total of 19 acres in the Near East Side project was devoted to public purposes. The Community Plaza consisting of the North Garage, Public Safety Building, and the Everson Museum covered 9.7 acres while the State Department of Mental Hygiene hospital took up 3.2 acres. The remaining 6.1 acres went to the City of Syracuse and Central Tech High School.

The Roman Catholic Diocese of Syracuse was expected to build a small office building on 0.2 acres in the Downtown One project area. This was the only tax-exempt development scheduled in this area.

And finally, the only tax-exempt project scheduled for Clinton Square was a federal office building on 2.7 acres.[8] Thus a total of only 21.9 acres of renewal land will be converted to tax-exempt status.

There was no noticeable relationship in Syracuse between urban renewal and land devoted to park and recreational uses. Syracuse has been hampered by a shortage of developable vacant land, which has, in turn, increased the intensity of land use, building coverage, and residential densities. The land shortages realistically limit the city's choices of action in land redistribution. Open space and recreational facilities are critically lacking in many areas of the city. High land costs and pressures for higher intensity land use have made park and recreation development in the city a slow process.[9]

Buffalo

Buffalo, like Syracuse, did not use urban renewal as a vehicle to effect the transfer of land from private to public use. If anything, the city tried to do just the opposite--transfer land from tax-exempt status to a revenue-producing situation. This approach was exemplified by the Maryland Street West project whereby urban renewal was the vehicle used to transfer an area making up one-third of the project area from public to private ownership. While Maryland Street exemplifies an approach not found in the other cities, the overall effect of urban renewal on land use patterns in Buffalo was negligible.

There was also no noticeable relationship between changes in the amount of city park land and urban renewal efforts. While Buffalo has been found to be "sadly lacking in usable neighborhood parks and play spaces,"[10] urban renewal was not related to any efforts to increase or decrease the amount of city park land.

Buffalo does, however, have some interesting plans for park land changes proposed for the period 1970 through 1975. First, the city found that two parks, Grover Cleveland and South Park, are located away from most residential neighborhoods and are too large to be efficiently utilized. The city, therefore, is considering converting part of the park land to land for housing. Table 6.5 shows the proposed reallocation of park resources.

TABLE 6.5

Recommended Disposition of South Park and Grover
Cleveland Park Land, Buffalo, New York

Site	Acres Remaining in Park Usage	Acres Converted to Housing	Acreage
South Park	72.3	90.0	162.3
Cleveland Park	31.6	80.0	111.6
Total	103.9	170.0	273.9

Source: Nathaniel S. Keith and Marcou, O'Leary and Associates, Inc., Buffalo Community Renewal Program Extension for the City of Buffalo, New York (Buffalo: City of Buffalo, N.Y., n.d.), p. 63.

A parallel proposal would provide replacement park land scattered throughout the city to balance off the 170-acre loss in South and Cleveland parks. A total of 13 sites encompassing 344.8 acres was proposed. This proposal is found in Table 6.6. Note that urban renewal (or NDP) is the proposed development mechanism for seven of the new sites.[11] Thus, while Buffalo park development was not related to renewal activities during the 1960s, planning for the 1970-75 period proposed urban renewal as a vehicle for substantial park developments.

TABLE 6.6

Replacement Acreage for Park Land Converted to Nonpark Use, 1970-75, Buffalo, New York

Location	Acreage Converted to Park Use	Existing Use	Development Mechanism
Site C	4.3 acres	vacant	urban renewal
Site F	31.8 acres	vacant	develop city-owned land
Site K	6.0 acres	vacant	renewal or private dedication
Site M	13.0 acres	vacant	private dedication
Site N	13.4 acres	vacant	city purchase and develop
Cold Spring	9.5 acres	residential/commercial	urban renewal
Model cities NDP	15.0 acres	residential/commercial	neighborhood development program
Ellicott project	16.0 acres	vacant/park	urban renewal
Waterfront project	21.0 acres	vacant	urban renewal
Other renewal action	5.0 acres	varies	urban renewal
Central model cities	15.0 acres	residential/commercial	model cities
Squaw Island	75.0 acres	vacant	city develop
15 percent of parks plan	119.8 acres	varies	varies
Total	344.8 acres		

Source: Nathaniel S. Keith and Marcou, O'Leary and Associates, Inc., Buffalo Community Renewal Program Extension for the City of Buffalo, New York (Buffalo: City of Buffalo, N.Y., n.d.), p. 65.

CONCLUSIONS AND CONTENTIONS

Two hypotheses were suggested concerning the relationship between public housing and urban renewal and the physical structure of the city. Specifically:

1. The amount of land devoted to public use is positively related to urban renewal expenditures.
2. Structural changes within cities are positively related to public housing construction and urban renewal expenditures.

Urban renewal success was found to be significantly and independently related to public land ownership while public housing was not. At the zero order level, however, both programs were related to land ownership patterns, but once controls were introduced only urban renewal was independently and negatively related to the private ownership of land. Unfortunately, data were not available to test the relationship between urban renewal and changes in land ownership patterns.

On the basis of the statistical evidence and the qualitative data furnished by renewal experience in Vallejo and Austin, urban renewal appears to be an effective vehicle for the transfers of land from the private to the public sector. There appears to be one major exception to this trend, however. This process apparently works only in cities where there are substantial amounts of vacant land available for development. In cities such as Buffalo and Syracuse renewal is not ordinarily used to permanently transfer land from the private to the public sector.

Another factor comes into play at this point also. Cities such as Austin, which are not forced to rely heavily on the property tax for income, appear to have less trouble and are apparently more willing to utilize urban renewal for public redevelopment purposes.

Renewal and housing were also expected to have a positive relationship with increases in park and recreation land. This relationship did not appear; in fact, high levels of renewal are independently related to low levels of park expansion. The Buffalo experience may point to a failure on the author's part to select an adequate unit of measure. Buffalo was planning to use urban renewal, not to increase the number of acres of park land, but to increase the total number of parks. It is thus possible that total quantity of park land was a poor measure and that renewal and housing might better be related to changes in the number of parks and recreation areas within a city rather than to changes in total acreage.

The most dramatic effect of urban renewal grants is the actual physical change in the face of the city brought about by redevelopment. Unfortunately, beauty cannot be quantified--thus there is no way to "prove" the second hypothesis. From an impressionistic viewpoint, however, the physical changes brought about by urban renewal are dramatic. Renewal in Vallejo changed the face of that city forever. While Jane Jacobs rightly deplores the destruction of Boston's North End, there is no question but that renewal is capable of transforming an area of blight and ugliness into pride and beauty--Vallejo, Austin, and Syracuse attest to that reality.

NOTES

1. Allen D. Manvel, "Land Use in 106 Large Cities," in Three Land Research Studies, National Commission on Urban Problems (Washington, D.C.: Government Printing Office, 1968), pp. 19-59.

2. George D. Butler, ed., Recreation and Park Yearbook 1961 (New York: National Recreation Association, 1961), pp. 47-119; U.S. Department of the Interior, Bureau of Outdoor Recreation, Volunteer Recreation Leaders and Recreation and Park Areas, Series AA, Report 301-303 and 306 (Washington, D.C.: unpublished computer printout, dated 04/19/71), and Recreation and Park Areas, Series AA, Report 604-615 (Washington, D.C.: unpublished computer printout, dated 04/15/71).

3. The difference between the 1960 and 1970 means does not equal 770. A total N of 274 was used to compute the 1960 mean and an N of 160 was used for the 1970 mean. Only 147 cities responded to both questionnaires so the mean change of 770 acres applies only to these 147 cities.

4. Computed from data on map of the Marina Vista Project, Bond and Dougherty, Inc., Vallejo, Calif., February 1969.

5. Ibid.

6. "Urban Renewal Special," Austin American-Statesman, August 27, 1972, pp. 4-5.

7. Chamber of Commerce, Community Profile: Austin, Texas (Austin: Chamber of Commerce, 1972).

8. Syracuse Governmental Research Bureau and Metropolitan Development Association, Profile of Central New York (Syracuse: Syracuse Governmental Research Bureau and Metropolitan Development Association, 1972), pp. 14-15.

9. A Workable Program for Community Improvement: 1968 Progress Report for the Elimination and Prevention of Slums and Blight in Syracuse, New York (Syracuse: City of Syracuse, 1968), pp. 15-16.

10. Nathaniel S. Keith and Marcou, O'Leary and Associates, Inc., Buffalo Community Renewal Program Extension for the City of Buffalo, New York (Buffalo: City of Buffalo, N.Y., n.d.), p. 61.

11. Ibid., pp. 61-67.

CHAPTER

7

SOCIAL
EFFECTS OF
PUBLIC HOUSING AND
URBAN RENEWAL PROGRAMS

Unquestionably, the most vocal criticisms of public housing and urban renewal programs in recent years have been directed at the social effects of the programs--both planned and spillover. A planned social effect of urban renewal, for example, has been the reduction of substandard housing. In attempting to attain this goal, however, renewal has justly been criticized as a program of "Negro removal." Thus a spillover effect has become a major consequence of the program. This chapter will examine some of the social effects attributed to renewal and housing in light of some of the major effects and criticisms of the programs.

IMPROVED HOUSING CONDITIONS

An aggregate approach to the examination of the effects of urban renewal and public housing on housing conditions in U.S. cities between 1960 and 1970 was made extremely difficult because of changes in the 1970 census of housing. It was initially expected that housing and renewal success could be correlated with the change between 1960 and 1970 in the percent of sound housing with all plumbing facilities. It was expected that urban renewal and public housing would be positively associated with an increase in this variable. Unfortunately, the Bureau of the Census changed its housing classifications and no longer reports dwelling units as sound, deteriorating, or dilapidated.

The census for both 1960 and 1970 did, however, contain data on plumbing that could effectively be used to measure the change in the percent of dwelling units without all plumbing facilities. It was expected that both urban renewal and public housing success would be related to a decrease in the percent of housing units lacking some or all plumbing.

The 1960 figure was created by adding the percent of sound housing with all plumbing facilities[1] plus the percent of deteriorating housing with all plumbing facilities[2] and subtracting from 100. The 1970 percent of housing lacking some or all plumbing facilities required no computation.[3] The change in the percent of housing lacking some or all plumbing facilities was then obtained by subtracting the 1960 figure from the 1970 figure.

In general the housing stock in cities with populations of 50,000 or more improved dramatically between 1960 and 1970. The percent of housing lacking plumbing facilities was reduced by an average (mean) of 7.09 percent during the 10-year period. The change ranged from a substantial reduction of 29.5 percent to a slight increase of 1.1 percent with a standard deviation of 5.3 percent. By 1970 an average (mean) of only 3.34 percent of the housing in cities over 50,000 lacked some plumbing facilities. Housing conditions varied widely from city to city with a high of 18.7 percent and low of 0.3 percent lacking some or all plumbing.

Surprisingly, neither urban renewal nor public housing success was found to be related to this change. Zero order product moment correlation coefficients were computed between housing and renewal and the change in the percent of housing units lacking some or all plumbing facilities between 1960 and 1970 (Table 7.1). Neither urban renewal nor public housing was significantly associated with this measure of change in housing quality.

TABLE 7.1

Zero Order Product Moment Correlation Coefficients between
Grant Use and Change in Housing Conditions, 1960-70

	Change in Percent Lacking Plumbing
Urban renewal	−0.059
Public housing	−0.058

Suspecting that the independent relationships between variables might be hidden by the influences of other variables in the model, partial correlation coefficients were computed controlling for the city profile factors and the political variables. The partials are found in Table 7.2. Neither relationship was significant at the .05

level. The importance of this lack of relationship cannot be understated. It was expected that both urban renewal and public housing
would have strong relationships with changes in the stock of substandard housing, but the relationship was not shown by either simple or
partial correlation.

TABLE 7.2

Partial Correlation Coefficients Showing Independent
Relationship between Grant Use and Change in
Housing Conditions, 1960-70

	Change in Percent Lacking Plumbing
Urban renewal	−0.020
Public housing	−0.081

Does this then mean the urban renewal and public housing programs do not affect the quality of housing within a community? Not
at all. The general improvement in housing conditions between 1960
and 1970 has already been noted. Urban renewal and public housing
unquestionably account for part of this change. The important finding
concerning the lack of relationship between renewal and housing and
changes in aggregate housing conditions concerns the meaning of the
relationship to cities not receiving substantial amounts of renewal
funds or constructing/leasing substantial numbers of public housing
units. Apparently these cities are able to improve the quality of
their housing without the aid of either federal program. It is likely
that state programs such as New York's housing program or California's renewal program, local code enforcement projects, and/or
private renewal and renovation serve to offset the predicted effects
of urban renewal and public housing.

CHANGE IN LOW-RENT HOUSING STOCK

Both urban renewal and low-income public housing are commonly suspected (or credited) as being major determinants of change
in the stock of low-rent housing. Public housing is usually credited
with increasing the supply of low-rent housing while urban renewal
is generally blamed for reductions in the number of low-rent housing
units. To test these propositions, two measures of the change in the

stock of low-rent housing were developed from 1960[4] and 1970[5] census data. These measures were the change in the number of contract rental units under $60.00 from 1960 to 1970, and the change in the percent of contract rental units (of total rental units) under $60.00 from 1960 to 1970.

A substantial decrease in low-rent (under $60.00) housing was expected simply because of inflationary factors. Such was the case. Cities showed a mean reduction of 8,991 low-rent housing units between 1960 (mean of 15,709) and 1970 (mean of 6,718). Changes ranged from a reduction of 605,902 units to a slight increase of 340 units with a standard deviation of 36,904.

A second indicator of change in low-rent housing was also computed--the change in the percent of rental units under $60.00 from 1960 to 1970. The percent of low-rent housing units also decreased dramatically during the 10-year period with an average (mean) reduction of 25 percent and standard deviation of 12 percent. Changes ranged from an increase of 65 percent to a reduction of 72 percent.

Both urban renewal and public housing were significantly related to large decreases in the total stock of rental housing under $60.00 (Table 7.3) with $r = -.75$ and $r = -.89$ respectively. Without controlling for city demographic variables, however, this figure has little meaning. Perhaps more meaningful is the low, but statistically significant, zero order relationship between urban renewal and the change in the percent of low-rent housing. In this case the positive relationship indicates that an increase (or small decrease) in the change in percent of low-rent housing is associated with urban renewal success.

TABLE 7.3

Zero Order Product Moment Correlation Coefficients between
Grant Use and Change in Low-Rent Housing Stock, 1960-70

	Number Rental Units under $60	Percent Rental Units under $60
Urban renewal	−0.748*	0.155*
Public housing	−0.892*	0.065

*Significant at the .05 level.

The relationships change considerably with the introduction of controls. When the city factors and political variables were held constant there was no significant relationship between renewal or housing and the change in the percent of low-rent housing. A weak but significant independent relationship does exist between housing ($r = -.26$) and renewal ($r = .13$) and the change in the total number of low-rent housing units. Table 7.4 shows these relationships. The slight positive relationship between urban renewal and change in the number of low-rent housing units indicates that urban renewal success is independently related to the least reduction in low-rent housing. On the other hand, public housing construction was independently related to large decreases in the total low-rent housing stock. Apparently cities experiencing serious declines in their total supply of low-rent housing react by increasing construction/leasing public housing units. However, this construction effort was not adequate to offset the decline in housing stock.

TABLE 7.4

Partial Correlation Coefficients Showing Independent
Relationship between Grant Use and Change in
Low-Rent Housing Stock, 1960–70

	Number Rental Units under $60	Percent Rental Units under $60
Urban renewal	0.132*	0.090
Public housing	-0.259*	0.041

*Significant at the .05 level.

These figures raise serious questions concerning the common contentions about the effects of urban renewal on the low-rent housing stock. Renewal does not appear to be as villainous as was heretofore believed. Table 7.5 shows the partial correlation coefficients between the renewal model variable and the change in the percent of rental units under $60.00 between 1960 and 1970. Only two of the relationships are significant at the .05 level with a perfect partial correlation coefficient of -1.0 between Size/Manufacturing and the change in low-rent housing stock. Thus urban renewal does not really determine the reduction in low-rent housing; it is city size and density measures that affect the cost of housing. The contention that urban renewal reduces the supply of low-cost housing probably resulted from examination of short-term case studies. There is no question but that massive clearance programs destroy low-cost housing in the short run. Over the long run, however, the data do not support this contention. The case studies presented later in this chapter appear to amplify this finding.

TABLE 7.5

Partial Correlation Coefficients Showing Independent
Relationships between Renewal Model Variables
and the Change in the Percent of Rental Units
under $60, 1960-70

	Change in Percent under $60
Status, Wealth, and Education (low)	−0.022
Central City	−0.108
Urban Density	−0.202*
Size/Manufacturing	−1.000*
Commuting/Growth	0.036
Model city	0.047
HUD office in state	0.030
Renewal difficulty	0.000
Years since 1949 for URA	−0.028
Years since 1960 for enabling legislation	0.037
Form of government	−0.010
Representation	−0.026
Type of election	0.019
Wallace vote	−0.001
Goldwater vote	0.071
Elazar's political cultures	0.035
Metro status	0.029
Urban renewal	0.060

*Significant at the .05 level.

QUALITATIVE ANALYSIS

Examination of the social effects of renewal and housing grants proved to be most difficult. Given the relatively short amount of time the author was able to spend in each city, heavy reliance had to be placed on secondary data sources. Fortunately, much information was available.

Alhambra

Of the six cities visited during the field observations, Alhambra was the only city operating a renewal or redevelopment program without federal assistance. For this reason, some of the social effects of Alhambra's program were examined for later comparison with programs operating under the restrictions imposed by federal law.

Alhambra tried a rather unusual approach to what little slum clearance (and it can hardly be called that) it has attempted. There were a number of low-value residential dwellings in commercial and industrial areas of the city. These dwellings were located on land that had been zoned for commercial or industrial use after the houses had been built. The city refers to these dwellings as "nonconforming residences." There were 124 nonconforming residences in commercial areas and 163 in the industrial area. While far from what one might consider "slum housing," for Alhambra these dwellings constituted the city's low-rent housing.

On August 2, 1966, with an effective date of September 8, 1966, the city council passed (5 to 0) an ordinance requiring, in essence, that wood frame dwellings used for residential occupancy that were over 35 years old and constituting a nonconforming structure would be removed within five years of the effective date of the ordinance.[6] This ordinance would have virtually eliminated low-rent housing in Alhambra by September 8, 1971. This date was later changed to November 18, 1972.[7] In 1971 a number of the residents of the nonconforming dwellings were able to apply enough pressure on the city council to have the date for the elimination of nonconforming dwellings changed to five years from January 14, 1972 (January 14, 1977).[8] Thus an attempt to legislate the removal of low-rent housing merely because it constituted a nonconforming use failed. Nonconforming structures in Alhambra are removed or demolished as a matter of course in the city--but generally only when another use for the property is planned.

The general appearance and condition (though not necessarily substandard) of the nonconforming dwellings violated the city norm concerning maintenance of private property. Though the attempt to "do away" with these structures failed, it was not so much the nonconforming nature of the dwellings that caused the attempt at elimination, but rather the appearance of the property. As a class, the owners and tenants of this property were in violation of an important community norm. The community responded in what was for it a logical manner.

Alhambra also provides an interesting contrast to the relocation requirements of federal law. Operating under the Community Redevelopment Law of the State of California, Alhambra's redevelopment plan called for the Redevelopment Agency to "assist all persons (including families, business concerns, and others) displaced by the Project in finding other locations and facilities."[9]

Toward this end, the agency would pay a maximum of $200.00 in moving expenses.[10] Relocation efforts consisted of assisting families (and occasionally businesses) in finding new homes--mainly through local realtors. There was no specific attempt made to keep the families in Alhambra; in fact, most relocated outside the city. A side benefit to redevelopment, as seen by the city, was the transfer of low-income families from Alhambra to adjacent communities.

Vallejo

The accusation that urban renewal is responsible for a reduction in the supply of low-rent housing is not substantiated by urban renewal activity in Vallejo. For one thing, two of the Vallejo projects involve very little clearance. The Flosden Acres project is primarily a program of residential rehabilitation rather than residential destruction. The same is true of the Concentrated Code Enforcement program-- 359 units will be brought into conformance with the city codes rather than being destroyed.

Only the clearance project, Marina Vista, might be accused of reducing the supply of low-rent housing. In the long run, however, Marina Vista substantiates the findings in Table 7.4. The Marina Vista project demolished over 600 major structures,[11] of which approximately 400 were residences. Administrators report anywhere between 160 and 350 residential relocations forced by the project. Even assuming that all of the 400 housing units demolished could have provided safe, decent, sanitary housing for low-income families, more low-rent housing was put into the Marina Vista project area than could possibly have been removed.

Table 7.6 shows the present residential redevelopment in the Marina Vista project. Note that 618 housing units are provided, whereas only 400 (maximum) were destroyed. In addition, another 100-unit high-rise apartment building for low-income elderly residents is planned for the area. Assuming, however, that the additional 100 units are never built, there still remain 466 subsidized units (all but the Carolina Apartments) in Marina Vista. Urban renewal in Vallejo, then, not only accounts for the upgrading of existing residential dwelling units, but in the long run is associated with an increase in the supply of low-rent housing.

Chapter 3 suggested a rather negative attitude on the part of the citizens and officials of Vallejo concerning federal housing programs for low-income families. The attitude is not as pervasive as it might originally have been perceived. There is no question but that the city is not interested in low-rent public housing; however, the use of a variety of federal programs to provide subsidized housing for low- and moderate-income families appears to be well accepted. Government programs to provide privately owned (or institutionally owned) low-rent housing at reduced rates is encouraged. Nowhere is this more evident than in the use of three such programs in the Marina Vista area. There thus appears to be a distinction on the part of Vallejo's citizens between providing for the "elderly and the working poor" on the one hand (acceptable) and the "welfare poor" on the other (unacceptable).

TABLE 7.6

Housing in the Marina Vista Urban Renewal Project
Vallejo, California

Ascension Arms (202)	75 units
Marina Vista Apartments [221(d)(3)]	236 units
Carolina Apartments	152 units
High-rise (236)	155 units
Total	618 units

Source: Redevelopment Agency of the City of Vallejo (Vallejo: January 19, 1973.

Austin

Austin provided an excellent opportunity to examine the social effects of urban renewal-forced relocations. The early relocations in Austin associated with the Kealing and Glen Oaks areas contributed substantially to the later difficulties the Urban Renewal Agency would experience in Blackshear. One former official reported that "the relocation of the people was really just a sham."

With field studies lasting approximately one week in each of the cities visited, it was impossible to study citizen attitudes (as opposed to elite and media opinions) in any depth. For this reason, every attempt was made to examine both published and unpublished secondary sources dealing with housing or renewal. Such an opportunity was available concerning the effects of relocations in Austin.[12]

Allen Williams randomly sampled 95 of the 182 households displaced from the Kealing urban renewal area between 1964 and

1968. In examining the housing condition of the relocatees, interviewers estimated the condition of the new dwellings and found that
almost one out of every three households moved into a new dwelling
that was classified as deteriorating or dilapidated.[13] Thus, almost
one-third of the families displaced from Kealing did not obtain a
decent home.

Williams also found that 70.5 percent of the relocated households were faced with an increased financial burden after relocation,
and 18.7 percent of those who owned their own homes in Kealing became renters after the move. Of the 44 families who were renting
in Kealing and continued renting after relocation, 67.4 percent were
faced with an average rental increase from $39.00 per month to
$52.00 per month.

Of the Kealing homeowners, 60.4 percent had paid for their
former homes. Five of the former homeowners became renters after
relocation, seven purchased and completely paid for new homes,
while the remaining 58.6 percent purchased other homes and were
making an average house payment of $77.00. Thus only 24.1 percent
of the former Kealing homeowners were able to relocate without increased housing costs.[14]

In addition to surveying the changing housing characteristics,
Williams attempted to examine the effects of urban renewal on the
social community. Concerning the physical characteristics of the
neighborhoods, the majority of those interviewed indicated that there
was little difference between Kealing and their new neighborhoods.
Similarly, the majority of respondents found little difference between
neighborhoods concerning convenience to facilities such as schools,
churches, transportation, or shopping. Of the 40 percent (approximate) reporting differences, however, roughly two-thirds considered
their old neighborhood more convenient.[15]

Data were available on the relocation addresses of 98.2 percent
(169 households) of those Kealing residents relocating in Austin.
None of these households relocated in a predominantly white neighborhood. Approximately 66 percent relocated within one mile of the
center of the Kealing area with the majority of the remaining families
moving further to the east but still remaining in the black community.
Furthermore, no white families moved into the redeveloped Kealing
area. The conclusion here is obvious--the Kealing project relocations in no way contributed to desegregation in the City of Austin.[16]

For a large number of those forced to relocate from the Kealing area (26.3 percent), factors associated with a loss of community
were salient, but these factors were not major complaints by the
majority. The strongest complaint was the forced disruption of
neighborhood friendships or kinship, although a secondary area
causing some problem was the difficulty in church attendance forced
on some by relocation.[17]

The Williams study provided important insight into the social effects of urban renewal in Austin--at least as far as the relocations forced by one project are concerned. The Kealing relocations undoubtedly helped many improve their housing conditions; however, a very high percentage of those relocated did not obtain suitable housing. The relocations also placed a financial burden in terms of increased housing costs on the vast majority of the former Kealing residents. There was some change in the social community as a result of relocation but this did not appear to be an important factor for the majority. And finally, renewal was not a useful tool in promoting racial integration within the city.

Syracuse

The first large urban renewal project in Syracuse, the Near East Side project, is a prime example of the reason renewal critics term urban renewal "black removal." This project forced the relocation of a substantial number of black families to make way for business and civic redevelopment. Relocations from this area required moving 800 to 900 families and 630 single persons to new homes over a five-year period.[18] In spite of the fact that the city attempted to coordinate the construction of public housing units to alleviate the burdens of relocation, it was not entirely successful. Far fewer low-income housing units were constructed in Syracuse than were razed by urban renewal. Over a 10-year period from 1959 through 1968, approximately 5,500 persons were displaced and relocated (a large number from freeway construction).[19]

Blaming urban renewal for all low-income housing problems and relocations in Syracuse, however, oversimplifies a complex social process. Outside of the Near East Side in the early 1960s, renewal has not been a significant cause of relocations. Table 7.7, for example, presents the city relocation estimates for a two-year period ending in March 1969. Note that the vast majority of relocations were not as a result of HUD-assisted projects. City and state programs were causing many more relocations in Syracuse in the late 1960s than was urban renewal. In 1960 approximately 20 percent of the housing in Syracuse was classified as substandard. In an effort to upgrade local housing quality the city embarked upon a large-scale code enforcement program. The program has substantially aided in upgrading housing quality, but it has not been without its negative effects--forced relocations.[20] Thus while renewal has received substantial, and often justified, criticism in Syracuse, the program has often served as a smokescreen for other culprits.

TABLE 7.7

Estimates of Displacements and Relocations for the Period April 1, 1967,
through March 31, 1969, in Syracuse, New York

Type of Government Action	Number of Families Displaced		Number of Families Relocated			
			In Standard Housing		In Substandard Housing	
	White	Black	White	Black	White	Black
HUD-assisted projects	8	4	8	4		
Code enforcement	50	100	47	90	3	10
Highway construction	15		15			
Mental hygiene	8	103	8	103		
Overincome in public housing	35		35			
Total	116	207	113	197	3	10

Source: A Workable Program for Community Improvement: 1968 Progress Report for the Elimination and Prevention of Slums and Blight in Syracuse, New York (Syracuse: City of Syracuse, 1968), Housing and Relocation Requirements, p. 6.

215

Buffalo

Rather than utilize urban renewal clearance and public housing
construction as major tools to eliminate slums and blight in residential neighborhoods, Buffalo adopted an approach much like Syracuse's.
Specifically, Buffalo is now concentrating its efforts on code enforcement. The city has initiated a Systematic Neighborhood Improvement
Program (SNIP) of code enforcement. The city's Division of Rehabilitation and Conservation will ultimately inspect for code compliance
every single dwelling unit in Buffalo. In areas designated for urban
renewal, inspections will only cover areas of immediate hazard.
Upon completion of the present SNIP program, the city will establish
a schedule that will result in biannual inspections of multiple dwellings and routine periodic inspections of all other dwellings at adequate intervals to insure continuing compliance.[21]
     In Buffalo, as in Syracuse, displacement by urban renewal has
been a problem. However, it does not account for even one-half of
the recent displacements in the city. Between October 1, 1967, and
September 30, 1969, HUD-assisted programs (primarily urban renewal) accounted for only 285 of the 475 forced family relocations
(Table 7.8). Again, highway construction and code enforcement accounted for approximately 60 percent of the relocations during the
period.[22]
     As of 1969 renewal accounted for the destruction of many more
low-income dwelling units than it created. In the long run, however,
this will not be the case. If present palns are put into effect, 5,150
low- and moderate-income dwelling units will be constructed during
the period 1970-75 in four urban renewal areas: Ellicott, Maryland
Street West, Waterfront, and Oak Street.[23]
     Thus while renewal is associated with a decrease in low-rent
housing in the short run, in the long run renewal will result in an
increased supply of low-cost homes. Had Buffalo's renewal program
progressed at a reasonable rate, renewal in Buffalo, like Vallejo,
would have probably provided increased low-rent housing during the
decade under study.

CONCLUSIONS AND CONTENTIONS

     The final hypotheses in this study examine the relationships
between housing and renewal and the expected social effects of the
program:

1. The quantity of low-cost housing is positively related to public
    housing construction.

TABLE 7.8

Number of Displaced Families and Relocations for the Two-Year Period Ending September 30, 1969, in Buffalo, New York

| | Number of Families Displaced | | Number of Families Relocated | | | |
| | | | In Standard Housing | | In Substandard Housing | |
	White	Minority	White	Minority	White	Minority
HUD-assisted projects	152	33	145	30	7	3
Code enforcement	60	80	58	75	2	5
Highway construction	57	93	55	89	2	4
Total	269	206	258	194	11	12

Source: Workable Program 1970/1972 (Buffalo: City of Buffalo, 1969), p. 13.

2. The quantity of low-cost housing is negatively related to urban renewal expenditures.
3. Improved housing conditions are positively related to public housing construction.
4. Improved housing conditions are positively related to urban renewal expenditures.

One of the most surprising results of this entire study was the lack of relationship found between both urban renewal and public housing and the 1960-70 change in the percent of local housing units lacking some or all plumbing. In cities throughout the nation, the percent of housing units lacking plumbing decreased dramatically during the decade. This decrease, however, was not specifically related to urban renewal or low-rent public housing construction/leasing. While housing and urban renewal, especially renewal, provide vehicles to improve the overall quality of housing, cities not electing to use urban renewal for this purpose are apparently able to find other equally successful methods to improve overall housing quality. Likewise, cities achieving substantial success in terms of urban renewal funds received may devote most of the funds to downtown or commercial renewal rather than toward housing improvement.

One of the major criticisms directed at urban renewal has been that it reduces the supply of low-cost housing in the city. On the other hand, it was expected that public housing construction would increase the supply of low-rent housing. In the long run this was not found to be true. Neither urban renewal nor public housing was found to be independently related to changes in the percent of low-rent housing. In fact, urban renewal showed a slight positive relationship with the change in the total number of low-rent housing units. Public housing, on the other hand, was negatively related to the change in the total number of rental units. It thus appears that public housing construction is brought about by the knowledge that there will be a reduction in the quantity of low-rent housing. The case studies have generally supported these findings. In the long run, renewal is probably associated with an increase in the supply of low- and moderate-rent housing. Renewal, then, may temporarily reduce the low-income housing supply, but in the long run it appears to increase it.

But what of the effects of renewal on the individuals directly involved? The findings of Allen Williams in Austin are probably very similar to what one would find in most U.S. cities: that minorities are the victims of urban renewal, that there is a disruption of the community (good or bad), that families forced to relocate generally move into improved housing but pay a higher price for that housing, and that renewal really does not do much to help the cause of racial integration.

The case studies did show, however, that while urban renewal may bear the brunt of the criticism concerning forced relocations, highway construction and code enforcement projects may be the real present-day villains.

NOTES

1. U.S. Department of Commerce, Bureau of the Census, County and City Data Book 1962 (Washington, D.C.: Government Printing Office, 1962), pp. 476-575.

2. Computed from data in U.S. Department of Commerce, Bureau of the Census, United States Census of Housing 1960, HC (1), separate volume for each state (Washington, D.C.: Government Printing Office, 1962), Table 12.

3. U.S. Department of Commerce, Bureau of the Census, Housing Characteristics for States, Cities, and Counties, Vol. 1, separate volume for each state (Washington, D.C.: Government Printing Office, 1972), Table 1.

4. Computed from data in Census of Housing 1960, Table 17.

5. Computed from data in Housing Characteristics, Table 10.

6. Ordinance No. 066-3334, City of Alhambra, Calif., August 2, 1966.

7. Ordinance No. 967-3383, City of Alhambra, Calif., October 10, 1967.

8. Ordinance No. 071-3546, City of Alhambra, Calif., December 7, 1971.

9. Alhambra Redevelopment Agency, Redevelopment Plan for the Industrial Redevelopment Project (Alhambra, Calif.: Alhambra Redevelopment Agency, May 26, 1969), p. 11 (Mimeographed).

10. Ibid.

11. Redevelopment Agency of the City of Vallejo, Marina Vista (Vallejo, Calif.: Gibson Publications, n.d.), p. 1.

12. J. Allen Williams, Jr., "The Effects of Urban Renewal Upon a Black Community: Evaluation and Recommendations," Social Science Quarterly 50 (December 1969): 703-12. J. Allen Williams, Jr., Blackshear Diagnostic Survey: A Description and Problem Analysis (Austin: The Urban Renewal Agency of the City of Austin, June 1968) (Mimeographed).

13. Williams noted that "the interviewers were not trained appraisers, but their judgments of structures in another urban renewal area compared favorably with those made by experts. For example, whereas the urban renewal agency classified 56.0 percent of the houses substandard, interviewers classified 53.6 percent substandard." Williams, "Effects of Renewal," p. 704.

14. Williams, "Effects of Renewal," pp. 704-5.

15. Ibid., pp. 706-7.

16. Ibid., 207-8.

17. Ibid., pp. 208-9.

18. "Action Asked in Urban Renewal Problems," Syracuse Post-Standard, July 30, 1961, pp. 1, 31.

19. Housing Committee of the League of Women Voters of Metropolitan Syracuse, Housing in Onondaga County: Present Facts and Future Goals (Syracuse: League of Women Voters, February 1969), pp. 1, 4.

20. A Workable Program for Community Improvement: 1968 Progress Report for the Elimination and Prevention of Slums and Blight in Syracuse, New York (Syracuse: City of Syracuse, 1968), Housing and Relocation Requirements, pp. 1-7.

21. Workable Program 1970/1972 (Buffalo: City of Buffalo, 1969), p. 3B.

22. Ibid., p. 13.

23. Nathaniel S. Keith and Marcou, O'Leary and Associates, Inc., Buffalo Community Renewal Program Extension for the City of Buffalo, New York (Buffalo: City of Buffalo, N.Y., n.d.), pp. 34-35.

8

SOME SUGGESTIONS
FOR THE FUTURE

This chapter will not attempt to present a detailed summary of the findings concerning the determinants of grant usage or grant effects; this has been done in the last section of each of the preceding chapters. The purpose here is to briefly summarize the broad findings within the framework of the model developed in Chapter 2 and to relate these findings to the overall framework of U.S. urban society.

Concerning the patterns of use of renewal and housing grant programs, the overwhelming dominance of a city's physical and socioeconomic profile as a determinant of grant use was noted. The profile factors operate through an intervening political framework consisting of federal, state, and local decisions as well as an environment consisting of the political attitudes of the local populace. Federal influence was not only felt within the framework of housing and renewal laws and project approvals, but through an apparent advantage of federally selected "model cities" or "demonstration cities" in urban renewal funding and housing authorizations.

State lawmakers also significantly affected the outcome of the grant programs. The rapidity with which state legislatures passed program-enabling legislation and the impediments placed in the way of program utilization by state laws substantially affected use by local governments.

The formal structure of local government (reform characteristics) was influential in determining public housing construction and leasing but had little effect on local use of urban renewal. On the other hand, local political attitudes (as measured) helped shape the urban renewal program but had no effect on the growth and development of public housing. In addition, this study tended to confirm that an overreliance on the individual case study might result in overestimating the importance of the political leader and program administrator in urban renewal and public housing grant use.

Both programs, but especially urban renewal, were business dominated and were often used to enhance the economic position of the city. Public housing construction appeared to have a slight effect on the short-term local employment picture, while urban renewal did not. While renewal and housing are used to enhance the city's economic position, there is no evidence that the programs are successful in this regard in the short run. It is possible, but undetermined here, that renewal and housing may benefit the community's economic position over the long run (perhaps 30 to 50 years); this study, however, notes little short-term success--except in rare cases such as that exemplified by Syracuse.

Both renewal and housing have little independent effect on local government employment. Renewal, however, was positively related to increased city tax revenues, expenditures, and debt. Urban renewal thus was found to be an effective tool for increasing the city's tax base.

Neither program showed the expected relationship with stability in the mayor's office. Other factors, particularly the form of government, were more important determinants of the mayor's reelection chances.

Urban renewal success was found to be greatest in cities devoting large amounts of land to public purposes, suggesting that urban renewal is an effective vehicle for transferring land from private to public use.

And finally, urban renewal and public housing were not related to the overall upgrading of local housing (plumbing facilities). Nor was renewal related to reductions in the supply of low-rent housing; in fact, it actually showed a weak but positive relationship to the number of rental units under $60.00. In the early stages of the program, urban renewal forced massive relocations, but by the end of the 1960s much more administrative care was being shown as the program moved away from the clearance concept toward one of renovation and restoration. Nonetheless, renewal is often still blamed for forced relocations while highway construction programs and local code enforcement projects may in fact be the major causes of these relocations. Evidence on the effects of relocations since 1968 (and the new benefits) is sketchy. Under the old relocation act, however, families and businesses forced to relocate were hurt much more than they were helped.

URBAN RENEWAL IN AN URBAN SOCIETY

While physical and demographic characteristics of cities (demand) are the prime determinants of whether a city will have an urban renewal program and how large it will be, local political factors determine how the program is shaped. Before discussing renewal within the framework of urban society, it is first necessary to discuss the limits placed upon the discussion of renewal and to examine two concepts not heretofore discussed: institutional racism and the concept of the zero-sum game.

Stokely Carmichael and Charles Hamilton, among others, make a distinction between individual racism and institutional racism. Individual racism involves individual whites acting in a racist manner against individual blacks, while institutional racism involves acts by the total white community against the black community. Individual racism

> consists of overt acts by individuals, which cause
> death, injury, or the violent destruction of property. This type can be recorded by television
> cameras; it can frequently be observed in the process of commission. The second type is less
> overt, far more subtle, less identifiable in terms
> of specific individuals committing the acts. But
> it is no less destructive of human life. The second type originates in the operation of established
> and respected forces in the society, and thus receives far less public condemnation than the first
> type.[1]

Institutional racism need not be conscious acts of the white community against the black. It relies on "the active and pervasive operation of anti-black attitudes and practices,"[2] conscious or unconscious.

Before examining urban development programs in light of this discussion of racism, it is necessary to consider the second major point: that renewal, from a local perspective, is a zero-sum game. That is, there are winners and there are losers in the renewal process. In a nonzero-sum game it is possible for all, or most, players to win (or lose). In a zero-sum game some win while others lose.

From a financial viewpoint, urban renewal is downtown oriented. Most projects are located in the central business district or in a "near downtown" area. They are oriented toward improving economic vitality although they may meet the legally defined residential requirements. Renewal, then, is generally associated with business or government (in the broad sense including schools, hospitals, universities, etc.) expansion. But resources for renewal are extremely limited in terms of local needs. Alan Altshuler notes that society allocates its resources in accordance with the "squeaky wheel" principle:

Resources are scarce, claims abundant; people are
selfish, the consensus on priorities weak. This is
not to say that the public lacks any sense of what is
right and proper, or that this sense can be ignored.
It is merely to say that this sense is extremely general, and is itself largely an indirect and lagged
product of power relationships.[3]

As urban renewal is applied to the squeaky wheel of physical
blight, economic decay, and social injustice in the city, certain segments of the community reap the benefits. Local government benefits through an expanded tax base. The community as a whole benefits through an improved physical appearance and increased public
land for parks, museums, universities, hospitals, etc. Certain
types of business interests benefit directly from the renewal process
while local businessmen in general may see themselves as benefiting
from renewal in the long run. (Whether they actually do or not is
open to debate.)

In a zero-sum game, however, there are always losers. The
losers here are the residents of the "near downtown" areas--Ameri-
ca's minorities. By Carmichael and Hamilton's definition, then,
urban renewal is a thoroughly racist program--not through design of
law, but through the manner in which it is implemented at the local
level. This does not mean that renewal administrators are racists--
most are capable and compassionate individuals. As long as the
poor, the powerless, and the black reside in the "near downtown,"
urban renewal will always work to their disadvantage, for rejuvena-
tion of the "near downtown" is foremost in the minds of those citizens and interest groups having the power to influence the renewal
process.

PUBLIC HOUSING

Low-rent public housing when viewed within a local framework
differs substantially from urban renewal in that it is not a zero-sum
game. Theoretically, everyone can benefit from public housing--
there need not be any losers. While there are those who object to
public housing sites in their particular neighborhoods on the basis
that it will reduce property values, there is little evidence to support this contention. There are, of course, specific instances in
which public housing could reduce adjacent property values. There
is undoubtedly not much demand for home sites adjacent to the former
Pruitt-Igoe project in St. Louis or to Buffalo's Talbert Mall or Ellicott Mall. This situation, however, has been the result of a lack of

awareness of the problems these high-density units would create rather than a deficiency in the low-income public housing program per se. High-density projects and housing developments located in such a manner as to be inaccessible to basic services are now known to be undesirable and to be major contributors to a city's social problems.

Virtually all segments of the society in U.S. cities can benefit from a properly developed public housing program. Architectural firms, construction companies, and suppliers all benefit from the construction of the housing itself, as does local employment. Banks and financial institutions benefit from the tax-exempt bonds issued to finance the project, and investors benefit from the purchase of the bonds. The projects cost the city nothing--the city government assumes no financial liability, and housing construction has been shown to be unrelated to city financial measures. In fact, the city indirectly benefits because the pressures operating to create additional slums and blight are relieved. And finally, the low-income segment of the population benefits from safe, decent, sanitary housing at rates they can afford.

Public housing, then, when viewed within the larger community can operate as a nonzero-sum game. That is, everyone benefits and nobody loses. Recall again that the major assumption of this contention is that the program is properly conceived, carried out, and administered. Pruitt-Igoe also was a nonzero-sum game--but everyone lost.

Former President Nixon was quite correct when he expressed the fear that the federal government was becoming a "nationwide slumlord."[4] Some housing projects are still "human cesspools . . . massive barracks for the destitute . . . a $20,000,000 slum."[5] However, this is not because the public housing concept is deficient, it is because such projects were built either without knowledge of, or without caring about, the consequences of the program.

THE FUTURE FOR PUBLIC HOUSING
AND URBAN RENEWAL

This is not an attempt to predict the political future of two highly controversial programs, but rather is an effort to suggest some ways that the negative effects of the programs might be minimized. As of this writing, both programs might well be eliminated by the Ford administration. A complete cost-benefit study might indicate that there are better ways to meet our housing and redevelopment goals. The future of public housing and urban renewal in its present form is thus highly uncertain.

From this author's perspective, drawn primarily from field observations of housing programs, there appears to be nothing wrong with the basic low-income public housing program that minor modifications could not alleviate.[6] It would be a simple task for Congress to extend tenant income limits or to raise the ceiling on per-unit construction costs. The legal changes that might be made to the present program, then, are technical details.

Properly administered, public housing operates to the benefit of all and the detriment of none when viewed from the local perspective. It is a nonzero-sum game and can operate to everyone's benefit. The major failing in the public housing program, and a critical failure, has been poor planning, design, and administration. Yet failure to utilize current knowledge in government programs is common practice. Social science research of the past 20 years in the arenas of housing and other social needs has been singularly ignored by local officials and HUD administrators alike.[7]

Local housing authority directors are generally appointed for considerations other than their knowledge of the housing and social needs of the local low-income population. This may be no problem so long as that needed input comes from somewhere; but in today's operation of the housing program it generally does not emerge from within the local community. Guidance should then come from the Department of Housing and Urban Development, but it does not. HUD is in a position, through its ability to give and/or withhold project approval, to insure that public housing projects are designed not only utilizing up-to-date building methods but utilizing social knowledge as well. A wealth of knowledge is available--and a wealth of knowledge is ignored.

While public housing may operate to everyone's benefit, urban renewal, in the context of Carmichael and Hamilton's definition of institutional racism, is a racist program. As a zero-sum game, urban renewal operates to the detriment of the urban minority population. In fact Congress recognized this in 1968 when it provided increased relocation payments for displaced households. An owner-occupant was eligible for a replacement housing grant of up to $5,000, while relocation payments of up to $1,000 could be made to renters over a two-year period.[8] The difficulty, however, was that the benefits were not always worth the disruption--especially to renters. There is some evidence that hostility to urban renewal under the 1968 benefits was not great among property owners who might stand to gain from the sale of their property to the urban renewal agency-- witness the emergence of the Blackshear Residents for Individual Property Rights, organized in opposition to the antiurban renewal forces in Austin. This organization was made up predominantly of local property owners anxious to sell their property to the urban renewal agency. However, Congress later recognized that these benefits were still too low. The Uniform Relocation Assistance and Real Property Acquisition Policies Act of 1970 substantially increased benefits to both owner-occupants and renters.[9] Owner-occupants are now eligible for grants of as much as $15,000 to cover the difference between the acquisition cost of the dwelling acquired under the federal program and the cost of a comparable replacement dwelling. Renters also benefited from the 1970 Act. Renters are now eligible to receive up to $4,000 ($83.33 per month) over a four-year period to lease or rent replacement housing. They are also eligible for a grant of up to $4,000 to make a downpayment on the purchase of a home. If the downpayment exceeds $2,000, however, the displaced renter must match any amount in excess of the $2,000 in making the downpayment.[10]

Current benefits, however, are still inadequate. To remove the racist overtones from urban renewal, several changes are necessary. First, Congress, HUD, and the general public must recognize the program for what it is--a program oriented (through its application) to downtown and near downtown redevelopment. There is no sin in utilizing urban renewal for this purpose, the sin is in not recognizing that this is the way the program is being operated. Without the urban renewal program, or some similar form of federal aid, there would be very little downtown redevelopment in U.S. cities. It is only in the "boom" cities such as Austin that private enterprise can afford to undertake downtown redevelopment projects on its own. In spite of the mistakes of the past (again, administrative errors) such as the destruction of Boston's West End,[11] urban renewal can do much to enhance U.S. cities--both physically and financially.

Once the true purpose of urban renewal is recognized, it is then necessary to change the program so that it is no longer racist in nature. This can be done by converting renewal to a nonzero-sum game so that everyone will benefit from the renewal process. As it stands now, the city and the business community are the winners in the renewal process while the black community and other minorities lose (an admitted oversimplification). If the black and minority communities were also winners in the renewal process, urban renewal would no longer operate as a zero-sum game and the program would no longer be racist in nature.

Most of affluent America's relocation is economic. When John Doe is told by his employer, IBM, that he is being transferred from Austin, Texas, to New York City he may not be very happy about it, but in the vast majority of instances he will make the move. Why? For economic considerations. IBM might tell Mr. Doe that he will lose his job if he does not accept the move, or more likely, IBM might offer him a large salary raise if he moves to New York. In either case, Doe moves for economic reasons, either because he wants to keep his job or because he finds the offer of more money attractive enough so that he willingly moves to New York City.

Such should also be the case with urban renewal. Just as John Doe is offered an economic profit to change locations for the convenience of his employer, so should urban renewal offer those displaced by renewal compensation for their forced relocations. This is already done in a limited manner for certain relocatees. An owner-occupant displaced by urban renewal may now be eligible for a replacement housing grant of up to $15,000, in addition to moving expenses plus the negotiated (or court-ordered) cost of the property to be acquired by the renewal agency. A renting family, on the other hand, is only eligible to receive an extra $83.33 per month for a four-year period plus moving expenses. What if the family unit is elderly, disabled, on welfare, or on some form of fixed income? After a four-year period in improved housing they must face another move to a home that they can afford.

If the true purpose of urban renewal is recognized (again, not its purpose according to law, but its purpose according to application), a correction of the inequities makes good sense. If people and businesses are displaced for reasons of government profit (increased property tax revenues) or business profit, why shouldn't they benefit in the same manner as John Doe when he is relocated by his employer? Such a move would change the concept of urban renewal from a zero-sum to a nonzero-sum game, where the program works to everyone's advantage. Why should owner-occupants be primary beneficiaries while the renter is not? If a cash grant of some reasonable size were offered to families in renewal areas as an incentive to move, a large majority might relocate with much less reluctance than they do today. This cash grant could take the form of a relocation allowance. While the federal government recognizes the increased financial burden associated with moves of its employees (military officers, for example, receive a dislocation allowance equal to one month's base pay, plus moving expenses), it does not recognize this burden in relation to renewal-forced relocations. In addition to present programs, a relocation allowance of $1,000-1,500 would not be excessive.

Urban renewal will always have its victims--people living most of their lives in a familiar neighborhood who have no wish to move at any price, but this group will likely be a small minority. People live in slums because they have to, not because they want to. A substantial grant acting as compensation for relocation should be as welcome to a family forced to relocate by urban renewal as is John Doe's move-associated pay raise. Since both Doe and renewal area family are forced to move for someone's profit, both should benefit in a similar manner.

In final summary, this study has examined the patterns of use and some of the effects of federal urban renewal and public housing programs in some detail. The findings have pointed out the overwhelming importance of the city's physical and socioeconomic characteristics in determining grant use. A number of the effects of these grants were noted and certain myths concerning grant effects were dispelled. It was suggested that the weakness in the low-rent public housing program was in its administration rather than in some basic program failure. On the other hand, it was argued that urban renewal operates as a zero-sum game and embodies the characteristics of institutional racism in its present form. Renewal would thus require a fundamental change in concept to be of real benefit to all segments of urban society.

NOTES

1. Stokely Carmichael and Charles V. Hamilton, Black Power: The Politics of Liberation in America (New York: Random House, 1967), p. 4.

2. Ibid., p. 5.

3. Alan A. Altshuler, Community Control: The Black Demand for Participation in Large American Cities (Indianapolis: Pegasus, 1970), p. 193.

4. "Nixon Says Crisis in Cities Is Over; Cities Dip in Crime," New York Times, March 5, 1973, pp. 1, 20.

5. Harrison Salisbury, The Shook-Up Generation (New York: Harper, 1958), p. 74.

6. In addition to the field studies, the author also draws on personal experience with the Oklahoma City Housing Authority, Oklahoma City, Oklahoma.

7. See, for example, J. Allen Williams, Jr., "The Multifamily Housing Solution and Housing Type Preferences," Social Science Quarterly 52 (December 1971): 543-59; and Oscar Newman, Defensible Space (New York: Macmillan, 1972).

8. For a short discussion of 1968 changes in relocation benefits see J. Allen Williams, Jr., "The Effects of Urban Renewal Upon a Black Community: Evaluation and Recommendations," Social Science Quarterly 50 (December 1969): 709-12.

9. Public Law 91-646, United States Statutes at Large, 91st Cong., 2d sess., 1970-71, Vol. 814, Part 2, pp. 1894-1907.

10. Ibid., pp. 1896-97.

11. Jane Jacobs, The Death and Life of Great American Cities (New York: Random House, 1961).

BOOKS

Advisory Commission on Intergovernmental Relations. Fiscal Balance in the American Federal System. Vol. 1. Washington, D.C.: Government Printing Office, 1967.

_____. Measures of State and Local Fiscal Capacity and Tax Effort. Washington, D.C.: Government Printing Office, 1962.

_____. State and Local Finances--Significant Features 1967 to 1970. Washington, D.C.: Government Printing Office, 1967.

Alford, Robert R., and Harry M. Scoble. "Political and Socioeconomic Characteristics of American Cities." In The Municipal Year Book 1965, edited by Orin F. Nolting and David S. Arnold. Chicago: International City Managers' Association, 1965.

Alhambra Chamber of Commerce. Alhambra California Facts. Alhambra: Chamber of Commerce, 1972.

_____. 1972-73 Community Factbook. Wittier, Calif.: Frank Clement, 1972.

Alhambra Industrial Directory. Alhambra: Chamber of Commerce, 1972.

Alhambra Redevelopment Agency. Redevelopment Plan for the Industrial Redevelopment Project. Alhambra, Calif.: Alhambra Redevelopment Agency, May 26, 1969 (Mimeographed).

Altshuler, Alan A. Community Control: The Black Demand for Participation in Large American Cities. Indianapolis: Pegasus, 1970.

Anderson, Martin. The Federal Bulldozer. Cambridge, Mass.: MIT Press, 1964.

Art. 12691-3, Section 3, Acts 1957, 55th Legislature, p. 704, Ch. 298. Vernon's Annotated Revised Civil Statutes of the State of Texas, Vol. 2B. Kansas City, Mo.: Vernon Law Book Company, 1963.

Austin Chamber of Commerce. Austin's Remarkable Growth Pattern. Austin: Chamber of Commerce, 1972 (Mimeographed).

_____. General Demographic Trends. Austin: Chamber of Commerce, 1972 (Mimeographed).

Austin, City of. 1972-1973 Workable Program. Austin: City of Austin, 1972.

Banfield, Edward C., and James Q. Wilson. City Politics. New York: Random House, 1963.

The Beaumont Jaycees. Beaumont Community Attitude Survey. Beaumont: The Beaumont Jaycees, March 15, 1968 (Mimeographed).

Bellush, Jewel, and Murray Hausknecht, eds. Urban Renewal: People, Politics and Planning. Garden City, N.Y.: Doubleday, 1967.

Berry, Brian J. L., Sandra J. Parsons, and Rutherford H. Platt. The Impact of Urban Renewal on Small Business. Chicago: Center for Urban Studies, The University of Chicago, 1968.

Bonjean, Charles M. "Dimensions of Power Structures: Some Problems in Conceptualization and Measurement." In Future Directions in Community Power Research: A Colloquium, edited by Frederick M. Wirt. Berkeley: Institute of Governmental Studies, University of California, 1971.

Brazer, Harvey E. City Expenditures in the United States. Occasional Paper No. 66. New York: National Bureau of Economic Research, 1959.

Break, George F. Intergovernmental Fiscal Relations in the United States. Washington, D.C.: Brookings Institution, 1967.

Brickhouse, J. Earl. A Low Cost Housing Study of Beaumont, Texas. Beaumont: Chamber of Commerce, April 25, 1972 (Mimeographed).

Brown, W. H., Jr., and C. E. Gilbert. Planning Municipal Investment: A Case Study of Philadelphia. Philadelphia: University of Pennsylvania Press, 1961.

"Buffalo." Encyclopedia Americana. Vol. IV. 1970.

Buffalo Municipal Housing Authority. Data on Occupied Projects Under Management, 1972. Buffalo: Municipal Housing Authority, August 1972 (Mimeographed).

Butler, George D., ed. Recreation and Park Yearbook 1961. New York: National Recreation Association, 1961.

Campbell, Alan K., and Seymour Sacks. Metropolitan America. New York: The Free Press, 1967.

Carmichael, Stokely, and Charles V. Hamilton. Black Power: The Politics of Liberation in America. New York: Random House, 1967.

Cartwright, Desmond S. "Ecological Variables." In Sociological Methodology 1969, edited by Edgar F. Borgatta. San Francisco: Jossey-Bass, 1969.

CCDC Newsletter 1. Beaumont: Central City Development Corporation, November 1972.

Central City Development Corporation. Beaumont Central City Analysis: Advance Information Kit. Beaumont, Texas: Central City Development Corporation, 1972 (Mimeographed).

Clark, Terry N., ed. Community Structure and Decision-Making: Comparative Analyses. San Francisco: Chandler, 1968.

Community Profile: Austin, Texas. Austin: Chamber of Commerce, 1972 (Mimeographed).

Dahl, Robert A. Who Governs? New Haven, Conn.: Yale University Press, 1961.

Davies, James Clarence, III. Neighborhood Groups and Urban Renewal. New York: Columbia University Press, 1966.

Denzin, Norman K., ed. Sociological Methods. Chicago: Aldine, 1970.

Department of City Planning and Department of Urban Improvement. A Community Renewal Program: Syracuse, New York. Syracuse: City of Syracuse, N.Y., n.d.

232

Derthick, Martha. The Influence of Federal Grants: Public Assistance in Massachusetts. Cambridge, Mass.: Harvard University Press, 1970.

Doxiadis, C. A. Urban Renewal and the Future of the American City. Chicago: Public Administration Service, 1966.

Duhl, Leonard J., ed. The Urban Condition. New York: Basic Books, 1963.

Dutcher, Margaret J., and Robert Studer. History of Alhambra. Alhambra: Chamber of Commerce, n.d.

Dye, Thomas R. Politics, Economics, and the Public: Policy Outcomes in the American States. Chicago: Rand McNally, 1966.

Easton, David. A Framework for Political Analysis. Englewood Cliffs, N.J.: Prentice-Hall, 1965.

_____. The Political System, An Inquiry Into the State of Political Science. New York: Knopf, 1953.

_____. A Systems Analysis of Political Life. New York: John Wiley, 1965.

Elazar, Daniel J. American Federalism: A View from the States. 2d ed. New York: Crowell, 1972.

_____. The American Partnership. Chicago: University of Chicago Press, 1962.

Eyestone, Robert, and Heinz Eulau. "City Councils and Policy Outcomes: Developmental Profiles." In City Politics and Public Policy, edited by James Q. Wilson. New York: John Wiley, 1968.

Fabricant, Solomon. The Trend of Government Activity in the United States Since 1900. New York: National Bureau of Economic Research, 1952.

Filstead, William J., ed. Qualitative Methodology. Chicago: Markham, 1970.

Fisher, Robert M. Twenty Years of Public Housing. New York: Harper, 1959.

Forstall, Richard L. "A New Social and Economic Grouping of Cities." The Municipal Year Book 1970. Washington, D.C.: International City Management Association, 1970.

Fowler, Edmund P., and Robert L. Lineberry. "Patterns of Feedback in City Politics." In Urban Political Analysis: A Systems Approach, edited by David R. Morgan and Samuel A. Kirkpatrick. New York: The Free Press, 1972.

Frederickson, H. George, and Linda Schluter O'Leary. Power, Public Opinion, and Policy in a Metropolitan Community: A Case Study of Syracuse, New York. New York: Praeger, 1973.

Freedman, Leonard. Public Housing: The Politics of Poverty. New York: Holt, Rinehart and Winston, 1969.

Freeman, Linton C. Patterns of Local Community Leadership. Indianapolis: Bobbs-Merrill, 1968.

Friedly, Philip H., Jerome Rothenberg, Jon E. Burkhardt, and James L. Hedrick. Benefit-Cost Applications in Urban Renewal: Summary of the Feasibility Study. Washington, D.C.: Government Printing Office, 1968.

Friedman, Lawrence M. Government and Slum Housing: A Century of Frustration. Chicago: Rand McNally, 1968.

Front Runner for the New Decade. Austin: Chamber of Commerce, January 24, 1972 (Mimeographed).

Galbraith, John Kenneth. The Affluent Society. New York: New American Library, 1958.

Gans, Herbert. The Urban Villagers. Glencoe, Ill.: The Free Press, 1962.

Goodwin, Leonard. Do the Poor Want to Work? Washington, D.C.: Brookings Institution, 1972.

Graves, W. Brooke. American Intergovernmental Relations. New York: Scribners, 1964.

Greer, Scott. The Urbane View: Life and Politics in Metropolitan America. New York: Oxford University Press, 1972.

_____. Urban Renewal and American Cities. Kansas City: Bobbs-Merrill, 1965.

Groberg, Robert P. Centralized Relocation: A New Municipal Service. Washington, D.C.: National Association of Housing and Redevelopment Officials, 1969.

Grodzins, Morton. The American System, A New View of Government in the United States. Chicago: Rand McNally, 1966.

Gruen Associates. Alhambra Industrial Redevelopment: A Design and Implementation Framework. Los Angeles: Gruen Associates, August, 1970.

Victor Gruen Associates. Alhambra 1985: A General Plan for Alhambra, California. Los Angeles: Victor Gruen Associates, 1965.

Hadden, Jeffrey K., and Edgar F. Borgatta. American Cities: Their Social Characteristics. Chicago: Rand McNally, 1965.

Haldi, John. "The Role of Analysis." In Program Budgeting and Benefit-Cost Analysis, edited by Harley H. Hinrichs and Graeme M. Taylor. Pacific Palisades, Calif.: Goodyear Publishing Company, 1969.

Hannah, James. Expenditures, Staff, and Salaries of Planning Agencies, 1971. Chicago: American Society of Planning Officials, April 1971.

Harman, Harry H. Modern Factor Analysis. 2d ed. Chicago: Universityof Chicago Press, 1967.

Hawkins, Brett W. Politics and Urban Policies. Indianapolis: Bobbs-Merrill, 1971.

Hawley, Amos H. "Community Power and Urban Renewal Success." In Community Structure and Decision-Making: Comparative Analyses, edited by Terry N. Clark. San Francisco: Chandler, 1968.

Hebert, F. Ted, and Richard D. Bingham. Personal and Environmental Influences upon the City Manager's Knowledge of Federal Grant-In-Aid-Programs. Norman: Bureau of Government Research, Universityof Oklahoma, 1972.

Hollingshead, August, and L. H. Rogler. "Attitudes Toward Slums and Public Housing in Puerto Rico." In The Urban Condition: People and Policy in the Metropolis, edited by Leonard J. Duhl. New York: Simon and Schuster, 1963.

Housing and Apartment Development: Austin, Texas. Austin: Chamber of Commerce, February 21, 1972 (Mimeographed).

Housing Committee of the Erie and Niagara Counties Regional Planning Board. Technical Report on Housing in the Erie-Niagara Region: First Year Study. Grand Island, N.Y.: Erie and Niagara Counties Regional Planning Board, June 1970.

Housing Committee of the League of Women Voters of Metropolitan Syracuse. Housing in Onondaga County: Present Facts and Future Goals. Syracuse: League of Women Voters, February 1969.

International City Management Association. The Municipal Year Book 1971. Washington, D.C.: International City Management Association, 1971.

Jacobs, Jane. The Death and Life of Great American Cities. New York: Random House, 1961.

Kaplan, Harold. Urban Renewal Politics. New York: Columbia University Press, 1963.

Keith, Nathaniel S., and Marcou, O'Leary and Associates, Inc. Buffalo Community Renewal Program Extension for the City of Buffalo, New York. Buffalo: City of Buffalo, N.Y., n.d.

John F. Kennedy Library. Vallejo, Calif.: Public Library System, n.d.

Leach, Richard H. American Federalism. New York: Norton, 1970.

Lindbloom, Carl G., and Morton Farrah. The Citizen's Guide to Urban Renewal. Rev. ed. West Trenton, N.J.: Chandler-Davis, 1968.

Lineberry, Robert L., and Ira Sharkansky. Urban Politics and Public Policy. New York: Harper & Row, 1971.

Lipsky, Michael. Protest in City Politics: Rent Strikes, Housing and the Power of the Poor. Chicago: Rand McNally, 1970.

Living At Its Best. Austin: Chamber of Commerce, n.d.

Long, Norton. The Unwalled City. New York: Basic Books, 1972.

Lowe, Jeanne R. Cities in a Race With Time. New York: Random House, 1967.

Manvel, Allen D. "Land Use in 106 Large Cities." Three Land Research Studies. National Commission on Urban Problems. Washington, D.C.: Government Printing Office, 1968.

Margolis, Julias. The Analysis of Public Output. New York: National Bureau of Economic Research, 1970.

Martin, Roscoe C., et al. Decisions in Syracuse. Bloomington: Indiana University Press, 1961.

Maxwell, James A. Financing State and Local Governments. Rev. ed. Washington, D.C.: Brookings Institution, 1969.

McCall, George J., and J. L. Simmons, eds. Issues in Participation Observation: A Text and Reader. Reading, Mass.: Addison Wesley, 1969.

Meltsner, Arnold J. The Politics of City Revenue. Berkeley: University of California Press, 1971.

Merewitz, Leonard, and Stephen H. Soznick. The Budget's New Clothes. Chicago: Markham, 1971.

Miner, Jerry. Social and Economic Factors in Spending for Public Education. Syracuse: Syracuse University Press, 1963.

Moore, William, Jr. The Vertical Ghetto: Everyday Life in an Urban Project. New York: Random House, 1969.

Morgan, David R. Handbook of State Policy Indicators. Norman: Bureau of Government Research, University of Oklahoma, 1971.

_____, and Samuel A. Kirkpatrick, eds. Urban Political Analysis: A Systems Approach. New York: The Free Press, 1972.

Morris, Peter. "A Report on Urban Renewal in the United States." In The Urban Condition: People and Policy in the Metropolis, edited by Leonard J. Duhl. New York: Basic Books, 1963.

Morrison, Denton E., and Ramon E. Henkel, eds. The Significance Test Controversy: A Reader. Chicago: Aldine, 1970.

Mushkin, Selma J., and John F. Cotton. Sharing Federal Funds for State and Local Needs. New York: Praeger, 1969.

National Association of Housing and Redevelopment Officials. Critical Urban Housing Issues: 1967. Washington, D.C.: National Association of Housing and Redevelopment Officials, 1967.

Newman, Oscar. Defensible Space. New York: Macmillan, 1972.

Nolting, Orin F., and David S. Arnold, eds. The Municipal Year Book 1960. Chicago: International City Managers' Association, 1960.

_____. The Municipal Year Book 1961. Chicago: International City Managers' Association, 1961.

Oakland Task Force. Federal Decision-Making and Impact in Urban Areas. New York: Praeger, 1970.

Olson, David M. Nonpartisan Elections: A Case Analysis. Austin: Institute of Public Affairs, University of Texas, 1965.

_____. "Austin: The Capital City." In Urban Politics in the Southwest, edited by Leonard E. Goodall. Tempe: Institute of Public Administration, Arizona State University, 1967.

The President's Committee on Urban Housing. The Report of the President's Committee on Urban Housing: A Decent Home. Washington, D.C.: Government Printing Office, 1968.

Rainwater, Lee. Behind Ghetto Walls: Black Family Life in a Federal Slum. Chicago: Aldine, 1970.

_____, and William L. Yancey. The Moynihan Report and the Politics of Controversy. Cambridge, Mass.: MIT Press, 1967.

Rapkin, Chester, and William G. Grigsby. The Demand for Housing in Racially Mixed Areas. Berkeley: University of California Press, 1960.

Redevelopment Agency of the City of Vallejo. Marina Vista. Vallejo, Calif.: Gibson Publication, n.d.

_____. Urban Design for Marina Vista: A Redevelopment Project for the Urban Renewal of Downtown Vallejo, California. Vallejo, Calif.: Gibson Publications, n.d.

Rossi, Peter H., and Robert A. Dentler. The Politics of Urban Renewal. New York: The Free Press, 1961.

Rothenberg, Jerome. Economic Evaluation of Urban Renewal. Washington, D.C.: Brookings Institution, 1967.

Rummel, R. J. Applied Factor Analysis. Evanston, Ill.: Northwestern University Press, 1970.

Salisbury, Harrison. The Shook-Up Generation. New York: Harper, 1958.

Sanford, Terry. Storm Over the States. New York: McGraw-Hill, 1967.

Scammon, Richard M., ed. America Votes 7. Washington, D.C.: Governmental Affairs Institute, 1968.

_____, ed. America Votes 8. Washington, D.C.: Governmental Affairs Institute, 1970.

Schnore, Leo F. The Urban Scene. New York: The Free Press, 1965.

Schoenberger, Robert A., ed. The American Right Wing: Readings in Political Behavior. New York: Holt, Rinehart, 1969.

Segal, Morley, and A. Lee Fritschler. "Emerging Patterns of Intergovernmental Relations." The Municipal Year Book 1970. Washington, D.C.: International City Management Association, 1970.

Sharkansky, Ira. The Politics of Taxing and Spending. Indianapolis: Bobbs-Merrill, 1969.

_____. Spending in the American States. Chicago: Rand McNally, 1968.

Stahl, Frank. Reflections: A Summary of Urban Renewal Activities in Buffalo, New York 1971/1972. Buffalo: Department of Urban Renewal, 1972.

Sundquist, James L., and David W. Davis. <u>Making Federalism Work:</u> <u>A Study of Program Coordination at the Community Level.</u> Washington, D.C.: Brookings Institution, 1969.

Syracuse Governmental Research Bureau and Metropolitan Development Association. <u>Profile of Central New York.</u> Syracuse: Syracuse Governmental Research Bureau and Metropolitan Development Association, 1973.

Talbot, A. R. <u>The Mayor's Game: Richard Lee of New Haven and the Politics of Change.</u> New York: Praeger, 1970.

U.S. Congress. House. Committee on Banking and Currency. <u>Basic Laws and Authorities on Housing and Urban Development.</u> Washington, D.C.: Government Printing Office, 1969.

U.S. Department of Commerce. Bureau of the Census. <u>City Government Finances in 1969-70.</u> Washington, D.C.: Government Printing Office, 1971.

_____. <u>County and City Data Book 1962.</u> Washington, D.C.: Government Printing Office, 1962.

_____. <u>General Social and Economic Characteristics: California.</u> Washington, D.C.: Government Printing Office, 1972.

_____. <u>General Social and Economic Characteristics: New York.</u> Washington, D.C.: Government Printing Office, 1972.

_____. <u>General Social and Economic Characteristics: Texas.</u> Washington, D.C.: Government Printing Office, 1972.

_____. <u>General Social and Economic Characteristics: U.S. Summary.</u> Washington, D.C.: Government Printing Office, 1972.

_____. <u>Housing Authorized by Building Permits and Public Contracts 1966.</u> Washington, D.C.: Government Printing Office, 1967.

_____. <u>Housing Authorized by Building Permits and Public Contracts 1968.</u> Washington, D.C.: Government Printing Office, 1970.

_____. <u>Housing Authorized by Building Permits and Public Contracts 1970.</u> Washington, D.C.: Government Printing Office, 1971.

_____. <u>Housing Authorized in Individual Permit-Issuing Places 1963.</u> Washington, D.C.: Government Printing Office, 1963.

_____. Housing Authorized in Individual Permit-Issuing Places 1964. Washington, D.C.: Government Printing Office, 1964.

_____. Housing Characteristics for States, Cities, and Counties. Washington, D.C.: Government Printing Office, 1972.

_____. New Housing Units Authorized by Local Building Permits, Annual Summary 1960-61. Washington, D.C.: Government Printing Office, 1962.

_____. United States Census of Housing 1960. Washington, D.C.: Government Printing Office, 1962.

U.S. Department of Housing and Urban Development. Consolidated Development Directory. Report S-11A. Washington, D.C.: U.S. Department of Housing and Urban Development, 1970.

_____. Urban Renewal Directory: As of December 31, 1970. Washington, D.C.: Government Printing Office, 1971.

U.S. Department of the Interior. Bureau of Outdoor Recreation. Recreation and Park Areas. Series AA, Report 604-615. Washington, D.C.: Unpublished computer printout, April 15, 1971.

_____. Volunteer Recreation Leaders and Recreation and Park Areas. Series AA, Report 301-303 and 306. Washington, D.C.: Unpublished computer printout, April 19, 1971.

U.S. Office of Economic Opportunity. Catalog of Federal Domestic Assistance. Washington, D.C.: Government Printing Office, 1970.

Vallejo Chamber of Commerce. Fact Card No. 8. Vallejo: Chamber of Commerce, n.d.

_____. Vallejo, California. Encino, Calif.: Windsor Publications, 1971.

_____. Vallejo, California. Vallejo: Solano County Board of Supervisors, n.d.

Vallejo Planning Department. Neighborhood Analyses: Vallejo, California. Vallejo: City of Vallejo, Calif., 1966 (Mimeographed).

_____. <u>1967 Special Census Release</u>. Vallejo: City of Vallejo, Calif., 1968 (Mimeographed).

Warren, Roland L., ed. <u>Politics and the Ghettos</u>. New York: Atherton, 1969.

Weaver, Robert C. <u>The Urban Complex</u>. Garden City, N.Y.: Doubleday, 1964.

Williams, Oliver P., and Charles R. Adrian. "Community Types and Policy Differences." In <u>City Politics and Public Policy</u>, edited by James Q. Wilson. New York: John Wiley, 1968.

Wilson, James Q., ed. <u>City Politics and Public Policy</u>. New York: John Wiley, 1968.

Wolf, Eleanor Paperno, and Charles N. Lebeaux. <u>Change and Renewal in an Urban Community</u>. New York: Praeger, 1969.

Wolman, Harold. <u>Politics of Federal Housing</u>. New York: Dodd, Mead, 1971.

<u>A Workable Program for Community Improvement: 1968 Progress Report for the Elimination and Prevention of Slums and Blight in Syracuse, New York</u>. Syracuse: City of Syracuse, 1968.

<u>Workable Program 1970/1972</u>. Buffalo: City of Buffalo, 1969.

Wright, Deil S. <u>Federal Grants-In-Aid: Perspectives and Alternatives</u>. Washington, D.C.: American Enterprise Institute for Public Policy Research, 1968.

Zisch, William E., Paul H. Douglas, and Robert C. Weaver. <u>The Urban Environment: How It Can Be Improved</u>. New York: New York University Press, 1969.

ARTICLES

Aiken, Michael, and Robert R. Alford. "Community Structure and Innovation: The Case of Public Housing." <u>American Political Science Review</u> 64 (September 1970): 843-64.

_____. "Community Structure and Innovation: The Case of Urban Renewal." <u>American Sociological Review</u> 35 (August 1970): 650-65.

Bahl, Roy W., Jr., and Robert J. Saunders. "Determinants of Changes in State and Local Government Expenditures." National Tax Journal 18 (March 1965): 50-57.

_____. "Factors Associated with Variations in State and Local Government Spending." Journal of Finance 21 (September 1966): 523-34.

Bellush, Jewel, and Murray Hausknecht. "Entrepreneurs and Urban Renewal: The New Men of Power." Journal of the American Institute of Planners 32 (September 1966): 289-97.

Bishop, George A. "Stimulative Versus Substitutive Effects of State School Aid in New England." National Tax Journal 17 (June 1964): 133-43.

Booms, Bernard H. "City Governmental Form and Public Expenditure Levels." National Tax Journal 19 (June 1966): 187-99.

Clark, Terry N. "Community Structure, Decision-Making, Budget Expenditures, and Urban Renewal in 51 American Communities." American Sociological Review 33 (August 1968): 576-93.

Cole, Richard L. "The Urban Policy Process: A Note on Structural and Regional Influences." Social Science Quarterly 52 (December 1971): 646-55.

Converse, Philip E. et al. "Continuity and Change in American Politics: Parties and Issues in the 1968 Election." American Political Science Review 63 (December 1969): 1083-1105.

Crew, Robert E., Jr. "Dimensions of Public Policy: A Factor Analysis of State Expenditures." Social Science Quarterly 50 (September 1969): 381-88.

Dales, Sophie R. "Federal Grants to State and Local Governments, 1967-68." Social Security Bulletin 32, no. 8. Washington, D.C.: Government Printing Office, August 1969, pp. 15-22.

Davis, Otto A., and George H. Haines, Jr. "A Political Approach to a Theory of Public Expenditure: The Case of Municipalities." National Tax Journal 19 (September 1966): 259-75.

Dawson, Richard E., and James A. Robinson. "Inter-Party Competition, Economic Variables, and Welfare Policies in the American States." Journal of Politics 25 (May 1963): 265-89.

Dye, Thomas R. "City-Suburban Social Distance and Public Policy." Social Forces 44 (September 1965): 100-06.

_____. "Income Inequality and American State Politics." American Political Science Review 63 (March 1969): 157-62.

Eulau, Heinz, and Robert Eyestone. "Policy Maps of City Councils and Policy Outcomes: A Developmental Analysis." American Political Science Review 62 (March 1968): 124-43.

Fisher, Glenn W. "Determinants of State and Local Government Expenditures: A Preliminary Analysis." National Tax Journal 14 (December 1961): 349-55.

_____. "Interstate Variation in State and Local Expenditures." National Tax Journal 17 (March 1964): 57-75.

Fried, Marc, and Peggy Gleicher. "Some Sources of Residential Satisfaction in an Urban Slum." Journal of the American Institute of Planners 27 (November 1961): 305-15.

Fritschler, A. Lee, B. Douglas Harman, and Morley Segal. "Federal, State, Local Relationships." Urban Data Service, December 1969.

Fritschler, A. Lee, and Morley Segal. "Intergovernmental Relations and Contemporary Political Science: Developing an Integrative Typology." Publius 1 (Winter 1972): 95-122.

_____, and John D. Norton. "Local Intergovernmental Coordinators." Urban Data Service. Washington, D.C.: International City Management Association, August 1970.

Gabler, L. R., and Joel I. Brest. "Interstate Variations in Per Capita Highway Expenditures." National Tax Journal 20 (March 1967): 78-85.

Gans, Herbert J. "The Failure of Urban Renewal: A Critique and Some Proposals." Commentary 39 (April 1965): 29-37.

Gold, Ronald B. "Fiscal Capacities and Welfare Expenditures of States." National Tax Journal 22 (December 1969): 496-505.

Gramlich, Edward M. "Alternative Federal Policies for Stimulating State and Local Expenditures: A Comparison of Their Effects." National Tax Journal 21 (June 1968): 119-29.

_____. "A Clarification and a Correction." National Tax Journal 22 (June 1969): 286-90.

Harlow, Robert L. "Sharkansky on State Expenditures: A Comment." National Tax Journal 21 (June 1968): 215-16.

Hartman, Chester. "The Housing of Relocated Families." Journal of the American Institute of Planners 30 (November 1964): 266-82.

_____. "Social Values and Housing Orientations." Journal of Social Issues 19 (April 1963): 113-82.

Hebert, F. Ted, and Richard D. Bingham. "The City Manager's Knowledge of Grants-In-Aid: Some Personal and Environmental Influences." Urban Affairs Quarterly 7 (March 1972): 303-06.

Henderson, James M. "Local Government: A Social Welfare Analysis." Review of Economics and Statistics 50 (May 1968): 156-63.

Hofferbert, Richard I. "The Relation Between Public Policy and Some Structural and Environmental Variables in the American States." American Political Science Review 60 (March 1966): 73-82.

Horowitz, Ann R. "Simultaneous Equation Approach to the Problem of Explaining Interstate Differences in State and Local Government Expenditures." Southern Economic Journal 34 (April 1968): 459-76.

Johnson, Gerald W. "Research Notes on Political Correlates of Voter Participation: A Deviant Case Analysis." American Political Science Review 65 (September 1971): 768-76.

Jones, K., and W. Jones. "Toward a Typology of American Cities." Journal of Reproductive Medicine: Lying-In 10 (August 1970): 20.

Kaufman, Walter C., and Scott Greer. "Voting in a Metropolitan Community: An Application of Social Area Analysis." Social Forces 38 (March 1960): 196-204.

Kurnow, Ernest. "Determinants of State and Local Expenditures Reexamined." National Tax Journal 16 (September 1963): 252-55.

Lineberry, Robert L., and Edmund P. Fowler. "Reformism and
Public Policies in American Cities." American Political
Science Review 61 (September 1967): 701-16.

Masten, J. T., and K. E. Quindry. "A Note on City Expenditure
Determinants." Land Economics 46 (February 1970): 79-81.

Maxwell, James A. "Federal Grant Elasticity and Distortion."
National Tax Journal 22 (December 1969): 550-51.

McIntyre, M. Charles. "Determinants of Expenditures for Public
Higher Education." National Tax Journal 22 (June 1969): 262-72.

Morse, Elliott R. "Some Thoughts on the Determinants of State and
Local Expenditures." National Tax Journal 19 (March 1966):
95-103.

Mushkin, Selma J. "PPB in Cities." Public Administration Review
29 (March/April 1969): 167-78.

_____, and Robert F. Adams. "Emerging Patterns of Federalism."
National Tax Journal 19 (September 1966): 225-47.

Nourse, Hugh O. "Redistribution of Income from Public Housing."
National Tax Journal 19 (March 1966): 27-37.

Oates, Wallace E. "The Dual Impact of Federal Aid on State and
Local Government Expenditures: A Comment." National Tax
Journal 21 (June 1968): 220-23.

O'Brien, Thomas. "Grants-In-Aid: Some Further Answers."
National Tax Journal 24 (March 1971): 65-71.

Osman, Jack. "The Dual Impact of Federal Aid on State and Local
Government Expenditures." National Tax Journal 19 (December 1966): 362-73.

_____. "On the Use of Intergovernmental Aid as an Expenditure
Determinant." National Tax Journal 21 (December 1968):
437-47.

Pogue, Thomas F., and L. G. Sgontz. "The Effect of Grants-In-
Aid on State-Local Spending." National Tax Journal 21 (June
1968): 190-99.

Rainwater, Lee. "Fear and the House-As-Haven in the Lower-Class." Journal of the American Institute of Planners 32 (January 1966): 23-30.

Reynolds, Harry W., Jr. "The Human Element in Urban Renewal." Public Welfare 19 (April 1961): 71-82.

Sacks, Seymour, and Robert Harris. "The Determinants of State and Local Government Expenditures and Intergovernmental Flow of Funds." National Tax Journal 17 (March 1964): 75-85.

Schmandt, Henry V., and G. Ross Stephens. "Local Government Expenditure Patterns in the United States." Land Economics, November 1963: 397-98.

Schmid, C. F. "Generalizations Concerning the Ecology of the American City." American Sociological Review 15 (April 1950): 264-81.

_____. "Urban Crime Areas: Part I." American Sociological Review 25 (August 1960): 527-42.

_____, E. G. MacCannell, and M. D. Van Arsdol. "The Ecology of the American City: Further Comparison and Validation of Generalizations." American Sociological Review 23 (August 1958): 392-401.

Sharkansky, Ira. "Economic and Political Correlates of State Government Expenditures: General Tendencies and Deviant Cases." Midwest Journal of Political Science 11 (May 1967): 173-92.

_____. "Economic Development, Regionalism and State Political Systems." Midwest Journal of Political Science 12 (February 1968): 41-61.

_____. "Government Expenditures and Public Service in the American States." American Political Science Review 61 (December 1967): 1066-77.

_____. "Regional Patterns in the Expenditures of American States." Western Political Quarterly 20 (December 1967): 955-71.

_____. "Some More Thoughts About the Determinants of Government Expenditures." National Tax Journal 20 (June 1967): 171-79.

_____. "The Utility of Elazar's Political Culture." Polity 2 (Fall 1969): 66-83.

Smith, David L. "Federal Grant Elasticity and Distortion: A Reply." National Tax Journal 22 (December 1969): 552-53.

_____. "The Response of State and Local Governments to Federal Grants." National Tax Journal 21 (September 1968): 349-57.

Staples, J. H. "Urban Renewal: A Comparative Study of Twenty-Two Cities, 1950-1960." Western Political Quarterly 23 (June 1970): 294-304.

Stephens, G. Ross, and Henry J. Schmandt. "Revenue Patterns of Local Governments." National Tax Journal 15 (December 1962): 432-37.

Teeples, R. K. "A Model of a Matching Grant-In-Aid Program with External Tax Effects." National Tax Journal 22 (December 1969): 486-95.

Thurow, Lester. "The Theory of Grants-In-Aid." National Tax Journal 19 (December 1966): 373-77.

Tropman, John E. "Critical Dimensions of Community Structure: A Reexamination of the Hadden-Borgatta Findings." Urban Affairs Quarterly 5 (December 1969): 215-32.

Wilde, James A. "The Expenditure Effects of Grant-In-Aid Programs." National Tax Journal 21 (September 1968): 340-47.

_____. "Grants-In-Aid: The Analytics of Design and Response." National Tax Journal 24 (June 1971): 143-55.

Williams, J. Allen, Jr. "The Effects of Urban Renewal Upon a Black Community: Evaluation and Recommendations." Social Science Quarterly 50 (December 1969): 704-12.

_____. "The Multifamily Housing Solution and Housing Type Preferences." Social Science Quarterly 52 (December 1971): 543-59.

Wilson, James Q. "Planning and Politics: Citizen Participation in Urban Renewal." Journal of the American Institute of Planners 29 (November 1963): 242-49.

Wolfinger, Raymond E., and John Osgood Field. "Political Ethos and the Structure of City Government." American Political Science Review 60 (June 1966): 306-26.

Wright, Deil S. "The States and Intergovernmental Relations." Publius 1 (Winter 1972): 7-68.

UNPUBLISHED MATERIALS

Amended Memorandum of Understanding. Austin: Urban Renewal Agency of the City of Austin, July 1, 1972 (Mimeographed).

"Dates of Enactment of State Housing Authority Laws." Attachment to letter from Deborah Greenstein, Program Analyst, Housing Management Research Division, Department of Housing and Urban Development, Washington, D.C., November 3, 1972.

"Dates of Enactment of State Urban Renewal Laws." Attachment to letter from Deborah Greenstein, Program Analyst, Housing Management Research Division, Department of Housing and Urban Development, Washington, D.C., November 3, 1972.

Denbow, Stefania, and Joseph Ohren. Housing in the Syracuse Community. Syracuse, N.Y.: March 1972 (Mimeographed).

Memorandum Opinion: Blackshear Residents Organization, et al. vs. Housing Authority of the City of Austin, et al. Civil Action No. A-70-CA-51. Austin: United States District Court, Western District of Texas, Austin Division, filed December 3, 1971 (Mimeographed).

Ordinance No. 071-3546. City of Alhambra, Calif., December 7, 1971.

Ordinance No. 967-3383. City of Alhambra, Calif., October 10, 1967.

Ordinance No. 066-3334. City of Alhambra, Calif., August 2, 1966.

Ordinance No. 070-3480. City of Alhambra, Calif., July 7, 1970.

Ordinance No. 071-3512. City of Alhambra, Calif., April 6, 1971.

Rafuse, R. W., Jr. "State and Local Fiscal Behavior Over the Post-war Cycles." Ph.D. dissertation, Princeton University, Department of Economics, 1963.

U.S. Department of Housing and Urban Development. "Execution Project Number by State." Transmittal Notice MC-24, February 1970 (Mimeographed).

Williams, J. Allen, Jr. Blackshear Diagnostic Survey: A Description and Problem Analysis. Austin: The Urban Renewal Agency of the City of Austin, June 1968 (Mimeographed).

NEWSPAPERS

Austin American, December 4, 6, 1959; March 23, April 7, 1969.

Austin American-Statesman, December 6, 1959; March 26, 1961; March 31, 1963; March 12, 1967; August 27, 1972.

Austin Statesman, December 1, 3, 4, 1959.

Beaumont Enterprise, April 3, May 3, June 1-4, 6-12, 1960; November 1, 3, 5, 8-10, 12, 14, 17, 19, 1967; May 10, 12, 15, 1968.

Buffalo Courier Express, November 1, 5, 8, 1961; June 2, 6, November 2, 3, 1963; November 4, 1964; October 19, 1965; November 6, 1968; November 5, 1969.

Buffalo Evening News, April 19, August 18, 1965; December 2, 1968.

Mossberg, Walter S. "A Blue-Collar Town Fears Urban Renewal Perils Its Way of Life." Wall Street Journal, November 2, 1970, pp. 1, 13.

"Nixon Says Crisis in Cities Is Over; Cities Dip in Crime." New York Times, March 5, 1973, pp. 1, 20.

Post-Advocate (Alhambra, California), November 2, 4, 1964; October 29, November 8, 1968.

Sunday Enterprise (Beaumont), November 19, 1967.

Sunday Times-Herald (Vallejo), April 4, 1965.

Syracuse Herald-American, January 2, 1966.

Syracuse Herald-Journal, April 23, 1959; May 31, 1965; July 16, 1968.

Syracuse Post-Standard, May 17, 29, 1956; July 30, November 2, 1961; November 2, 1962; January 12, April 15, November 4, 1964; August 12, December 9, 1966; November 6, 1968; November 1, 5, 1969.

Vallejo Times Herald, April 5, 1961; April 1, 2, 1963; November 4, 1964; April 20, 1969.

unemployment, 160, 162, 167, 168, 170

urban renewal, criticisms of, 224, 226-229; definition, 69-70; effects on city finances, 56, 180-182, 184-185, 187-188, 189-190, 222; effects on government employment, 174-178, 190-191, 222; effects on improved housing conditions, 56-59, 204-206, 214, 216, 218, 222; effects on intergovernmental transfers, 179, 190; effects on land use patterns, 55, 193-194, 196-197; effects on local business, 51-53, 222; effects on political stability, 55-56, 182-184, 187, 188-189, 191; effects on supply of low-rent housing, 56-59, 204-205, 211, 213, 214, 216; goals, 35; history, 30-37; operations, 29-30, 33, 35; projects, 28, 36; types of programs, 29

urban renewal programs, determinants of use, 38, 81-82, 144-145

Vallejo, Calif., general, 79, 108-109; grant effects in, 165-166, 184-185, 198, 211-212; grant use, 118-121; physical characteristics, 116-118

Wallace, George, 43
Wallace vote, 86-88, 91, 149
Warren, Mich., 43
Weaver, Robert, 53
Wilde, James, 24
Wolf, Eleanor, 57, 59
workable program, 32, 35

zero-sum game, 223-225

ABOUT THE AUTHOR

RICHARD D. BINGHAM is Assistant Professor of Political Science at Marquette University, Milwaukee, Wisconsin. He is a former American Political Science Association Urban Intern and recipient of the Woodrow Wilson Foundation Dissertation Grant. He recently was awarded a National Science Foundation grant to study the adoption of technological innovation by local government.

Dr. Bingham's previous publications and papers are in the areas of state and local government and public policy analysis. He is author of several monographs published by the Bureau of Government Research of the University of Oklahoma and his work has appeared in the Urban Affairs Quarterly on several occasions.

Dr. Bingham holds a B.S. from Boston University and an M.A. and Ph.D. from the University of Oklahoma.

PROBLEM TENANTS IN PUBLIC HOUSING:
Who, Where, and Why Are They?
Richard S. Scobie

MANDATORY HOUSING SUBSIDIES:
A Comparative International Analysis
Morris L. Sweet and
S. George Walters

HOUSING MARKETS AND CONGRESSIONAL GOALS
Ernest M. Fisher

URBAN INCENTIVE TAX CREDITS:
A Self-Correcting Strategy to
Rebuild Central Cities
Edward M. Meyers and
John J. Musial